INEQUALITY AND GLOBALIZATION

THE GORMAN LECTURES IN ECONOMICS

Richard Blundell, Series Editor

A series statement appears at the end of the book.

Inequality and Globalization

IMPROVING MEASUREMENT THROUGH
INTEGRATED FINANCIAL ACCOUNTS

ARCHAWA PAWEENAWAT

ROBERT M. TOWNSEND

PRINCETON UNIVERSITY PRESS
PRINCETON & OXFORD

Published by Princeton University Press

41 William Street, Princeton, New Jersey 08540
99 Banbury Road, Oxford OX2 6JX
press.princeton.edu

All Rights Reserved

ISBN 978-0-691-21102-2
ISBN (e-book) 978-0-691-25804-1

British Library Cataloging-in-Publication Data is available

Editorial: Hannah Paul and Josh Drake
Production Editorial: Jenny Wolkowicki
Jacket design: Karl Spurzem
Production: Erin Suydam
Publicity: William Pagdatoon
Copyeditor: Bhisham Bherwani

Jacket image: nattanai chimjanon / Alamy Stock Photo

This book has been composed in Arno Pro

Printed in the United States of America

10 9 8 7 6 5 4 3 2 1

CONTENTS

v

ILLUSTRATIONS

Figures

Tables

Appendix

ACKNOWLEDGMENTS

ARCHAWA PAWEENAWAT GRATEFULLY acknowledges financial support from the Thailand Research Fund. Robert M. Townsend gratefully acknowledges financial support from the Eunice Kennedy Shriver National Institute of Child Health and Human Development (NICHD) under grant R01 HD027638 and the Bill & Melinda Gates Foundation through the Chicago Consortium on Financial Systems and Poverty and support for the Townsend Thai surveys from the Puey Ungphakorn Institute for Economic Research (PIER), the Bank of Thailand, and the Thailand Research Fund. We are grateful for permission from Cambridge University Press to reproduce in Chapter 2, with some editing, Samphantharak, Krislert, and Robert M. Townsend (2009), *Households as Corporate Firms: An Analysis of Household Finance Using Integrated Household Surveys and Corporate Financial Accounting*, Econometric Society Monographs, Cambridge; New York: Cambridge University Press. We are also grateful for permission from the Western Economic Association International to reproduce in Chapter 5, with edits, Samphantharak, Krislert, Scott Schuh, and Robert M. Townsend (2018), "Integrated Household Surveys: An Assessment of U.S. Methods and an Innovation," *Economic Inquiry* 56 (1): 50–80, Western Economic Association International. The opinions expressed are those of the authors and should not be attributed to the Puey Ungphakorn Institute for Economic Research or the Bank of Thailand. We thank Narapong Srivisal for his contributions to additional material in Chapter 2 and Deborah Jamiol for her excellent assistance in preparing this manuscript.

INEQUALITY AND GLOBALIZATION

1

Introduction

THE TITLE AND SUBTITLE to this monograph juxtapose two seemingly different subjects and approaches. The title is exciting, timely, and important for political debates and policy decisions: inequality, the impact of trade and manufacturing shocks, financial liberalization and repression, and the impact of the COVID-19 virus pandemic. The subtitle, referring to measurement through integrated financial accounts, may seem tedious if not off-putting.

Yet, the title and subtitle are intimately linked. The measurements of phenomena fueling debates and policy actions are actually disturbingly imperfect. Yet, states of affairs are reported as factual, with accuracy not much questioned. Perceived facts reinforce political positions and have consequences through important policy actions.

Integrated financial accounts have the property that the flows in income statements, including savings and investments, are consistent with the changes in financial assets and liabilities in the balance sheet. Increasing income inequality is taken as synonymous with the rich getting richer, with a tailored financial sector serving that group, consistent with the Main Street vs. Wall Street dichotomy. But the United States and most countries do not actually have consistent measures of wealth and income. Inequality in wealth has to be estimated. Researchers are passionate about measurement, realizing its importance for policy questions, but they do not have anything close to ideal data sets. None of the U.S. micro household surveys are constructed in such a way that the income statements and balance sheets are consistent with each other. At the macro level, GDP is very well measured in the United States by the Department of Commerce's Bureau of Economic Analysis (BEA), and wealth is very well measured by the Federal Reserve Board through Flow of Funds Accounts. But these efforts typically are not linked. A wonderful integration occurs with an inter-agency project creating Integrated Macro Accounts.[1] But the discrepancy between flows and changes in stock are acknowledged there, pointing to a relatively large errors-and-omissions line item. The single biggest problem is that we do not have consistent measures of wealth and income; that is, no single data set has income, consumption, and wealth.

These limitations show up in a variety of research efforts, for example, to assess the impact of increasing imports to the United States from China and to assess the longer-term sectoral decline in U.S. manufacturing. Via careful analysis with existing data, one can deduce that there are adverse effects on income and employment, and indeed correlations with the opioid problem (Autor, Dorn, and Hanson, 2013; and also Charles, Hurst, and Schwartz, 2018). We can also see from existing data the interstate trade and state-level current account deficits (Ehrlich, Fukui, and Townsend, 2021). But without integrated, consistent regional financial accounts, we cannot as yet look at the entire picture of financial balance sheet outcomes, the impact on assets and liabilities, even though exact accounting identities tell us they must be there.

Likewise, for the United States, the uneven impact of the COVID-19 pandemic is inferred through the measurement of payment flows, but economics and logic, and some rare examples from specialty surveys, tell us that what matters for impact and welfare is the balance sheet position of the impacted households. And we know even less about the liquidity positions of small businesses.

To give these comments a more positive spin, this monograph focuses on what can be done with consistent data. It features the impact of trade and financial liberalization, the flip side of repression. In Thailand, a growing emerging market country, we have created consistent integrated financial accounts at the individual household and small enterprise levels. These can then be aggregated up to create village and local income and product accounts, flow of funds associated with changes in line items of assets and liabilities, and balance of payment accounts. We can link anecdotal stories of individual households to their financial accounts, document the actual real impact on them from growth, and assess what would have happened to them if the liberalization in trade and financial flows had not been allowed. The data and model feature important heterogeneities in productivity and wealth, with precision about winners and losers, even within villages. We try to be constructive

---

1. See https://www.bea.gov/data/special-topics/integrated-macroeconomic-accounts.

and conclude the monograph with concrete suggestions for what can be done in the United States to allow for this kind of analysis.

In this introductory chapter we now go over some of these aspects in more detail.

1.1 High Inequality in Income and Wealth

In this section we focus first on the inequality situation in the United States, then adopt a larger cross-country perspective, and finally consider the role of geography.

1.1.1 *Situation in the U.S.*

Though the extremes in income and wealth are an important, age-old topic, Piketty, Saez, and Zucman (2018) have drawn renewed attention to them. In the United States, the share of wealth of the top ten percent increased in the 1920s, dropped during the Depression, and, after a period of stability, took off again, reaching 50%. The share of income of the top 1% has a similar U-shape, but also highlights the increasing contribution of income from capital (dividends, interest payments, and capital gains) for that top group. Indeed, when the rate of return on capital exceeds the rate of growth, the rich benefit and income inequality tends to rise. Relatedly, inequality in wealth increases.

1.1.2 *An International, Advanced Country Perspective: Inequality with a Large but Inefficient Financial Sector*

Hildebrand (2019) constructs annual national financial balance sheets and production accounts for twelve advanced economies since 1850. Financial assets relative to output have more than quadrupled in the past 150 years, since 1860. After 1980, the financial asset-to-output ratio skyrocketed, reaching 523% of gross domestic product in 2009, compared to just 223% thirty years earlier. Yet, ironically, it does not appear from Hildebrand's analysis that financial intermediation has become more efficient. Profits and the markups of banks are stable, and the share of investment funded by internal savings remains largely constant.

These observations are consistent with the boom in the financial industry observed by Piketty, Saez, and Zucman (2018), with rising inequality in Canada, the UK, and Australia. Since 1980, the share of overall income going to the top 1% has risen sharply in these countries. Recent experience (at the time of this writing) also raises questions, with equity market prices breaking new records while COVID-19 ravages various sectors and income groups in the real economy.

1.1.3 The Geography of Inequality Is Part of the Mix

While focusing on health and earned wages, Agrawal and Phillips (2020) note that London, with its financial industry, stands out. According to the IFS Deaton Review summary[2] of Agrawal and Phillips (2020): "Productivity and earnings in London are one-third to one-half times higher than the UK average. Mean property and financial wealth increased by 150% in London in the ten years prior to 2016–18, compared with only 50% across Great Britain as a whole."

In France, a new increase in inequality started around 1983. The income share of the top 1% rose significantly between 1983 and 2007, from less than 8% of total income to over 12% over this period, thus by more than 50% (Garbinti, Goupille-Lebret, and Piketty, 2018).

By 2018, a protest movement arose, with the yellow vests holding weekly demonstrations against rising fuel prices and uneven burdens of taxes. They succeeded in getting a major fuel tax reversed. But the movement was stalled at first by violence and then by the COVID-19 pandemic (Wikipedia 2021).

For the United States, Smith, Zidar, and Zwick (2019) provide state-level estimates of wealth. The data reveal vast disparities in wealth across regions. In the Northeast, wealth exceeds $450K per capita, whereas in the poorest states in the South, wealth is less than $200K. Further, and much more to the point, disparities are increasing. The coastal states have experienced increased wealth-to-income ratios between 100% and 300% since 1980, in contrast to more modest growth inland.

1.1.4 Repressive Policies Follow

With globalization, trade, and capital flows thought to underlie the inequality phenomena, repressive and/or distorting policies have followed. The United States renegotiated NAFTA with quotas and protectionist targets for specific industries. The United States also pulled out of the Trans-Pacific Partnership

---

2. See https://ifs.org.uk/inequality/geographical-inequalities-in-the-uk/

(TPP), imposing sanctions on China, with American farmers and consumers caught in the middle. Tax policy in the United States under the previous Republican administration seemed to target individual states as a function of past voting patterns. The 2020 election continued to highlight an urban/rural divide, with Democrats seeming to favor a continuation of some protectionist Trump policies (e.g., buy American), while also pushing for a higher minimum wage and increased social benefits.

The EU works at maintaining the monetary union while debating financial integration across countries. Britain under Brexit has pulled out of the trade union. Yellow jacket protestors in France have called for lower fuel taxes, a reintroduction of the solidarity tax on wealth, and a minimum wage increase.

1.1.5 Yet the Measurement of Inequality Is Problematic, despite All the Above Perceived Facts and Policy Actions

Piketty, Saez, and Zucman (2018), much to their credit, articulate quite clearly some of the problems and limitations of policy guidance. They focus on the absence of "distributional accounts" corresponding to measured national income.

> We still face three important limitations when measuring income inequality. . . . There is a large gap between national accounts—which focus on macro totals and growth—and inequality studies—which focus on distributions using survey and tax data, usually without trying to be fully consistent with macro totals. This gap makes it hard to address questions such as: What fraction of economic growth accrues to the bottom 50%, the middle 40%, and the top 10% of the distribution? How much of the rise in income inequality owes to changes in the share of labor and capital in national income, and how much to changes in the dispersion of labor earnings, capital ownership, and returns to capital? Second, about a third of U.S. national income is redistributed through taxes, transfers, and public good spending. Yet we do not have a good measure of how the distribution of pre-tax income differs from the distribution of post-tax income, making it hard to assess how government redistribution affects inequality. (p. 554)

Piketty, Saez, and Zucman (2018) seek to overcome the limits of existing series by computing better inequality statistics for the United States, creating these needed distributional national accounts.

As they note, though, this is not a new concept:

The first national accounts in history—the King's famous social tables produced in the late seventeenth century—were in fact distributional national accounts, showing the distribution of England's income, consumption, and saving across 26 social classes—from temporal lords and baronets down to vagrants—in 1688. (p. 558)

1.1.6 An Obvious Remedy to the Measurement Problem: Integrated Financial Accounts

Not having the necessary data is simply an artifact of the way U.S. data are collected. Ironically, to construct integrated accounts, all one needs to do is follow the steps outlined in U.S. Department of Commerce (1985). If one were able to start at the level of individual household and/or firm accounts, then one would be getting measures of individual income and contribution to production. This would happen along with consistent balance sheets and income flows from assets. Such complete financial accounts are termed "integrated," comprising balance sheets, income statements, and cash flow statements that are consistent with each other. In other words, the financial accounts are naturally integrated in the measurement of flows and stocks. Finally, the integrated accounts allow aggregation from micro to macro. One does not need to distribute national income. Indeed, accounting logic is the other way around. National income is the sum of individual incomes. And all of Piketty, Saez, and Zucman (2018)'s questions can be answered. Given all of this, and their importance to policy, it is startling that the United States, like most countries, does not have integrated financial accounts.

Both U.S. national income accounts and inequality studies often use the same data sets, such as the CPS data, as one example. The issue is making micro and macro consistent with each other, whether the approach be top-down or bottom-up. That requires a conceptual framework and associated measurement. Complete financial accounts for a surveyed population in Thailand are presented in Samphantharak and Townsend (2009), here reported in Chapter 2, and the aggregation, here in Chapter 3.

1.1.7 Where Do the Current Inequality Facts Come from?

At the micro level, measurement of inequality in wealth in the United States is currently done by mechanically linking income to the balance sheet. Thus, the measurement of wealth inequality in the United States inevitably involves assumptions and extrapolations. Typically, authors use a rate of return approach. Essentially, observed income is discounted to get the present value of wealth, mechanically. More specifically, using aggregated IRS data, measures of dividends and interest income are used to infer the balance sheet of financial assets, with the same formula applied uniformly across income classes and regions. Smith, Zidar, and Zwick (2019) improve on this by allowing heterogeneity in rates of return across wealth classes and activities. This matters for orders of magnitude, as they summarize:

> Accounting for heterogeneity reduces the growth in top shares since 1980 by half. . . . Our approach also alters the composition of top wealth. We find a larger role for private business wealth and a smaller role for fixed income wealth, consistent with the composition of top wealth in the SCF [the Survey of Consumer Finances] and estate tax data. Less than half of top wealth takes the form of liquid securities with clear market values. (Smith, Zidar, and Zwick, 2019, p. 3)

1.1.8 Integrated Macro Accounts in the U.S.: The Conceptual Framework Is Correct and Clear

The Integrated Macro Accounts (IMAs) integrate flows from available data from the Bureau of Economic Analysis with changes in balance sheet items, the stocks, of the Federal Reserve Board. The IMA is (an unfortunately rare) joint project, featured on both the FRB and BEA websites. But inevitably it comes with errors and omissions. The problem of divergent measurement is recognized by both agencies.

Still, the concept of IMA is identical to the one underlying the complete integrated financial accounts.

> This article introduces a set of macroeconomic accounts that relate production, income and saving, capital formation, financial transactions, and asset revaluations to changes in net worth between balance sheets for major sectors of the U.S. economy. These new accounts should help economists gain a better understanding of major developments in the U.S. economy by providing a comprehensive picture of economic activity within an integrated framework in which consistent definitions, classifications, and accounting conventions are used throughout the presentation. (Bond et al., 2007, p. 14).

Unfortunately, the change in net lending or net borrowing from the integrated macro "current account" flows is different from the net lending or net borrowing in the financial account changes in the balance sheet. The former comes from income minus consumption data, as with the BEA. The latter is net lending from the financial accounts, that is, measured by observing the changes in actual assets and liabilities using flow of funds and the SCF. When comparing the two—the flows vs. changes in stocks—discrepancies can be quite sizable.

1.2 Implications for Policy, What We Can Say Currently but with Limitations: The China Shock and Manufacturing Shocks

As noted, trade policies are formulated around inequality concerns and the aggravating impact of globalization. In what follows, we set the stage for a discussion of what we know from the literature and associated problems that stem from a lack of integrated financial accounts. The main limitation is our inability to assess, quantify, and compare mitigating mechanisms; standard accounting identities do not add up as data come from different sources.

1.2.1 *The Adverse Impact of Trade and Manufacturing Shocks*

In deservedly much cited work, Autor, Dorn, and Hansen (2013) summarize their findings:

> We analyze the effect of rising Chinese import competition between 1990 and 2007 on U.S. local labor markets, exploiting cross-market variation in import exposure stemming from initial differences in industry specialization and instrumenting for U.S. imports using changes in Chinese imports by other high-income countries. Rising imports cause higher unemployment, lower labor force participation, and reduced wages in local labor markets that house import-competing manufacturing industries. In our main specification, import competition explains one-quarter of the contemporaneous aggregate decline in U.S. manufacturing employment. Transfer benefits, payments for unemployment, disability, retirement, and healthcare, also rise sharply in more trade-exposed labor markets. (Autor, Dorn, and Hansen 2013, p. 2121)

Likewise, from Charles, Hurst, and Schwartz (2018):

> Using data from a variety of sources, this paper comprehensively documents the dramatic changes in the manufacturing sector and the large decline in

employment rates and hours worked among prime-aged Americans since 2000. . . . We find that manufacturing decline in a local area in the 2000s had large and persistent negative effects on local employment rates, hours worked and wages [and] that declining local manufacturing employment is related to rising local opioid use and deaths. . . . Given the trends in both capital and skill deepening within this sector, we further conclude that many policies currently being discussed to promote the manufacturing sector will have only a modest labor market impact for less educated individuals. (Charles, Hurst, and Schwartz 2018, p. 2)

1.2.2 The China Shock and Manufacturing Shocks through the Lens of Open Economy Accounting Identities

The China shock can be analyzed through the conceptual lens of accounting identities at the state level: trade flows, current accounts including gifts and public/private transfers, and associated potential adjustments on the financial side. But currently this has to be done without the benefit of integrated accounts. In particular, the disconnect between flows and changes in stocks hampers the ability to study all potential mitigating adjustment mechanisms.

As an analogy, when the U.S. macro economy runs a trade deficit against another country, the latter country is accumulating U.S. assets. Likewise, if a state runs a trade deficit, exporting less of previously manufactured goods, the state receives private and/or public transfers or runs down financial claims on other states, or both. The accounting identities are:

- Financial flows (baseline measurement)

$$\text{Current Account}_{st} = \text{Trade Balance}_{st} + \text{Net Income Transfers}_{st}$$
$$\text{Trade Balance}_{st} = \text{Exports}_{st} - \text{Imports}_{st}$$
$$\text{Net Income Transfers}_{st} = \text{Gross State Income}_{st} - \text{Gross State Product}_{st}$$
$$\text{Private Transfers}_{st} = \text{Net Income Transfers}_{st} - \text{Public Transfers}_{st}$$

A second set of financial flows is based on the premise that positive changes in net worth correspond with increases in claims on other states, except that increases in the housing stock and other capital investments are within-state (with the obvious change in sign for running a current account deficit on the left and a corresponding decrease in claims on other states).

TABLE 1.1. Data sources.

Variables	Data source
State-level trade flows	Commodity Flow Survey
State-level gross income and product	BEA regional accounts
State-level public transfer receipts	BEA regional accounts
State-level housing stock	American Community Survey
State-level house price	Federal Housing Finance Agency
State-level stocks and bonds	IRS tax record
State-level wage, dividends, interest income	IRS tax record
State-level capital stock	Yamarik (2013)
State-level household debt	NY Fed Consumer Credit Panel
State-level Chinese shock	Autor, Dorn, and Hanson (2013)
State-level manufacturing shift share	Charles, Hurst, and Schwartz (2018)

Source: Recreated from Ehrlich, Fukui, and Townsend (2021).

- Financial flows (alternative measurement) (from Ehrlich, Fukui, and Townsend 2021)

$$\text{Current Account}_{st}^{alt} = \text{Net worth}_{it} - \text{Net worth}_{i,t-1} - \text{Capital Investment}_{it}$$
$$- \text{Housing Investment}_{it}$$
$$\text{Net worth}_{it} = \text{Housing net worth}_{st} + \text{Stocks}_{st} + \text{Bonds}_{st} - \text{Debt}_{st}$$

But currently, we do not have consistent state-level aggregated regional accounts. Thus, following the literature and using a variety of independent data sets (see list in Table 1.1), Ehrlich, Fukui, and Townsend (2021) create synthetic accounts, which, not unlike Integrated Macro Accounts, come sometimes with substantial errors.

To gauge the impact of the China shock and the manufacturing decline, one utilizes these accounting identities and the data estimation, via seemingly unrelated regressions (SUR). The overall impact is summarized in Table 1.2, which shows that state-level exports decline under both shocks and the current account deteriorates under the China shock. Private transfers increase in both instances.

Though the financial flows ought to counterbalance the current account deficit, we currently find a counterintuitive increase in the housing stock. We have been unable to find other financial adjustment mechanisms, though when the current account deteriorates, as noted, there must be some adjust-

TABLE 1.2. Summary of the effect of shocks on the variables in the accounting identities.

	China shock	Manufacturing Bartik
Real current account	–	Insignificant
Trade balance	–	–
Exports	–	–
Imports	Insignificant	Insignificant
Transfers	+	+
Private transfers	+	+
Public transfers	+	+

Source: Recreated from Ehrlich, Fukui, and Townsend (2021).

ment, by definition, but not due to construction of the data. The accounting errors may be insurmountable without attacking the problem directly.

1.2.3 Integrated Financial Accounts in an Emerging Market Setting

In Thailand, we have measured from transactions data the flow of funds exactly as in the accounting identities. In Chapter 3, we will discuss the construction of the data, and in Chapter 4 we will look at the trade and financial liberalization that has happened over time. Specifically, using relatively high-frequency, long-duration panel data, we construct integrated household financial accounts that are consistent with income and wealth, that is, with changes in stocks and flows. Relevantly here, we also construct village and regional economic accounts and the associated balance of payments accounts. If a village runs a current account surplus, we see all of the adjustment mechanisms. By construction, everything adds up properly.

Chapter 4 presents a heterogeneous-agent/occupational-choice/trade model with financial frictions built and calibrated around micro and regional facts, that is, at both the individual level and the aggregate level. With this in hand, one can conduct counterfactual policy experiments. One of these determines the effect of isolationist policies that could have impeded trade and/or capital flows across regions by looking at wedges in relative prices and interest rates.

Impacts can be large and vary with policy. They are significantly heterogeneous, with both gains and losses and non-monotone movement across wealth classes and occupations, even allowing for occupation shifts which a priori might have mitigated impact. This is the advantage of having data consistent from the ground up.

1.3 Implications for Policy: The Limitations of What We Can Say Currently in the U.S. regarding the Impact of COVID-19

There are a variety of important measurement efforts underway to assess the impact of the COVID-19 shock on the U.S. economy as policymakers formulate their policy response. Notable among them are those of Chetty et al. (2020) and the Philadelphia Fed.[3] In addition, there are some revealing specialty studies and reports from the JPMorgan Chase Institute (for example, see Cox et al., 2020).

Chetty et al. (2020) build a publicly available platform that tracks economic activity at a granular level in real time using anonymized data from private companies. This illustrates how real-time economic tracking can help rapidly identify the origins of economic crises and facilitate ongoing evaluation of policy impacts. They report weekly statistics on consumer spending, business revenues, employment rates, and other key indicators disaggregated by county, industry, and income group. Their original paper featured impacts as of spring 2020, with the most recent data available on their website (https://trackthere covery.org/).

They show that high-income individuals reduced spending sharply in mid-March 2020 in areas with high rates of COVID-19 infection and in sectors that require physical interaction. This greatly reduced the revenues of small businesses in affluent zip codes that cater to high-income households. This led to a surge in unemployment claims in affluent areas. State-ordered re-openings had little impact in that stimulus payments to low-income households increased consumer spending sharply but had modest impact on employment in the short run.

The Philadelphia Fed has made a comprehensive effort to assemble data. This includes their own survey[4] as well as their utilizing Fiserv payments processing data. These efforts show that the share of those with severe income loss has slowed, but roughly a third of the population is quite adversely impacted. The fraction of respondents seeking assistance from family and friends, seeking

3. See the FRB-Philadelphia for their collection of research briefs at https://www .philadelphiafed.org/the-economy/covid19.

4. For example, https://www.philadelphiafed.org/-/media/frbp/assets/consumer-finance /reports/cfi-covid-19-survey-of-consumers.pdf

credit card and other loans, and deferring payments on mortgages and utilities increased sharply.

However, there is little balance sheet information in either the Chetty/ Hendren assemblages of data or the Philadelphia Fed sources. Higher income households that reduced their spending arguably accumulated liquid assets. But because we are not looking at the balance sheets of small businesses, we do not know how many can or will recover. Cox et al. (2020) report on a deteriorated cash position for small businesses.

For lower income households, Baker et al. (2020) explore responses to stimulus payments and individual heterogeneity in marginal propensities to consume (MPCs) by using high-frequency transaction data from SaverLife, a nonprofit that had been helping working families develop long-term saving habits and meet financial goals. In their data, individuals linked their financial accounts so that the authors would have access to de-identified bank account balances and transactions data. The point is that here one sees both flows and changes in assets consistently.

With this, Baker et al. (2020) document sharp and immediate responses to the stimulus payments. Greater income, larger income drops, and less liquidity are all associated with larger MPCs out of the stimulus payments. Liquidity on the balance sheet is the strongest predictor of such MPCs.

In contrast, the JPMorgan Chase Institute's report on the household data from its clients paints a different picture (Cox et al., 2020). Even low-income clients increased their liquid asset balances, relatively more than others. In addition to sample selection issues, one notes for the JP Morgan Chase data that there are few measured items on the balance sheets and there is no effort to reconcile income with balance sheet changes.

1.4   Inequality and Liberalization in Developing Countries: The Same Questions in Reverse

Simon Kuznets, who pioneered the development of national income accounts, is also a pioneer in the study of inequality. Of course, as noted, both strands come together here. The Kuznets curve is based on the idea that inequality is likely to increase along the development path as relatively few benefit much, but then inequality declines in a catch-up phase with rising levels of wages, education, and financial access. Data from some countries, such as Thailand, support the hypothesis, but not from others.

One does see in data that, over time, emerging market countries are becoming more open in trade and financial flows, both externally and internally—and hence are becoming more liberal. Still, key questions are raised. One seeks to disentangle the impact of real factors (movement in relative sectoral prices, which determine production and trade) from financial factors (lower interest rates, more liberal credit/asset ratios). One seeks to do this not only for households providing wage labor but also for households running farm/business projects, and in the context of diverse, heterogeneous village and regional economies. There is a parallel with the earlier policy discussion, except that here actuals and counterfactuals are reversed relative to that discussion. Above, the reference to policy concerned the impact of tariffs and what might have happened had they not been imposed. Here, we assess the impact of the observed liberalization on GDP and the distribution of income, but ask, what if the liberalization had not been allowed to happen? What if internal domestic restrictions on trade and financial flows had been imposed?

1.5   Outline of the Monograph

Here we summarize the flow of the monograph, starting first with a detailed summary of the work in Thailand, where we have the desired data and can use those data in models answering policy questions, and then moving to work in the United States, including what is being done on important policy questions with the more limited data, and, finally, what we would like to do in terms of constructing better data.

1.5.1   Thailand

To begin, we take advantage of the unusual data for Thailand. We proceed in two broad steps. The first, in Chapter 2, is to describe the creation of complete integrated financial accounts at the household and SME level. The second step, in Chapter 3, illustrates the power of this information for the generation of village-level national accounts and flow of funds. Chapter 4 develops an economic model of trade and financial integration, as if running a China shock in reverse.

More specifically, we: (1) use the preexisting complete financial accounts from a comprehensive, integrated survey for the sampled households (income statement, balance sheet, and cash flow statement), of which many are running small and medium enterprises, and we embrace the concept of financial accounting for firms, for all sectors; (2) create the village economic System of National Accounts (SNA) and balance of payments accounts from the detailed balance sheets and income statements made available from the first step; (3) generate stylized facts on within-village heterogeneity in wealth and productivity; (4) generate stylized facts on cross-regional variation in factor prices, factor intensities, financial obstacles, and openness; (5) compare the regional measures to national events and numbers; (6) construct a two-sector occupation-choice/trade/financially constrained open-economy model for each of the regions, grounded carefully around the observed micro and regional heterogeneity; (7) estimate/calibrate key parameters and unobserved variables, different across the diverse regions; (8) simulate and judge model performance against the data; (9) disentangle the contribution of real or financial factors by freezing one group or the other at their initial values and comparing them to the baseline simulations; and (10) impose real and financial frictions, or wedges, one at a time.

We find that the impact of real and financial factors can be heterogeneous and large, generating both gains and losses and non-monotone impacts across wealth classes and occupations, even when allowing for occupation shifts. We are able to map and quantify impacts back onto featured case-study households, to bring the analysis to life, going beyond anecdotal stories and conjectures.

More about the data: Townsend Thai surveys are stratified random samples covering rural and semi-urban areas. We use the monthly data from January 1999 to December 2005, annualized, so we have six years in total. We have a reasonably large sample of households for each village, and we aggregate up to the county level (with four randomly selected villages for each county). Two counties are in the agrarian Northeast and two are relatively close to Bangkok and the industrialized central core. These economies reflect the diversity within the country; e.g., the Northeast not only specializes in agriculture but also has relatively less real capital, and tends to be less open to trade flows. The Townsend Thai surveys illustrate how much can be done with relatively small samples, and can serve as a prototype for a similar effort in the United States.

From these data, we review and utilize the framework developed in Samphantharak and Townsend (2009), which created the balance sheet, income statement, and statement of cash flow for each of the households/businesses. These accounts are integrated in the sense that changes of stocks in the balance sheet and flows in income statements are consistent with each other, without any error.

We then follow the steps laid out in U.S. Department of Commerce (1985) to create integrated village economic accounts for Thailand. As noted, no agency has done this yet for the United States. In particular, we create the production account, appropriation account, saving-investment account, and balance of payments account. We are mindful that our data are not perfect, in particular, that there can be sampling error and that we cannot distinguish the source (village production vs. import) of all consumption data. We also need to decide in the end which variables to feature and use in the model, for example, real capital vs. financial assets such as cash, how to account for land, and so on. And, of course, there is the measurement error in the measured variables themselves to account for.

In terms of stylized facts, we feature movement over time as the country evolves with structural transformation and public policy. We look at the value of outstanding loans and the loan/wealth ratios, which, as anticipated, have been increasing, especially in the Northeast; the declining price of manufactured goods relative to agriculture; declining and converging real interest rates; rising and diverging real wages, especially in the Central region; and rising wage to interest rate ratios. We distinguish between labor-intensive agricultural production and capital-intensive manufacturing production; present evidence of constraints, in terms of credit and the heterogeneity of the marginal product of capital across high and low wealth households; and document varying degrees of openness. We stress that we have measures of the distributions of wealth and income, already anticipated in the discussion of distributional accounts in the United States and their shortcomings.

To calibrate the model, we act as if interest rates are accurately measured and taken as given (small open economy). We do not believe we see accurate measures of local relative prices, of agricultural vs. manufactured goods, or of borrowing limits. Relative prices are determined at the sector level, but the particular types of goods in the capital-intensive and labor-intensive sectors vary by region; available price indices are not sufficiently disaggregated to reflect this regional variation or shipping costs. Borrowing limits are an approximation to implicit and formal credit contracts, which are not modeled in detail here. Thus, these two variables—relative prices and borrowing limits—are calibrated to match the sectoral profit shares and the wage rates, respectively. We are able to match quite well.

To judge the performance of the model, we compare the model's predictions on occupations, income, and wealth with those of the actual households in the Townsend Thai data. We do a reasonable job predicting the occupational choices and the levels of total income and fixed assets of the sampled households, which we detail in a sample of case studies.

We run two counterfactual exercises, namely, freezing real (relative prices) and then financial factors (interest rates and borrowing limits) at their initial values, with the other variables (financial and then real, respectively) allowed to vary freely. We compare this in turn to the baseline simulations, where both real and financial factors are allowed to vary to match the wage rates and profit shares we see in the data. When only financial factors are allowed to vary, as, for example, in a counterfactual for the province Lopburi in Thailand's central corridor, the profit share of the capital-intensive sector is higher, whereas when we vary only relative prices, the profit share is lower. Under either of these counterfactual scenarios, the wage rate is higher than what we observe in the data.

In a more austere counterfactual, we impose trade frictions or financial frictions on the economy, one at a time. When trade frictions are imposed, the price of imported goods must increase relative to that of exported goods. So, it matters whether the local economy was initially importing labor-intensive goods or capital-intensive goods, raising the price of the factor that is used relatively intensively in the imported goods. The counterfactual with trade frictions can thus cause the wage rate to drop, if, for example, the price of the labor-intensive goods is lowered, with the lost demand for exports of those goods. Of course, similar arguments can be made for capital-intensive goods. When financial frictions are imposed, the interest rate will decrease (or increase) if the economy had been exporting savings or lending (or borrowing from abroad, out of the region). Thus, owners of capital experience large losses (or gains).

Finally, our model shows heterogeneous effects on the households' welfare. In these exercises, whether households are better off or worse off also depends on where they are in the ability and wealth distributions. For example, if trade frictions increase the price of capital-intensive goods relative to the price of labor-intensive goods, this will, in turn, lower the wage rate as there is less demand for labor. Then, high-ability, high-wealth households, comprising entrepreneurs in the capital-intensive sector hiring laborers, will benefit from trade frictions. On the other hand, the low-ability households comprising wageworkers will be worse off. Also, the very-high-ability households, comprising entrepreneurs in the labor-intensive sector, could face worse prices.

1.5.2 *Summary of Work in the U.S.*

We take the framework of Samphantharak and Townsend (2009) to well-known and widely used U.S. surveys in two ways. First, in Chapter 5, we assess the degree of integration in U.S. household surveys. We do this by creating complete financial accounts of surveyed households in each of the selected surveys, running code over measured variables. We also assess the degree of coverage of each survey. But our main point is that the errors between the changes in the balance sheet and the flows from the income statement are a measure of integration of the accounts, and unfortunately these errors typically are not small. Unlike the effort in Thailand, survey answers were not cross-checked with the integrated accounts in mind.

Second, also in Chapter 5, we then merge the framework of Samphantharak and Townsend with the Federal Reserve Bank of Boston surveys on payments to create a comprehensive statement of liquidity accounts, generalizing the notion of cash flow. Though we do this for households, the conceptualization would apply to other sectors of the National Income and Product Accounts (NIPA) and Flow of Funds Accounts.

In Chapter 6, we present the Integrated Macro Accounts of the United States, a joint effort of the Federal Reserve Board and the Bureau of Economic Analysis. These integrated accounts are consistent in principle with the integrated and complete financial accounts in Samphantharak and Townsend (2009). But, as the data are gathered by different agencies from different sources, lack of integration shows up in nontrivial discrepancies.

The final chapter envisions the next logical step, creating integrated financial accounts for the United States, from the ground up. This would come from a household and SME survey that combines field research with financial transactions data, then integrated with other data. A related top-down approach works with Federal Reserve Board and Bureau of Economic Analysis data to help bridge the gaps in what would be integrated regional accounts, in turn guiding the coordination of data and further survey efforts.

2

Townsend Thai Surveys
and Financial Accounts

IN THIS CHAPTER,[1] we outline various types of household surveys featuring financial aspects and then turn to the Townsend Thai data that is the basis of the work done in Thailand.

2.1 Household Surveys and Household Finance

Household surveys are essential to researchers for understanding household behavior and to governments for designing and evaluating policies. In principle, researchers should design a survey to reflect the objectives of their study. There are generally two broad types of household surveys. The first is a survey that is specific and limited to certain issues. The second, called a multi-topic or an integrated survey, contains a series of questionnaires that spans multiple topics. Examples of the integrated surveys include the World Bank's Living Standards Measurement Study (LSMS) surveys and the Family Life Surveys.

As reported in Grosh and Glewwe (2000), only 17 out of the 32 countries with LSMS surveys have repeated surveys, and the resurveys were not conducted on a high-frequency basis. Family Life Surveys have been conducted in Indonesia, in four waves, and in Mexico, in three.

1. Narapong Srivisal is a co-contributor of this chapter. We gratefully acknowledge permission from Cambridge University Press to reproduce, with edits, parts of Chapters 2, 3, and 4 from Samphantharak, Krislert, and Robert M. Townsend (2009), *Households as Corporate Firms: An Analysis of Household Finance Using Integrated Household Surveys and Corporate Financial Accounting*. Econometric Society Monographs. Cambridge; New York: Cambridge University Press.

Integrated household surveys generally consist of modules for households, communities, and prices. The household module generally asks for individual household information on demographic factors such as: composition, fertility, and migration; education; health; employment; production activities and income; consumption; savings; and financing (credits and transfers). Modules on communities and prices include environmental and geographic measurements (e.g., of rainfall and temperature), names of institutions (e.g., local banks and schools), and prices of inputs and outputs sold in the community. The information on community and prices may come from secondary sources (e.g., government statistics), direct observations of the field enumerators, or interviews of key informants of the community (e.g., a village head).

Another household survey that collects detailed information on household financial situations and transactions at a high frequency is the Financial Diaries project. The financial diary method was originally used by Rutherford (2002), who tracked the financial flows of several dozen households in Bangladesh every two weeks for a year. His objective was to collect information on the financial lives of poor people. He asked the households about their income and expenditure as well as how they saved and protected themselves against risks. Subsequently, Ruthven's (2002) study of households in India improved the method by adding new features into the project, namely the construction of a balance sheet for each household, and the inclusion of in-kind transactions in the questionnaire. However, the financial diaries were still mostly unstructured interviews and open-ended discussions. Recently, Collins (2005) made the financial diaries more structured, using a combination of closed-ended and open-ended questionnaires. Her study of approximately 180 households in South Africa during 2003–2005 was at the time the biggest set of data from surveys using financial diaries. There is now a 300-household study in Kenya. In total, financial diaries have been implemented in eight countries.

The Financial Diaries Project starts with an initial survey that documents the condition of the households at the beginning of the survey. Frequent revisits then gather additional information about what has occurred since the previous interview. Unlike integrated household surveys, the Financial Diaries project mainly focuses only on financial aspects of the households. The questionnaire is comprised of questions about a series of transactions related to household income, expenditure, financing, and savings. The expenditure, financing, and savings transactions are broken down to a very detailed level, such as spending on bedding, towels, and blankets, or on burial plans (funeral insurance). However, the questions about transactions on production activities and income are broad, asking, in the aggregate, about regular wages, business revenues, agricultural income from livestock, and agricultural income from crops. Information on nonfinancial aspects of the households is minimally collected (Morduch and Schneider, 2017).

2.2 Townsend Thai Data

The data used here come from the monthly household-level panel survey, which is a part of the larger Townsend Thai project. The monthly survey was conducted in two provinces in the Central region, Chachoengsao and Lopburi, and in two provinces in the Northeast region, Buriram and Sisaket. In each province, counties (tambons) were randomly picked, and then four villages in each county were chosen at random as well. For the chosen county of the monthly survey, approximately 45 households per each of the four villages of the county were sampled at random. The survey began in August 1998 with the baseline survey, which collected the data on the status of the sampled households, including their composition, wealth, and the occupations of their members. Then, in the monthly resurvey, the same households were interviewed for activities within them, including changes in their wealth, inputs, outputs, and any income received during the previous month. The resurvey started in September 1998. The results reported are drawn from an 84-month period (months 5–88). This period covers January 1999 to December 2005.

At the beginning of the survey, there are, again, approximately 45 households per village. However, during the 88-month period covered in our survey, the migration of village residents is unavoidable.[2] For every household in our survey that moves out of the village, a replacement household is added. However, for the purpose of constructing the village accounts, we decide to use the balanced panel data and to consider only households that stay for the entire 88-month period.

Villages in the Central provinces are relatively richer than villages in the Northeast provinces. The average net worth of households in Chachoengsao and Lopburi in 1999 was approximately $112,000 and $46,000, respectively,

2. We observe migration at individual and household levels. However, as will be shown, there are persistent differences in wage rates across regions. According to data from the Community Development Department (CDD), the fraction of households with migrants during 1988–1999 was between 22–32%.

while the average net worth of households in Buriram and Sisaket was approximately \$22,600 and \$18,600, respectively. Villages in the Central provinces also participate more in the capital-intensive production activities (e.g., operating fish and/or shrimp ponds, raising livestock), while villages in the Northeast focus on the labor-intensive activities (e.g., being rice farmers or wageworkers).

2.3 Households as Corporate Firms: Financial Statements of Individual Households

Samphantharak and Townsend (2009) propose a framework to create balance sheets, income statements, and statements of cash flow for households in developing countries. As they point out, many households in developing countries not only behave as consumers, supplying factors of production and consuming output, but also as firms in production activities. Conceptualizing a household as an analogue to a corporate firm, Samphantharak and Townsend (2009) use and modify the standards of corporate financial accounting to create household financial statements.

But the point goes beyond understanding the financial situation of a given household, which is also potentially running a business. The standards of corporate financial accounting allow the construction of consistent integrated measurements of wealth and income, integrated accounts, a subject to which we return, incorporating work in the United States.

Again, households in developing countries are not simply consumers supplying factor inputs and purchasing and consuming outputs. Many are also engaged in production through both farm and nonfarm activities. In essence, these households function as firms. To understand this analogy, we discuss first in what business activities a typical firm is engaged. Then we present the analogy of households as corporate firms. This analogy serves as our conceptual framework for the construction of integrated household financial accounts.

Following Hart (1995), and finance more generally, we define a firm as a collection of assets. To obtain these assets, a firm has to get the necessary financing. The two main sources of funds are the creditors and the owners. The owners of a firm are the shareholders. Funds from the creditors are the liabilities of the firm, while funds from the owners are the contributed capital from the shareholders. The firm uses its assets in production activities that potentially generate revenue. After deducting all costs of production, including the corporate income tax, the firm is left with net income. The firm then uses its net income to pay dividends to the shareholders. The remainder of net income goes back to the firm in the form of retained earnings. Retained earnings add to contributed capital, constituting the total shareholders' equity, which is the total claim of the owners on the firm's assets.

Similarly, a typical household performs several activities. A household owns assets such as a house, farmland, livestock, and a tractor.[3] Again, to acquire these assets, a household gets funds from two main sources: the creditors and the owners. The owners of a household are the *household members*. Funds from the creditors (i.e., the household's debts) are the liabilities of the household. Funds from the owners are the contributed capital from the household members. The household uses its assets in production activities that potentially generate revenue. These activities could be cultivation, aquaculture, livestock raising, provision of labor services, or other business. Subtracting all costs of production and the personal income tax, the household is left with the after-tax net income (i.e., the household's *disposable income*). The household then uses its disposable income to pay "dividends" to the owners. The dividends come in the form of the *consumption* of household members. The remainder of the net income (i.e., the "retained earnings") is the household's *savings*. Savings add to the contributed capital or initial wealth, making the total *wealth* of the household, which is the total claim of the household members over the household assets. With positive savings, household assets increase by the same amount as the increase in wealth. Wealth is the residual claim, the assets of the household in excess of its liabilities to the creditors.

To be clear, households are by nature different from firms, especially in terms of their organizational structure and components. One difference is the definition of the household versus the firm. Usually, corporate financial accounting uses a legal definition to identify a corporate firm. A firm is a business entity registered with the government and considered as a judicial person. Unlike a registered firm, a household consists of a collection of individuals. Although each individual does register with the government as a member of a given household, this criterion does not coincide with the definition of household in a typical household survey, where individuals are considered to be in the same household if they live in the same housing structure

---

3. More generally, household assets also include financial assets such as deposits at commercial banks and from informal lending.

for at least a certain number of days or if they share certain common expenses together.[4]

However, despite the definition, a household could be viewed as an organization analogous to a corporate firm. Furthermore, we could view an extended household as a conglomerate with multiple divisions, and a nexus of households related by kinship as a business group. Also, the size of a household changes when members migrate into or out of the household. Migration into a household, possibly by marriage, with the introduction of personal assets that contribute to the total household assets, is analogous to the issuing and selling of shares to new shareholders in order to capitalize, or analogous to a business merger or takeover. Likewise, a divorce in or the dissolution of a household could be seen as a spin-off.

Another difference concerns ownership and dividends. The ownership of a registered corporate firm is well defined. Each shareholder owns the firm proportionally to the number of shares she holds. Dividends are usually paid on or defined by a per-share basis. But ownership within a household may be ambiguous. Although we can think of household members as the owners of the household, typically it is not clear what proportion of the household's assets is owned by each household member. Similarly, "dividends" paid to each household member in the form of consumption is not typically measured and may not be determined by the member's ownership over the household's assets. Note that the implication of considering a household as a monolithic entity is that we assume that the household is a decision making unit, and we ignore any within-household decision making and bargaining processes.

2.4 Overview of Financial Accounting

Once we have a conceptual framework that views households as corporate firms, the next step is to modify corporate financial accounting to apply it to the households. Standard financial accounting presents the financial situation of a firm in three main accounts: (1) the balance sheet, (2) the income statement, and (3) the statement of cash flows. This section provides an overview of corporate financial accounting concepts, describing what they are and why we need each of them. We also discuss how each account is related to the study of

4. For example, the Townsend Thai Monthly Survey defines an individual as a household member if he or she lives in the same housing structure for at least 15 days since the previous monthly interview.

household finance. This background is necessary for the construction of financial statements from a household survey that we present later in this monograph. Unless stated otherwise, the concepts and methods used in this monograph are standard and follow those presented in Stickney and Weil (2003).

2.4.1 Balance Sheet

The balance sheet of a firm presents the financial position of the firm at a given point of time. The major items in the balance sheet are assets, liabilities, and shareholders' equity. Assets are economic resources with the potential to provide future benefit to a firm. Liabilities are creditors' claims on the assets of the firm. Shareholders' equity shows the amount of funds the owners have provided to the firm, which is also their claim on the assets of the firm. Claims on assets coming from shareholders' equity are the excess of assets beyond those required to meet creditors' claims. As a firm must invest somewhere the resources it gets from financing, the balance sheet shows the obvious identity that total assets must equal the sum of total liabilities and shareholders' equity.

For households, the balance sheet consists of three major items—*household assets, household liabilities,* and *household wealth.* Examples of household assets are cash on hand, financial claims such as deposits at financial institutions or informal lending, various types of inventories, and fixed assets such as land, building, and equipment. Household liabilities are debts, borrowed from both financial institutions and people, formally and informally. The residual claim of household members over household assets in excess of liabilities is the wealth of the household. The wealth of the household changes over time due either to savings out of household net income or to other transactions such as gifts. These savings and gifts could be positive or negative.

2.4.2 Income Statement

The income statement is the statement of revenues, costs, gains, and losses over a period of time, ending with net income during the period. Net income is total revenue minus total costs. Revenues are in essence net assets flowing into a firm when it sells goods or provides services. Costs are in essence net assets utilized by a firm in the process of generating revenue. The income statement therefore presents the performance of the operating activities of a firm over a specified period of time.

There are two approaches to the income statement. The cash basis of accounting looks at the revenues and the expenses of a firm as it receives or spends cash. This approach is acceptable when (1) a firm has small changes in inventories and (2) the purchase of inputs, the production, and the sale of outputs occur in the same period. Otherwise, cash inflows from sales in one, given period could relate to the production and cash outflows from the purchase of inputs in preceding periods. An alternative approach is the accrual basis of accounting, where revenues and costs are realized (charged) when the firm sells the output. Therefore, since the revenues and the costs of one period relate to the output from the same activity or asset, the accrual-basis income statement tells more accurately the performance and profitability of the firm in its use of assets rather than the possibly more volatile cash-basis income statement.

Households engage in activities that take several months or years to complete. This is especially the case for households in developing countries, where agricultural cultivation and livestock raising are common practices. Also, inventories could play an important role, particularly for agricultural production, which has high fluctuations of input and output prices over the year. These problems are more acute the more frequently the data are gathered. We thus choose to follow the accrual basis of income when we construct accounts for households in developing countries, as in this monograph. It is important to keep in mind that the net income of the household presented here is not necessary the *cash* income the household receives. However, we can retrieve the cash income from the statement of cash flows, which we will discuss below.

2.4.3   *Statement of Cash Flows*

The statement of cash flows is a schedule or record of an entity's cash receipts from and payments to outsiders over a period of time. The basic idea is that each cash transaction implicitly involves either cash incoming or cash outgoing. The cash-inflow transactions are positively recorded while the cash-outflow transactions are negatively recorded. Summing the values of all transactions yields the net change in the stock of cash held by the firm over the period of time. Usually, the transactions are classified according to their functions: operating, investing, or financing.

There are two main reasons why we need the statement of cash flows in addition to the balance sheet and the income statement. First, as just noted, the net income from the income statement under the accrual basis of accounting is not equal to the net inflow of cash from operations. Usually firms have expenses on inputs (cash outflow) before the period of revenue from the sale of the associated outputs (cash inflow). These mismatched flows of funds could lead to a shortfall of cash, or in short, a liquidity problem. The balance sheet and the income statement do not provide information on the liquidity of the firm. Second, and relatedly, cash inflows and cash outflows may not be from production. Investing and financing activities are also involved in cash flows. Examples of these activities include accumulation of fixed assets, lending and borrowing, dividend payouts, and capitalization by issuance of new shares.

By definition, the total cash outflows must equal total cash inflows plus a decrease in cash holding of the firm, i.e., the firm's spending must be financed from somewhere. A firm's financing could be from either (1) internal sources such as operating income or cash on hand, or (2) external sources such as borrowings or the sale of newly issued shares. This identity is commonly known as the cash-flow constraint in corporate finance literature. Equivalently, we could say that total funds from internal and external financing must be spent somewhere.

Analogously, a household faces a similar constraint, as stated in its budget equation. Household spending during a particular period must be financed from somewhere—internal or external. We classify each household transaction as falling into one of three categories: (1) production, (2) consumption and investment, and (3) financing. Equation (2.1), below, illustrates a simple budget constraint of a typical household in period t:

$$C_t + I_t = Y_t + F_t \qquad\qquad (2.1)$$

The left-hand side is the spending of the household, consisting of consumption expenditure, C_t, and investment in fixed assets or capital expenditure, I_t. The right-hand side is the source of funds of the household, consisting of the household's cash flow from production, Y_t, and various financing devices, F_t, such as cash, deposits at financial institutions, borrowings, and gifts.[5] It is sometimes ambiguous how to classify a transaction into these categories. Investment transactions deserve special attention. Conventionally, investment in real fixed assets is considered as a cash outflow in the investment category, called capital expenditure,

5. Interest revenues and expenses are included in the total net income, and hence are cash flows from production.

while investment in financial assets (e.g., loans) is entered as cash outflows in the financing category. Note that an income-generating production activity is separate from financing activity. In other words, if we subtract the cash flow from production Y_t from the left-hand side of the equation (2.1), we define a budget deficit D_t, the excess of cash consumption and investment expenditures over cash flow from production, to be financed in some way, F_t.

To calculate the cash flow from production, Y_t, we use household net income from the income statement and make the following relevant adjustments. These adjustments are transactions that involve production activities but are not cash-related. First, we subtract any increase in inventory and any increase in accounts receivable from net income. An increase in inventory is a cost of multi-period production (including storage activity) that typically involves cash outflow, but that has not yet entered the current period net income calculation. An increase in accounts receivable, on the other hand, is embedded in the revenue and net income, even though they have not yet been paid in cash. Second, we add depreciation and an increase in accounts payable back into net income. Depreciation was deducted as cost of production even though there was no actual cash paid out. Similarly, an increase in accounts payable reflects the costs that the household has not actually paid to the suppliers yet. Third, we subtract unrealized capital gains and add unrealized capital losses to net income. Unrealized capital gains were a part of positive income although there was no actual cash inflow. Unrealized capital losses were a part of negative income while there was no actual cash outflow. Finally, we subtract consumption of household-produced outputs from net income to separate the within-household transactions from transactions with the market, as the former do not affect household liquidity. Consumption of household-produced items is a part of household income, but it is not a cash inflow.

2.5 Household Consolidated Financial Statements

Household consolidated financial statements consider a household's financial situation in aggregate and do not distinguish between different production activities the household performs. The household consolidated balance sheet represents the total wealth of the household. Total assets of the household consist of real assets and financial assets. Real assets are used in agriculture, business, livestock (including the animals themselves), fish/shrimp farming, and other household activities. Financial assets such as informal loans and formal savings at financial institutions are generally not logically allocated to any particular production activity. The total liability of the household is its indebtedness, which mostly consists of borrowings. Household debts could be either for consumption or for production, and in the consolidated account we need not distinguish between the two. The household members' wealth is equal to the total assets of the household net of the household members' indebtedness. The household consolidated income statement is the total net income of the household. Again, it is possible that a particular household may be involved in more than one production activity. For example, a farming household may grow crops and raise chickens at the same time. In this case, the household acts as a diversified conglomerate. Similarly, the household consolidated statement of cash flows presents the net flows of cash between the household and other entities outside the household. Again, we do not distinguish between transactions of family members within the household.

We use three accounting identities to confirm that our aggregate accounts are constructed correctly: (1) In the consolidated balance sheet, household total assets must equal the sum of household total liabilities and household wealth. (2) An increase in household wealth from the consolidated balance sheet must equal the sum of gifts received and savings, where gifts received are from the consolidated statement of cash flows, and savings are the difference between accrued net income (from all production activities) and household consumption from the consolidated income statement. (3) The net change in cash from the consolidated statement of cash flows must equal the change in cash from the consolidated balance sheet.

2.6   Constructing Household Financial Statements from a Household Survey

Several transactions are unique to households in developing countries. Therefore, some modifications of the financial accounts are needed.

2.6.1   Tangible Assets, Liabilities, and Wealth

To construct a balance sheet for each household, we need information on tangible assets and liabilities. As argued by Stickney and Weil (2003), corporate financial accounting has never satisfactorily defined the distinction between tangible and intangible assets. Typically, accountants define intangibles by giving an exhaustive list, and everything not on the list is tangible. Here, however, we explicitly define tangible assets to include physical and financial assets. Intangible assets are education and health human capital as well as other assets that are not tangible.

Many household surveys get information on initial assets from a baseline survey. For example, the Townsend Thai Monthly Survey questionnaires ask whether a household owns a television, a motorcycle, an automobile, a tractor, a sprinkler, a water pump, a chicken coop, a building, or other valuable assets. Households are asked when each asset was acquired and the value of the asset at acquisition. A depreciation formula can then be used to get current values. Exceptions are land and fishponds, which in the Townsend Thai Monthly Survey are not depreciated. Alternatively, as in the Living Standards Measurement Study (LSMS) surveys, respondents are asked how much they could obtain for an asset if it were sold at the time of the interview. Financial assets such as deposits at financial institutions and loans to other households are typically given nominal values as amounts owned or due, distinguishing principal from interest. Questions are also administered in the Townsend Thai baseline instruments about crop inventories and business inventories. A decision was made not to ask about initial cash holding or the value of jewelry or gold as this was viewed as too intrusive and could put the rest of the survey at risk. As for liabilities, the household is asked in the initial baseline for an enumeration of principal and interest due.

Interviewers go back to the households and update panel data with current information from events since the last interview. In the Townsend Thai Monthly Survey, households are asked about acquisition of assets, e.g., purchases, gifts, and the birth of livestock, and disposal of assets, e.g., sales, losses, disbursements of assets, and the death of livestock. The survey also asks about the values associated with each asset transaction. Deposits and withdrawals of savings are tracked. Questions are asked about changes in inventory. New borrowings since the last interview and repayment of previously held debt are measured. If the resurvey questionnaires distinguish between in-kind and cash transactions, then one can estimate changes in cash holdings. If we make an arbitrary guess about initial balances, then we can enter cash on hand on the balance sheet each month.

Following a convention in corporate financial accounting, financial assets and liabilities appear on the balance sheet at their net present cash value. Nonmonetary assets such as land, building, and equipment appear at acquisition cost. We then adjust downward the nonmonetary assets, except for land, to reflect depreciation. The acquisition value of land may underestimate the current value of a household's total assets. However, this problem is minor in the Townsend Thai Monthly Survey, as we do update the value of land when there is a major change on the plot, such as the construction of a new road nearby or some other land improvement (e.g., the building of a pond). We think that the approach we propose in this manuscript is less subject to measurement error than estimating the present value of the land every month. The main reason for this is that the market for land is thin, making the current price of land unavailable or unreliable. This is also the reason why standard corporate financial accounting adopts the acquisition value rather than evaluate the present value of land.[6]

2.6.2 *Gifts and Transfers*

Gifts and transfers received by a household are special transactions, since they contribute to the wealth of the household without being directly related to the production process. That is, gifts are not part of net income from production activities per se. In this section, we first provide our general treatment of these transactions, and then discuss issues related to two special types of gifts and transfers to a household that deserve further attention, namely remittances and government transfers.

2.6.3 *General Treatment of Gifts and Transfers*

In corporate financial accounting, donations received by a firm are credited to shareholders' equity under a special line item called donated capital.[7] They, however, do not enter the income statement of the firm, since they do not impact the profits or losses of a firm's production activities. National Income

---

6. In fact, we do ask the households in our survey about their assessment of the value of land. However, their assessment does not change much over time unless there are substantial improvements on land, which we have already taken into account. This is consistent with the fact that land market in rural areas is not liquid, so the current market price is not available.

7. The term *donated capital* is used in order to distinguish donations from contributed capital. Gifts or donations involve assets flowing into the firm without the issuing of shares or the compromising of other owners' equity interest in return. Although we define contributed capital as total initial wealth of the household without distinguishing whether the initial wealth was from past savings of the household or from gifts received in previous periods, subsequent gifts received by the household are recorded in a separate accounting item as cumulated net gifts received. As we discuss later in this section, a person who provides gifts to a household may have claims over the household's assets, although the claims are implicit.

and Product Accounts (NIPA) treat gifts and transfers to a household differently. Although gifts are not related to production and are not included in the national product calculation, they are a part of the personal income of a household in the personal income and outlay account of NIPA. Here, the accounts follow the guideline from corporate financial accounts, i.e., of not treating gifts and transfers as income, for two reasons. First of all, we are interested in the productivity of the household enterprise, which argues for using net income derived only from production activities. Also, gifts are commonly observed in developing economies as a financing mechanism, which argues for the treatment of gifts and transfers as cash inflows from financing.

Specifically, when a household receives a gift, for example, in the form of cash, we record it as a cash-inflow transaction in the statement of cash flows. Simultaneously, the cash on hand of the household increases by the same amount, so we add the value of this gift to the cash on hand item on the asset side of the balance sheet. Unlike borrowings, the gift is not a household's liability, as it is not a simple debt. Also, as noted, the gift is not a part of the household income from production, so it is not a part of the savings of the household either. Instead, we create a new line item under household wealth called cumulative net gifts received. Any gifts received are added to this item in the balance sheet. In the end, an increase in cash holding in the current period relative to the previous period on the asset side is identical to an increase in household wealth on the liability and wealth (equity) side. This increase in cash is also identical to the change in cash in the statement of cash flows as a cash inflow from financing. Likewise, giving cash to others is considered as a cash outflow in the statement of cash flow, and is also subtracted from cash holding and cumulative net gifts received on the balance sheet. Note again that this transaction never enters the income statement.

An incoming gift is interpreted as an increase in wealth, and it is comparable to new equity issued to shareholders as part of a firm's capitalization activity. The new shareholders have claims on the (additional) assets of the firm. Similarly, non-altruistic gift providers, who naturally expect reciprocity, also have *implicit* claims on household assets. However, the claims of gift providers may have less seniority than the claims from creditors and members of the household. They have such low seniority that laws do not protect them.[8]

---

8. In fact, the household may provide gifts back voluntarily in expectation to receive more gifts in the future, or the household may be forced to reciprocate because of social norms.

Note that since we list gifts and transfers as a separate item in the household's statement of cash flows (under financing activities), we can compute household personal income directly from our accrued net income plus net gifts received. Consequently, an increase in household wealth comes from two sources: gifts received and household savings. Again, in our context, household savings are defined as accrued net income less household consumption. This definition of savings for our households is therefore slightly different from that defined for households in NIPA, i.e., personal income less consumption. Our savings, however, are consistent with retained earnings in corporate financial accounts, which make a distinction between an increase in shareholders' equity from retained earnings and an increase from donations or transfers.

2.6.4 Remittances

Remittances are resources given to a household by someone who lives in a distant location and does not reside in the same building structure as the household. By our definition of the household in the survey, the person could be a migrant, and therefore is not considered as a household member, even though the person might well be a relative. Examples of these individuals in the Townsend Thai surveys include children of the household head who live and work in Bangkok or other provinces, and occasionally send money back to their parents living in the village. Consequently, we have to treat remittances in the same way as other gifts. They are not entered into the household income statement. They are simultaneously recorded as an increase in cumulative net gifts received and an increase in assets in the balance sheet, and as cash inflow under the financing category in the statement of cash flows.

Alternatively, some household surveys may attempt to follow individuals even when they have moved out and no longer live in the household's building structure. This is the case with the Yale Economic Growth Center surveys in Ghana and Tamil Nadu, India. In such cases, the definition of a surveyed household could be changed so that the household would still include a member who lives at a distance but sends money back home, given that the household members share the pool of resources and make certain household decisions collectively. The remittances from this person would therefore be counted as a part of household labor income.[9] The bottom line is that the

9. This is similar to remittances from a national citizen working abroad being counted as national income in NIPA.

treatment of remittances as gifts versus labor income depends on the definition of households in the survey.

2.6.5 Inventories

Many households in developing economies are engaged in farm and nonfarm
production activities that span over more than one period. These activities
include inventory storage and multi-period production. We consider each of
them in this section.

For households that hold inventory as working capital (say, retail business or
even agricultural households with work-in-process inventory), changes in inventory are to some extent exogenous, and dictated by a product cycle, supply conditions, or market demand. In this case, the ultimate sale of inventory should be
considered as income. For households that hold inventory strategically (say,
agricultural households that hold crops in inventory, waiting for the crop price
to rise), the sale of inventory should also be considered as income-generating
activity, as storage provides a risk-bearing service. Here, in the construction of
the accounts we treat the change in inventory as related to cash flow from production and treat the capital gain or loss from holding inventory as a revenue or
cost of a storage activity. Inventory is not treated as a buffer stock.

The following are types of inventories: cultivation input inventory (such as
fertilizer), cultivation work-in-process inventory (such as not-yet-harvested
crops), cultivation finished-goods inventory (such as harvested rice grains),
livestock input inventory (such as animal feed), livestock work-in-process inventory, livestock finished-goods inventory (such as chicken eggs), fish input
inventory, fish work-in-process inventory, fish finished-goods inventory, business input inventory (such as cloth for a tailor), business work-in-process inventory
(such as unfinished furniture for a carpenter), business finished-goods inventory (such as pottery and local liquor), and business goods for resale (for a retail
store). These inventories are a part of working capital of businesses, held for the
purpose of business as usual, and therefore are not considered as fixed assets.

2.6.6 Multi-period Production: Cultivation, Livestock,
and Non-retail Business Activities

The LSMS and other integrated household surveys do not measure net income
directly in a single module but gather information on revenues and costs in a
series of activity modules: cultivation, aquaculture (fish and shrimp), livestock

activity, personal or family business, and labor services. In order to take into account the difference in the timing of acquisitions, uses, harvests, and sales of inventories, the Townsend Thai Monthly Survey asks first for the (value and quantity of) inputs acquired since the previous interview, and then for the actual (value and quantity of) inputs used on land plots. Likewise, the survey asks first for the (value and quantity of) outputs harvested since the previous interview, and then the (value and quantity of) sales, household consumption, gifts, and storage. An inventory account can thus be constructed. These issues of timing, inputs purchased and used, and outputs produced and sold are not trivial, and lie at the heart of the distinction between accrued income and cash flow from production.

2.6.6.1 MULTI-PERIOD PRODUCTION: MERCHANDISING RETAIL BUSINESS

For the nonagricultural, merchandising retail business households, such as those with local convenience stores, keeping track of the in-transactions and out-transactions of business inventory is very difficult, if not impossible. This is mainly due to the heterogeneous types of inventory and a large number of transactions daily (and hence monthly). These problems could exacerbate measurement errors if we adopt the transaction-based questionnaire described above. De Mel, McKenzie, and Woodruff (2008) suggest that it is better to ask for the revenues and the average markups of sales over input costs to adjust for timing mismatch. With this information we can compute the gains and losses between acquisitions and sales. By coincidence, this is essentially the method we use in the Townsend Thai Monthly Survey when we compute profits from a household's nonagricultural business. We, however, compute the markups using the total revenue from sales over the past three months, divided by the total cost of input inventory over the same period. This calculation implicitly assumes that the average number of days that goods are in inventory is less than three months.[10]

---

10. The Townsend Thai Monthly Survey did not ask explicitly about the markups of households' retail business enterprises.

2.6.6.2 OUTPUTS FROM ONE PRODUCTION
ACTIVITY AS INPUTS IN OTHERS

A household is typically engaged in many production activities. Many households use outputs produced from one production activity as inputs in other production activities. We treat this transaction as if the household sold the outputs from one activity (in a market), and then repurchased the same commodity at the same value (from the same market) as the inputs for the other activities. For example, a household may raise chickens and use their eggs as an input for food sold in its restaurant. If the net income from the second activity is realized in the same period, there is no change in both total household net income and total cash flow from production because the revenue from one activity is completely offset by the cost from the other activity.

However, the net income of the second activity may not be realized in the same period. For example, a household may use manure from livestock as fertilizer in crop production. For the income statement, the effect is nontrivial. We act as if the household sold the manure and therefore record the transaction in the current period income statement. The repurchase of the manure will not enter the income statement until the harvest period of the crop. There is no change in the total cash flow from production because there was no cash involved in these household transactions, or technically because the cash inflow from manure is offset by the cash outflow for the increase in inventory held by the household, both in the statement of cash flows. Finally, in the balance sheet, this transaction is recorded simultaneously as an increase in household cumulative savings (income without consumption) and an increase in work-in-process inventory.

2.6.7 Consumption of Household-Produced Outputs and Other Consumption Expenditures

It is common for agricultural households to consume crops grown on their plots or animals raised on their farms. At a smaller scale, households usually grow vegetables in the backyard. As already noted, in the household financial statements, the consumption of household-produced outputs is recorded under both consumption and production activities, as if the household produced and sold the product to the market, and then repurchased and consumed it. Thus, output produced and eaten is treated both as income and consumption. Households also catch and consume fish, gather and consume herbs, and gather wood to produce charcoal. All of these are entered as income from other production activities as well as (food or nonfood) consumption.

Households may purchase goods (such as rice) in large amounts, put them in inventory, and gradually consume them over time. As before, we view storage as another type of multi-period production technology, though in this case it is storage of purchased goods. When a household consumes goods from inventory, we treat the transaction as if the household sold the goods in a market and simultaneously repurchased them back as consumption goods, and we record the transaction in the income statement. If the value of the goods at the time of the consumption is the same as the value at the time of the purchase, then the net income (from storage) is zero. If the values are not the same, the difference will be reflected as a capital gain or loss. Note that purchasing goods and putting them in inventory in the earlier month is considered a cash outflow, as reflected by an increase in inventory during the month of the purchase. However, consuming out of inventory does not affect the total cash flow from production during the month of the consumption. This is because net profit (from capital gain and loss), decrease in inventory, and consumption of household-produced (stored) items completely cancel out.

Many consumption items do not require unusual treatment. Many purchases within a month are equivalent to their uses. Examples of these purchases are those of perishable items and utility payments. Ideally, consumption items distinguish between value and quantity, so as to measure prices. Questions are asked about each item individually, at a fine level of disaggregation, depending on the survey. This disaggregation allows us to categorize food versus nonfood items, and durable goods such as clothing versus nondurable commodities.[11]

Some items such as gasoline, electricity, and other utilities are easy to record as expenditures, but raise obvious issues. They could be considered as household consumption expenses or cost of production in household production activities like cultivation or business. With limited information in the Townsend Thai Monthly Survey, we treat all of these expenses as a household's nonfood consumption expenditure in this monograph.

---

11. Recall that usually there is also a separate module for household fixed assets.

2.6.8 In-Kind Transactions

Noncash transactions are not included in the standard statement of cash flows for a corporate firm since they do not change cash holdings. These noncash trans-actions are reported in a separate note schedule.[12] In our framework, however, we decide to include both cash and noncash transactions with outside entities in the statement of cash flows. We do this for several reasons. First, barter ex-changes are common in developing economies. Rice, frequently bartered, is like commodity money. Other in-kind transactions such as in-kind loans and gifts are also observed. As we are interested in the overall financing of household budget, including both cash and in-kind transactions in the budget analysis seems essential. Dropping noncash transactions would imply that we discard some useful information from our analysis. For example, if household consumption were entirely from gifts (maybe from relatives), the standard statement of cash flows would show both consumption and gifts of this household as zeros whereas in some sense both are positive. The problem is similar when the household uses inputs (such as fertilizer) acquired as gifts (say, from the government). Second, the assumption of liquidity as reflected by cash alone is not entirely appropriate for households in developing coun-tries. The ability to use commodities as a medium of exchange may help households mitigate the problem of a cash-only budget constraint.[13]

For these reasons, we treat all outside-household transactions in the standard household budget equation as if they were in cash. In the case that a transaction is not cash-related, we view the transaction as a combination of two cash-equivalent transactions. For example, if a household consumes rice borrowed from its neighbor, we will act as if the household borrows cash from its neighbor and uses that cash to purchase the rice. In effect, there is a cash outflow for con-sumption and, simultaneously, there is a cash inflow from borrowing. Therefore, despite changes in the entries in the statement of cash flows, there is no real change in the bottom line—the cash held by the household is unaltered.[14]

12. See Stickney and Weil (2003) p. 183.

13. In practice, it is a judgment call as to which objects are commonly accepted and liquid enough to be used as media of exchange. Lim and Townsend (1998) provide discussion on this issue.

14. Again, although the net change in cash is zero, the change in cash flows from consump-tion and investment and the change in cash flows from financing are nonzero. They exactly cancel each other out.

2.6.9 Depreciation of Fixed Assets

The common approach used for depreciation in corporate financial accounting is the straight-line method. Under this method, depreciation is deducted equally (in value) over time until the value of assets becomes zero. Applying this method to a large household survey is extremely complicated because it requires a separate account to trace the current value of *each* asset of each household in each period. To incorporate depreciation into our accounts, we decided to use a constant depreciation rate method instead. This method is relatively simple to implement in the household data. Specifically, one can assume a constant depreciation rate for a given category of assets, and then use it to compute depreciation value (in dollars) based on the value of the assets in the previous period. For the Townsend Thai Monthly Survey, we arbitrarily assume a 10% annual depreciation of fixed assets other than land.

As for the account entries, depreciation is simultaneously deducted from the assets and cumulative savings in the balance sheet, i.e., it is treated as an expense in the income statement. As discussed earlier, depreciation does not involve any actual cash (or in-kind) flow out of the household, so we add depreciation back, as a cash inflow, when we adjust the net income to get the cash flow from production in the statement of cash flows.

2.6.10 Livestock

Livestock raises a unique issue. In some cases, household revenues are from selling the outputs produced by the animals (such as chicken eggs or cow milk), and in other cases revenues are from selling the animals themselves (such as chickens or cows). To address this issue, we consider the animals as one type of household asset and distinguish between the two different incomes generated by the livestock. For example, when a household sells milk, we treat the transaction as revenue from livestock activity. Likewise, spending on animal feed and vaccine is recorded as a cost of livestock activity. However, if the household sells the cows, alive or dead, we consider the income as capital gain (or loss, if the sale price is lower than the purchase price) from livestock assets.

Relatedly, as we consider livestock as an asset, we depreciate the livestock as they age. The depreciation rate is computed from the average life expectancy of the animal and is different for different types of animals, based on field experience and conversations with the villagers. For example, in this monograph we assume that a mature cow depreciates at a constant rate of 1% per month, or approximately 12% per year. This rate implies that an average mature cow lives for approximately 8 years. When an animal dies prematurely, we treat it as capital loss. When a new animal is born or when a young animal becomes mature, we consider it as capital gain within the total livestock asset category.

2.6.11 Loan Payments, Principal Repayments, and Interest Payments

Unlike formal credits with financial institutions, much of the lending and borrowing in developing countries is informal. Although household surveys usually ask detailed questions about repayment of loans, it is sometimes impossible to distinguish between the interest payment and the principal repayment in the compositions of the periodic payments of these loans. For example, a household may know just how much it has to repay the lender in a particular period and for how many periods, but the household does not know what portion of the payment is the interest and what portion is the principal repayment.

To our knowledge, there is no obvious way to deal with this problem. An alternative is that, for each loan, one could compute the total payment over the loan life and use it to infer the effective interest rate charged on the principal. This method allows a researcher to compute an amortization schedule for each loan, decomposing the periodic payments into interest payments and principal repayments. However, this method poses a problem for loans that have not yet reached maturity, since we cannot compute the total payment. Instead, we follow another method and assume that all payments go to principal repayment first. Once the principal has been fully paid, the remainder is treated as interest payment. The obvious drawback of this approach is that the interest payments will not enter the statement of income until the principal is fully repaid, making it lumpy. Note that the way we decompose the periodic loan payments also affects the net income and the cash flow from production because the interest payments are recorded period-by-period as interest expense (for the borrowers) or interest revenues (for the lenders). In sum, we should be very cautious when we analyze households with interest revenues or expenses if these accounts form a large part of net income and cash flow.

Finally, our treatment of interest and principal repayment acts as if loans are simple debt, not state-contingent securities. In practice, the principal of a loan may be adjusted if the borrower is suffering from adverse events. In some data, the lender gets repaid more if the lender is suffering from adverse events (Udry, 1994). These contingencies are unfortunately not clearly enumerated beforehand, and it is difficult to distinguish lower or higher total repayment due to adverse events on the part of the borrower or lender from interest rates, which vary over time and by loan. Nevertheless, our method for treating the interest expense category captures in part the premium (a higher than typical rate for the lender with adverse shocks) and the indemnity (a lower than typical rate for a borrower having difficulties) that flow from implicit insurance arrangements.

2.7 Transaction-Based Accounting

In this section we select some transactions commonly made by households in developing economies and show how to record them in the household financial statements. The examples are shown in Table 2.1. The first column describes the transaction. The second column shows an example of the questions in survey questionnaires associated with the transaction. These questions are taken from the Townsend Thai Monthly Survey. The third, fourth, and fifth columns show the corresponding entries on the balance sheet, income statement, and statement of cash flows, respectively. The last column contains remarks crucial to understanding the entries of the transaction to various accounts.[15]

2.8 Financial Statements of Example Households

In this section, we illustrate the financial statements by looking at example households. We will also come back to these particular households when we look at the impact of the trade and financial counterfactuals that we consider.

---

15. The detailed algorithm for constructing household financial statements for those surveyed in the Townsend Thai Monthly Survey is presented in Pawasutipaisit et al. (2010).

TABLE 2.1. Examples of transactions and their records.

Transaction	Example of corresponding survey questions	Balance sheet	Income statement	Statement of cash flows	Remarks
Receive wage income in cash	**JM4D** What is the total amount of cash payments that you received since the last interview for doing this job? Include the value of any cash tips, bonuses or overtime payments. If no cash payments were received, record 0.	Increase in cash; increase in cumulative savings	Revenue from labor	Net income (cash inflow)	
Use cash to pay telephone bill	**XM1A** [6] Since the last interview, have you or members of your household made any cash purchases of [telephone and telecommunication services]? If yes, what is the total amount that you and members of your household have spent on [telephone and telecommunication services] since the last interview?	Decrease in cash; decrease in cumulative savings	Consumption	Consumption (cash outflow)	
Deposit cash with the production credit group	**SM3B** How much have you deposited to [the production credit group] in total since the last interview?	Decrease in cash; increase in deposits at financial institutions		Increase in deposits at financial institutions (cash outflow)	
Sell calves for cash	**IM7C** What is the value of [the baby cows] you got rid of in this transaction? **IM7E** What kind of transaction was this? (1 = sell live animal for cash or credit) **IM7F** How much cash did you receive in total for this livestock? (If no cash was received, record 0)	Increase in cash, decrease in livestock assets; increase in cumulative savings	Capital gain from livestock	Net income (cash inflow); decrease in livestock assets (cash inflow)	1. We consider milk cows as livestock assets similar to fixed assets. 2. Increase in cumulative savings = Capital gain from livestock. 3. Total cash inflows = Total cash revenue.

(continued)

Event	Survey question	Accounting entry	Category	Income / cash flow	Notes
Lose value of mature milk cows due to their depreciation (from getting older)	*See last column of this row*	Decrease in livestock assets; decrease in cumulative savings	Livestock depreciation	(Negative) net income (cash outflow); depreciation (cash inflow)	1. We assume a constant depreciation rate, computed from the fact that a regular mature milk cow lives for about 8 years. 2. No net change in cash holding.
Lose mature cows due to their death	**IM7C** What is the value of [the mature cows] you got rid of in this transaction? **IM7E** What kind of transaction was this? (13=animal died and was not eaten/sold/etc.)	Decrease in livestock assets; decrease in cumulative savings	Capital loss from livestock	(Negative) net income (cash outflow); decrease in livestock assets (cash inflow)	No net change in cash holding.
Cash purchase of chemical fertilizer for rice plot	**CM5Q** How much cash did you pay in total to acquire [chemical fertilizer]? (If no cash was used, record 0)	Decrease in cash; increase in input inventory		Increase in input inventory (cash outflow)	
Use of chemical fertilizer on rice plot	**CFO4F1** What is the approximate total cash value of [chemical fertilizer] you used on this crop-plot since the last interview?	Decrease in input inventory; increase in work-in-process inventory		Decrease in input inventory (cash inflow); increase in work-in-process inventory (cash outflow)	1. No net change in cash holding. 2. No net change in total inventory.
Harvest rice and put in inventory	**CFO10E** What is the total value of [rice] that you have harvested since the last interview? *Enumerator: Be sure to include this product in the Inventory of Storable Crop module.*	Decrease in work-in-process inventory; increase in finished-goods inventory, increase in cumulative savings	Revenue and cost from cultivation	Net income, decrease in work-in-process inventory (cash inflow); increase in finished-goods inventory (cash outflow)	1. No net change in cash holding. 2. No net change in total inventory.
Consume rice from household's inventory	**MM4A1** Since the last interview, have you or members of your household eaten any of [rice stored in inventory]? **MM4A2** If so, how many kilos did you eat?	Decrease in inventory; decrease in cumulative savings	Capital gain, consumption	Capital gain, decrease in inventory (cash inflow); consumption (cash outflow)	1. For capital loss, transaction is recorded as cash outflow. 2. No net change in cash holding.

(continued)

TABLE 2.1. (*continued*)

Transaction	Example of corresponding survey questions	Balance sheet	Income statement	Statement of cash flows	Remarks
Use rice to feed household's chickens	**MM4B1** Since the last interview, have you or members of your household fed any of [rice stored in inventory] to livestock? **MM4B2** If so, how many kilos did you feed to livestock?	Decrease in finished-goods inventory; increase in work-in-process inventory		Decrease in finished-goods inventory (cash inflow); increase in work-in-process inventory (cash outflow)	1. No net change in cash holding. 2. No net change in total inventory.
Purchase animal feed on credit from suppliers	**VM3P** How did you acquire this [animal feed]? **VM3S** If acquired other than through purchase, what is the approximate total cash value of the [animal feed] you acquired?	Increase in inventory; increase in account payables		Increase in inventory (cash outflow); increase in account payables (cash inflow)	No net change in cash holding.
Resell animal feed on credit	**LF3E** Which of the following describes this loan? (E = sold goods on credit) **LF3J** What is the total value of [the animal feed that you sold on credit]?	Decrease in inventory, increase in account receivables; increase in cumulative savings	Revenue and cost from business activity	Net income (cash inflow); decrease in inventory (cash inflow); increase in account receivables (cash outflow)	No net change in cash holding.
Receive cash repayment for credit sales of animal feed	**LM6B** What is the total amount of repayment that you received on [credit sales of animal feed]? **LM6H** How much of the total amount repaid since the last interview was principal? **LM6I** How much of the total amount repaid since the last interview was interest? *Enumerator: If the borrower has made an "extra payment" please include that amount here.*	Increase in cash; decrease in account receivables, increase in cumulative savings	Interest revenue	Net income (cash inflow); decrease in account receivables (cash inflow)	Net income = interest revenue.

(*continued*)

Receive cash as gifts	**GM4C** Since the last interview, how much have you received in total from this type of organization? **GM5C** Since the last interview, how much have you received in total for this type of event? **GM6A3** (**GM6B3**) [Besides the gifts and contributions from organizations and those that are related to specific events that we have already talked about,] what is the total value of the gifts or remittances that you or members of your household have received since the last interview from people in (outside) the village?	Increase in cash; increase in cumulative gifts received	Gift (cash inflow)	
Receive rice as gifts	**MM3E1** Since the last interview have you or members of your household received any of [rice] as a gift? **MM3E2** If so, how many kilos did you receive as a gift?	Increase in finished-goods inventory; increase in cumulative gifts received	Increase in finished-goods inventory (cash outflow); gift (cash inflow)	No net change in cash holding.
Use of charcoal made from wood gathered from nature	**XM1C** [3] Since the last interview, have you or members of your household [produced and consumed (i.e., not purchased) wood and charcoal]? If yes, what is the total value of the home produced [wood and charcoal] that you and members of your household have consumed since the last interview?		Other revenue; consumption	Net income (cash inflow); consumption (cash outflow)	No net change in cash holding.

Notes: Examples of corresponding questions are based on the Townsend Thai Monthly Survey. The code in front of each question indicates the number of the question referenced.

Source: Recreated from Table 4.1 from Samphantharak and Townsend (2009).

TABLE 2.2. Statement of income and retained earnings of household A.

Uses		Sources	
Expenses from production		Revenues from production	
Cultivation	0	Cultivation	0
Livestock	181	Livestock	340
Fish and shrimp	0	Fish and shrimp	0
Business	0	Business	0
Labor	0	Labor	91,150
Other	730	Other	260
Interest expense	10,000	Interest revenue	0
Depreciation	3,435	Capital gains	0
Insurance premium	0	Less: Capital losses	0
Property tax	0	Insurance indemnity	0
Net income before tax			
Income tax	0		
Consumption	54,076		
Savings	23,329		
Charges against total revenue	91,750	Total revenue	91,750

Source: Townsend Thai Project; authors' calculations.

2.8.1 Household A

For the first example, we consider a typical working household in Lopburi. In 1999, this household consisted of a male household head, his wife, and a four-year-old daughter. The household head was 38 years old, while his wife was 34 years old. Both the household head and his wife only had primary-level education (4 years and 6 years, respectively). In 2000, this household had another daughter. The statement of income and retained earnings of this household in 1999 is reported in Table 2.2.

The composition of household A's income over time is shown in Panel (a) of Figure 2.1. In 1999, both adult members worked at a shoemaking factory. Later that year, the household head switched jobs to work as a construction worker. The next year, the wife started to work at a garment company making knitted dresses. From 2001, both adult members changed their jobs several times. This pattern is quite common in Thai rural villages and suggests high

TABLE 2.3. Balance sheet of household A.

Assets		Liabilities and net wealth	
Current assets		Current liabilities	
Financial assets		Accounts payable	0
Cash	22,992	Other borrowing	37,417
Accounts receivable	0	Household's net wealth	
Other lending	0	Contributed capital	118,192
Deposits	5,560	Current retained earnings	50,779
ROSCA (net position)	14,125	Gifts (net transfer)	−1,602
Inventories	1,777		
Prepaid insurance	0		
Livestock	1,081		
Fixed assets			
Household assets	69,251		
Agricultural assets	0		
Business assets	0		
Land and other fixed assets	90,000		
Total assets	204,786	Total liabilities and net wealth	204,786

Source: Townsend Thai Project; authors' calculations.

job mobility among Thai wage workers. This household also raised a small flock of chickens and ducks. In 2001, it branched out to cultivation activity and grew chilis. And in 2005, it invested in a friend's cantaloupe farm. However, labor income has always been the main source of this household's income.

Table 2.3 reports the average balance sheet of this household in 1999. Household A held most of its wealth in land and household assets. With the average value of fixed assets of 159,251 baht (69,251 baht excluding land) in 1999, household A was ranked at the 24th percentile within the province by the value of fixed assets (the 33rd percentile if land is excluded). Therefore, household A had relatively low wealth by the Lopburi standard.

The composition of household A's wealth over time is shown in Panel (b) of Figure 2.1. In the early years (1999–2002), household A's liability level is quite stable, and the increase in household A's asset level comes from the increase in household A's savings. From 2003, on the other hand, household A

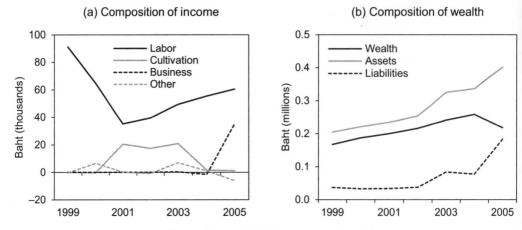

FIGURE 2.1 Composition of household A's income and wealth.
Source: Townsend Thai Project; authors' calculations.

also used loans to finance its asset accumulation. Table 2.4 reports the statement of cash flow of household A.

2.8.2 Household B

Next, we consider another household in Lopburi. In 1999, the members of this household consisted of a male household head, his wife, a seven-year-old daughter, and a two-year-old son. Both the household head and his wife were relatively young (30 years old and 26 years old, respectively). The household head had a lower-secondary education (9 years), while his wife had a primary education. The daughter was in kindergarten, while the son was not in school yet. Table 2.5 reports the statement of income and retained earnings of household B in 1999.

The composition of household B's income over time is shown in Panel (a) of Figure 2.2. The main source of income for this household was cultivation activity. In early years, the crops grown by this household included corn, sunflower, and peanuts. In later years, this household also diversified its crops to include chili and cotton. Both adult members also worked occasionally as wageworkers on their neighbors' farms. Moreover, this household also raised cattle (i.e., beef cows) but faced losses in most years.

Table 2.6 shows the average balance sheet of this household in 1999. Household B holds most of its wealth in land, livestock, and agricultural assets, respectively. The average value of this household's fixed assets in 1999

TABLE 2.4. Statement of cash flow of household A.

Change in cash holding	−11,479
Cash flow from production	**84,096**
(+) Income from production	87,447
(+) Depreciation of assets	3,435
(+) Change in accounts payable	0
(−) Change in accounts receivable	0
(−) Change in inventory	−40
(−) Consumption of household production	−6,746
(−) Net capital gains from production	−90
Cash flow from financing, investment, & consumption	**−95,575**
(+) Net capital gains from financial assets	0
(−) Capital expenditure on fixed assets	−10,795
(+) Net interest income	−10,000
(−) Tax expenditure	0
(−) Consumption expenditure	−47,330
(−) Insurance premium	0
(−) Capital expenditure on livestock	250
(−) Change in deposit at financial institutions	−940
(−) Change in ROSCA position	−10,750
(−) Lending	0
(+) Borrowing	−14,000
(+) Net gifts and transfer	−2,010
(+) Change in contributed capital	0
(+) Insurance indemnity	0
Statistical discrepancy	**0**
Change in cash holding from balance sheet	**−11,479**

Source: Townsend Thai Project; authors' calculations.

was 486,067 baht (191,150 baht excluding land), and household B was ranked at the 40th percentile by the value of fixed assets (the 64th percentile if land is excluded). Therefore, household B has medium wealth by the Lopburi standard.

The composition of household B's wealth between 1999 and 2005 is shown in Panel (b) of Figure 2.2. Like that of household A, the liability level of household B was stable from 1999 to 2004, and the increase in household B's

TABLE 2.5. Statement of income and retained earnings of household B.

Uses		Sources	
Expenses from production		Revenues from production	
Cultivation	14,717	Cultivation	370,000
Livestock	25,898	Livestock	0
Fish and shrimp	0	Fish and shrimp	0
Business	0	Business	0
Labor	1,000	Labor	28,540
Other	4,070	Other	50
Interest expense	47,627	Interest revenue	0
Depreciation	9,535	Capital gains	0
Insurance premium	700	Less: Capital losses	0
Property tax	0	Insurance indemnity	0
Net income before tax			
Income tax	0		
Consumption	65,301		
Savings	229,742		
Charges against total revenue	398,590	Total revenue	398,590

Source: Townsend Thai Project; authors' calculations.

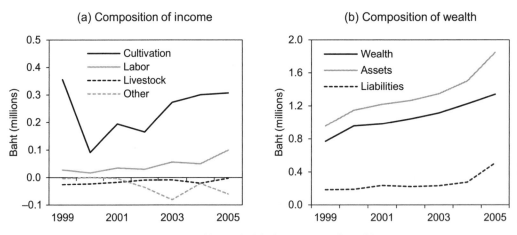

FIGURE 2.2 Composition of household B's income and wealth.
Source: Townsend Thai Project; authors' calculations.

TABLE 2.6. Balance sheet of household B.

Assets		Liabilities and net wealth	
Current assets		Current liabilities	
Financial assets		Accounts payable	0
Cash	70,936	Other borrowing	185,550
Accounts receivable	0	Household's net wealth	
Other lending	0	Contributed capital	840,679
Deposits	6,266	Current retained earnings	−68,660
ROSCA (net position)	89,480	Gifts (net transfer)	−1,249
Inventories	90,677		
Prepaid insurance	0		
Livestock	212,893		
Fixed assets			
Household assets	68,239		
Agricultural assets	122,911		
Business assets	0		
Land and other fixed assets	294,917		
Total assets	956,319	Total liabilities and net wealth	956,319

Source: Townsend Thai Project; authors' calculations.

asset level came from the increase in its savings. Also, household B used loans to finance its investment in 2005. The statement of cash flow of household B is reported in Table 2.7.

2.8.3   Household C

As the last example, we consider another entrepreneurial household from Lopburi. In 1999, this household included a male household head, his wife, a fourteen-year-old son, a ten-year-old son, and a three-year-old daughter. Both the household head and his wife were 36 years old and had 8 years of education each. In 1999, the elder son was in grade 8, while the younger son was in grade 3. In 2001, the elder son moved to a school in another province for three years before coming back in 2004. Table 2.8 reports the statement of income and retained earnings of household C in 1999.

The composition of household C's income over time is shown in Panel (a) of Figure 2.3. This household received income from several activities. The primary

TABLE 2.7. Statement of cash flow of household B.

Change in cash holding	−76,344
Cash flow from production	**−26,034**
(+) Income from production	369,269
(+) Depreciation of assets	9,535
(+) Change in accounts payable	0
(−) Change in accounts receivable	0
(−) Change in inventory	−401,328
(−) Consumption of household production	−3,509
(−) Net capital gains from production	0
Cash flow from financing, investment, & consumption	**−50,310**
(+) Net capital gains from financial assets	0
(−) Capital expenditure on fixed assets	−42,670
(+) Net interest income	−47,627
(−) Tax expenditure	0
(−) Consumption expenditure	−61,792
(−) Insurance premium	−700
(−) Capital expenditure on livestock	9,200
(−) Change in deposit at financial institutions	189
(−) Change in ROSCA position	−12,000
(−) Lending	0
(+) Borrowing	107,400
(+) Net gifts and transfer	−2,310
(+) Change in contributed capital	0
(+) Insurance indemnity	0
Statistical discrepancy	**0**
Change in cash holding from balance sheet	**−76,344**

Source: Townsend Thai Project; authors' calculations.

source of income of this household was its business, which was making compressed straw. The secondary source of this household's income was livestock (i.e., dairy cows and chickens). Household C also received a small amount of income from cultivation (i.e., growing grass for cattle feeding).

Table 2.9 reports the average balance sheet of this household in 1999. The average value of household C's fixed assets was 5,519,800 baht (1,094,300 baht excluding land), and household C was ranked at the 98th percentile by the

TABLE 2.8. Statement of income and retained earnings of household C.

Uses		Sources	
Expenses from production		Revenues from production	
Cultivation	5,928	Cultivation	41,600
Livestock	406,591	Livestock	548,772
Fish and shrimp	0	Fish and shrimp	0
Business	310,149	Business	801,120
Labor	70	Labor	12,000
Other	710	Other	105,200
Interest expense	4,500	Interest revenue	19,550
Depreciation	53,841	Capital gains	0
Insurance premium	0	Less: Capital losses	0
Property tax	0	Insurance indemnity	0
Net income before tax			
Income tax	0		
Consumption	142,170		
Savings	604,284		
Charges against total revenue	1,528,242	Total revenue	1,528,242

Source: Townsend Thai Project; authors' calculations.

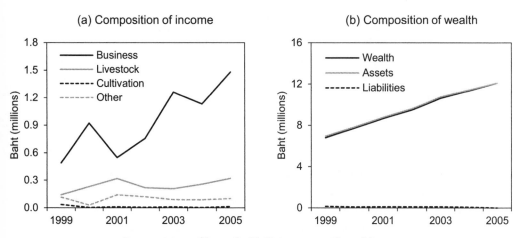

FIGURE 2.3 Composition of household C's income and wealth.
Source: Townsend Thai Project; authors' calculations.

TABLE 2.9. Balance sheet of household C.

Assets		Liabilities and net wealth	
Current assets		Current liabilities	
Financial assets		Accounts payable	0
Cash	365,886	Other borrowing	150,000
Accounts receivable	0	Household's net wealth	
Other lending	40,833	Contributed capital	6,467,045
Deposits	99,385	Current retained earnings	345,964
ROSCA (net position)	29,483	Gifts (net transfer)	−11,908
Inventories	20,382		
Prepaid insurance	0		
Livestock	875,330		
Fixed assets			
Household assets	520,380		
Agricultural assets	573,920		
Business assets	0		
Land and other fixed assets	4,425,500		
Total assets	6,951,101	Total liabilities and net wealth	6,951,101

Source: Townsend Thai Project; authors' calculations.

value of fixed assets by both measures (including and excluding land). Therefore, household C had very high wealth.

Household C held most of its wealth in land, followed by livestock, agricultural assets, and household assets. The level of household C's liabilities was insignificant relative to its wealth (see Panel (b) of Figure 2.3), suggesting that household C finances most of its investment using savings. Table 2.10 reports the statement of cash flow of household C.

2.9   Local Heterogeneity

In the Townsend Thai data, households' production activities can be classified as one of four sectors: business, cultivation, fish and shrimp, or livestock. The revenues and expenses of these activities, plus the labor revenue and expense, are recorded in the financial accounts introduced earlier in this section.

The production activities are also different across provinces. Villages in Chachoengsao have diverse sources of income, including through operating

TABLE 2.10. Statement of cash flow of household C.

Change in cash holding	447,068
Cash flow from production	**990,154**
(+) Income from production	859,393
(+) Depreciation of assets	53,841
(+) Change in accounts payable	0
(−) Change in accounts receivable	0
(−) Change in inventory	81,804
(−) Consumption of household production	−4,884
(−) Net capital gains from production	0
Cash flow from financing, investment, & consumption	**−543,086**
(+) Net capital gains from financial assets	0
(−) Capital expenditure on fixed assets	−273,900
(+) Net interest income	15,050
(−) Tax expenditure	0
(−) Consumption expenditure	−137,286
(−) Insurance premium	0
(−) Capital expenditure on livestock	117,000
(−) Change in deposit at financial institutions	6,450
(−) Change in ROSCA position	800
(−) Lending	−60,000
(+) Borrowing	−200,000
(+) Net gifts and transfer	−11,200
(+) Change in contributed capital	0
(+) Insurance indemnity	0
Statistical discrepancy	**0**
Change in cash holding from balance sheet	**447,068**

Source: Townsend Thai Project; authors' calculations.

fish and shrimp ponds, livestock, cultivation, and labor. Cultivation, livestock, and labor income are the main sources of income for villages in Lopburi. Labor income was the main source of income for villages in Buriram until 2002, when the income from businesses became equally large. For Sisaket, the main sources of income are cultivation, labor, and businesses. Here and below, when we refer to a province, we are utilizing all the data across villages in that province.

2.9.1 Productivity and Its Distribution

Even within the activities defined above, there are differences across provinces, especially for household cultivation and business activities. For example, many households in Lopburi grow corn, while those in Buriram grow rice. Household businesses could also range from operating a food stall or a small grocery store to selling trucks and tractors. All of these differences could lead to the productivity difference across provinces. However, when we estimate the production function, we group households' production activities into four broadly defined activities (i.e., business, cultivation, fish and shrimp, and livestock) for the purpose of fitting into the model. And we pick the two most common activities, namely, business and cultivation, to represent the two sectors in the model.

We estimate the production function of each activity using the following specification:

$$\ln(Y_{it}) = \delta_K \ln(K_{it}) + \delta_L \ln(L_{it}) + \varepsilon_{it}, \tag{2.2}$$

where Y_{it} denotes the output of household i in period t, and K_{it} and L_{it} denote the capital and the labor used by household i in period t. The error term ε_{it} captures the productivity of household i in period t. We allow the household's production function to have decreasing returns to scale (DRS), and therefore there are positive entrepreneurial rents.[16]

If the households in our data expand their production size when they observe positive productivity shocks, the levels of capital and labor used might be correlated with the error term and the OLS estimators could be biased. Therefore, we use the estimation method in Levinsohn and Petrin (2003) to obtain consistent estimators and use the level of intermediate input as a proxy variable. Panel (a) of Table 2.11 reports the estimated elasticities. Cultivation activity is the most labor-intensive, while fish and shrimp activity is the most capital-intensive.

---

16. On the other hand, if we impose the constant-returns-to-scale technological constraint, then only the most productive producers will produce, until they reach their borrowing limits. Then, the second most productive producers will take over, and so on. However, in this case, the more productive producers could also have positive profits.

(a) Actual distribution

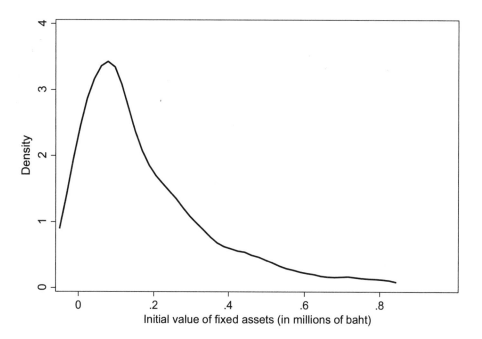

(b) Calibrated distribution

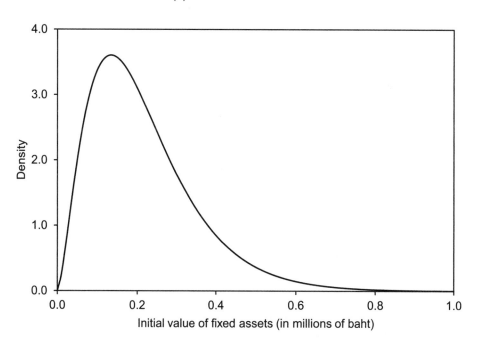

FIGURE 2.4 Actual and calibrated distributions of households' fixed assets in Lopburi in 1999.
Source: Townsend Thai Project; authors' calculations.

To estimate sector-average total factor productivity (TFP) and a household's entrepreneurial ability, we start by estimating household-specific TFP from the regression residual as follows:

$$a_i = \frac{1}{T} \sum_{t=1}^{T} \varepsilon_{it},$$
(2.3)

where a_i denotes the log TFP of household i. Then, we decompose the household-specific TFP into the sector-average TFP and the household's entrepreneurial ability, i.e.,

$$a_i = \bar{a} + z_i,$$
(2.4)

where z_i is assumed to have a normal distribution with mean zero and standard deviation σ_z.[17] Panel (b) of Table 2.11 reports the sector average TFP and σ_z for each activity.

2.9.2 The Distribution of Household Wealth

In the model, the distribution of capital endowment is assumed to follow the distribution of fixed assets, excluding land, in the data. If we do not take out land, the wealth level of households will be too high, and most of the household's capital will be lent out (in the model). This is partly because according to the estimated production function, the marginal product of capital is quite low, and the villages face high interest rates in the early years. So, it is better to just lend capital to someone else than use capital in production activities.

The initial distribution of a household's capital is assumed to follow a gamma distribution:

$$f(x; k, \theta) = x^{k-1} \frac{e^{-x/\theta}}{\theta^k G(k)},$$
(2.5)

where $G(\cdot)$ is the gamma function. We calibrate the parameters, k and θ, for the distribution to match that of the household's fixed assets in 1999. The calibrated

---

17. We assume that a household's entrepreneurial ability, z_i, is common to all production activities. In our case studies, if a household participates in more than one activity and has multiple estimated z_i, we pick the highest one. Of course, the multiple z_i suggest that we should have used Roy's model (as in Roy, 1951). However, we cannot estimate productivities for sectors a household was never in.

TABLE 2.11. Estimated parameters.

	Cultivation	Business	Livestock	Fish & shrimp
Panel A: Estimated elasticities				
δ_K	0.2313	0.3061	0.3099	0.5306
	(0.0390)	(0.0975)	(0.1967)	(0.1892)
δ_L	0.4564	0.3922	0.2260	0.0660
	(0.0375)	(0.0873)	(0.1052)	(0.0963)
Panel B: Average sectoral productivities and ability dispersion				
$\bar{a}$	4.1244	3.7464	4.6071	3.1648
σ_z	0.8409	0.9644	1.4057	1.8448

Note: Standard errors are in parentheses.

Source: Townsend Thai Project; authors' calculations.

values for k and θ are 2.6205 and 0.08267, respectively. Figure 2.4 compares the actual initial distribution of a household's fixed assets in the Lopburi data to the calibrated distribution in the model.

To put our case-study households in Lopburi in this context, household A is an average ability household ($z_i = 0$) with very low initial capital level (i.e., at the 10th percentile of the wealth distribution). Household B is a high-ability household ($z_i = 1.58\sigma$) with intermediate initial capital level (i.e., at the 50th percentile of the wealth distribution). And household C is a very-high-ability household ($z_i = 2.07\sigma$) with very high wealth (i.e., at the 99th percentile of the wealth distribution).[18]

2.10   Financial Frictions and Borrowing Limits

Pawasutipaisit and Townsend (2011) find strong differences in marginal products across households in the Townsend Thai data, high for low wealth households, which points to the existence of financial frictions. Due to an imperfect financial market, the amount of capital that an entrepreneur can utilize depends on the level of his own capital. We will assume that an entrepreneur i, whose capital level is W_{it}, cannot use capital in his production activity during period t more than $\eta_t W_{it}$. In other words, we assume that an entrepreneur i can borrow at most $(\eta_t - 1)$ times his capital level.

---

18. We have tested and found that, in the Townsend Thai data, the initial level of a household's wealth or fixed assets is mostly uncorrelated with the level of the household's ability.

Suppose that in each period, households consume according to the following consumption function:

$$C_{it} = C^* + \gamma(\pi_{it} - C^*), \qquad (2.6)$$

where C_{it} denotes the consumption of household i in period t, π_{it} denotes the net income (profit) of household i in period t, and C^* denotes the subsistence level of consumption. Household i then puts a fraction ω of its savings in cash and invests the rest in fixed assets.[19] The values of C^*, γ, and ω are estimated to match the patterns of consumption, cash holding, and investment at the provincial level. More specifically, we first estimate the consumption function above using the provincial-level income and consumption over a 7-year period. Then, we calculate ω from the ratio of savings in cash to investment in fixed assets at the provincial level. The estimated values of C^*, γ, and ω for Lopburi are 54,099, 0.1989, and 0.6462, respectively. The numbers suggest that, on average, the subsistence consumption level of households in Lopburi is 54,099 baht per year, the marginal propensity to consume is approximately 20%, and the average household saves approximately 65% of its unconsumed income in cash, as opposed to in fixed assets.

Figure 2.5 compares the predicted level of consumption based on the estimated consumption function above with the actual consumption level of our case-study households. The results suggest that the case-study households tend to save more (consume less) than the provincial-average household.

Panel (a) of Figure 2.6 shows the average value of outstanding loans per household in each province, while Panel (b) of Figure 2.6 shows the average loan-to-wealth ratio in each province. The values of outstanding loans have been increasing, including the year of the million-baht fund intervention. Indeed, the loan-to-wealth ratios have been increasing in Northeast provinces. This pattern suggests that the households in Buriram and Sisaket have indeed gained better access to the credit market over time. On the other hand, the loan-to-wealth ratios in Central provinces are relatively flat. We thus treat loan-to-wealth ratios as something we try to explain rather than as an exogenous policy shock.

Figure 2.7 shows the loan-to-wealth ratios of the case-study households. The loan-to-wealth ratios of household A and household B were much higher

---

19. This allocation would be optimal for a household maximizing the within-period utility function, $U = (C_{it} - C^*)^\gamma (i_{it}^K)^\alpha (i_{it}^{Cash})^\beta$, where i_{it}^K denotes the household's investment in fixed assets, i_{it}^{Cash} denotes the household's savings in cash, and $\omega = \dfrac{\beta}{\alpha + \beta}$, assuming that $\pi_{it} > C^*$.

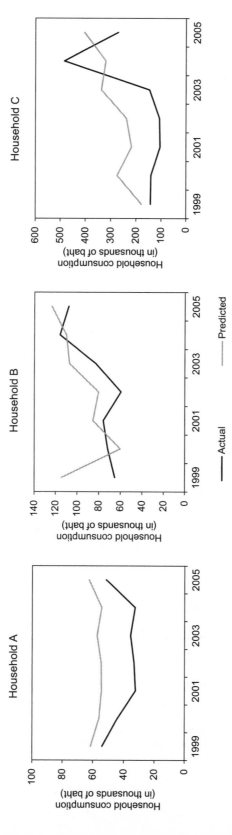

FIGURE 2.5 Actual and predicted values of consumption for case-study households.
Source: Townsend Thai Project; authors' calculations.

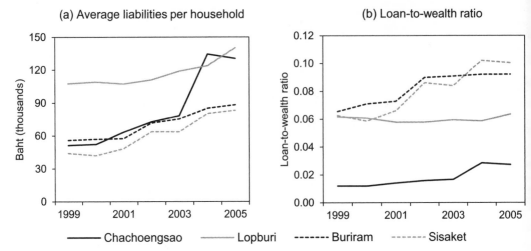

FIGURE 2.6 Average liabilities and loan-to-wealth ratios in all four provinces.
Source: Townsend Thai Project; authors' calculations.

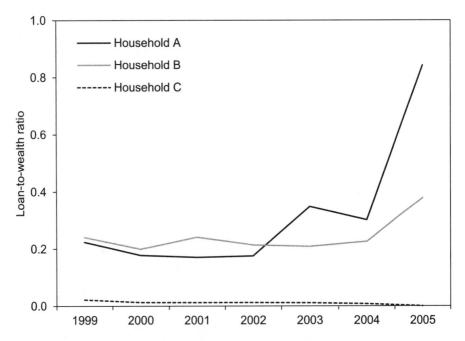

FIGURE 2.7 Loan-to-wealth ratios of case-study households.
Source: Townsend Thai Project; authors' calculations.

than the provincial average, especially in 2005. On the other hand, household C, which had higher wealth, had a lower loan-to-wealth ratio than the provincial average.

Figure 2.8 shows the movements in fixed assets and cash holdings of the case-study households over time. The results confirm the provincial pattern that cash holdings grow faster than fixed assets.

2.11 Revisions to the Construction of Household Financial Accounts

In this section, we will describe our recent revisions to the construction of household financial accounts described earlier and provide case studies to illustrate the reasons for these revisions.

2.11.1 *Remittances, Gifts, and Transfers*

In Samphantharak and Townsend (2009), there are three sources of household wealth: contributed capital, cumulative savings, and cumulative insurance indemnity. Contributed capital includes household initial assets net of liabilities from the baseline month, net assets brought into the household from the migration of household members, remittances from members living outside the household, and net gifts and transfers from organizations or individuals outside the household. In this framework, remittances, gifts, and transfers (in short, transfers) will not be counted toward the household's revenues or expenditures. In contrast, in the standard accounting framework, incoming and outgoing transfers are counted toward revenues and expenses, respectively, in the income statement, and net transfer contributes to cumulative savings in firms' balance sheets. However, to include net transfers in households' cumulative savings could also be misleading, especially for those interested in the economics of the household. This is because, unlike retained earnings, these transfers are not related to the households' productivity. If net transfers and retained earnings are both included in cumulative savings, households that rely mainly on remittances from relatives living outside the household could be mistakenly regarded as high-productivity households, with income from few assets, while, in fact, these households rarely engage in any production activities. This problem could be especially severe in the northeastern part of Thailand, where many households have only elderly and child members and are dependent on transfers.

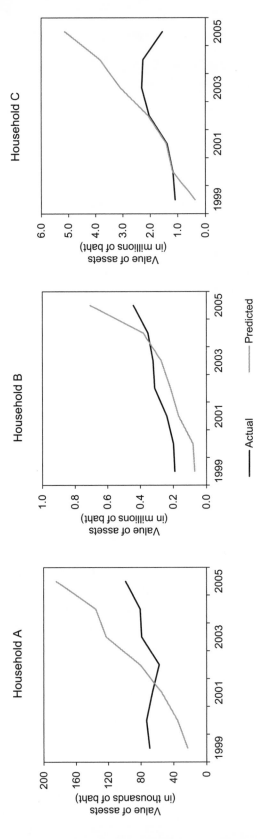

FIGURE 2.8 Values of fixed assets and cash holdings of case-study households.
Source: Townsend Thai Project; authors' calculations.

Therefore, to make household accounts more consistent with the goals of the standard accounting framework and to facilitate the use of household accounts in economic research, we decided to separate remittances, gifts, and transfers from contributed capital and have two different line items for cumulative savings in the balance sheet. Retained earnings will be recorded in cumulative savings from operations, while remittances, gifts, and transfers will contribute to cumulative savings from non-operations. In addition, all transfers will also be recorded in the income statement.

2.11.2   Depreciation of Assets

In Samphantharak and Townsend (2009), assets are depreciated at two different rates. Livestock are depreciated at 12% per year, while other fixed assets are depreciated at 5% per year.[20] However, by assuming the same depreciation rate for all other fixed assets, there could be discrepancies between the actual and the estimated values because certain assets (e.g., cellphones, computers, and cars) depreciate at a much faster rate than other assets (e.g., buildings). Therefore, we classify livestock and other fixed assets based on their recovery period according to the general depreciation system under the Modified Accelerated Cost Recovery System recommended by the Internal Revenue Service, and then use the 150% declining method to calculate the depreciation, i.e.,

$$Depreciation\ Rate = \frac{1.5}{Recovery\ Period}.$$

For example, the recovery period of a pickup truck is 5 years. Therefore, we depreciate the value of a pickup truck 30% per year (or 2.5% per month).

Another asymmetry in Samphantharak and Townsend (2009) is that, in the original financial accounts, the depreciation of livestock is included in livestock expenses. On the other hand, the depreciation of all other fixed assets is included with other expenses, which are separated from the cost of production. However, most households' fixed assets other than livestock are either used in production activities (e.g., agricultural assets and business assets) or used for domestic consumption (e.g., household assets). Therefore, we decided to

---

20. In Samphantharak and Townsend (2009), land and land improvements are not depreciated. In this version of financial accounts, we depreciate land improvements but do not depreciate lands.

reallocate the expense line items related to the depreciation based on the underlying assets. For example, the depreciation of livestock is still included in livestock expenses. The depreciation of agricultural assets and the depreciation of business assets are included in agricultural expenses and business expenses, respectively. In contrast, the depreciation of household assets, such as televisions or mobile phones, is considered as the flow of services from durable goods and is included in households' consumption.

2.11.3 *Capital Gains and Losses*

In Samphantharak and Townsend (2009), livestock capital gains and losses are counted toward total production revenue and total cost of production, respectively. On the other hand, capital gains and losses of other fixed assets are not included in production income but contribute to households' net income.

As in the case of asset depreciations, we decide to treat capital gains and losses differently for different underlying assets. Livestock capital gains and losses are included in livestock revenue and livestock expense, respectively, and contribute toward net income from production. Capital gains and losses from production, which include capital gains and losses from assets used in production activities (i.e., agricultural assets and business assets), are also included in net income from production. On the other hand, capital gains and losses from assets not related to production activities (e.g., household assets, land, or other financial assets) are included in other (net) operating income.

2.11.4 *Insurance Premium and Payments to Funeral Funds*

An insurance premium is a prepaid payment for future coverage. Therefore, in the standard accounting framework, when households pay premiums for insurance, they pay for an asset (labeled prepaid insurance) of which the value decreases over time as the remaining coverage period shortens. And the decrease in the value of prepaid insurance (as well as household wealth) in the balance sheet needs to be consistent with the income statement, and so should also be recorded as an expense in the income statement.

However, it is quite difficult to follow the framework just described for several reasons. First, we need to know the beginning and the length of coverage for each insurance policy that a household owns to be able to calculate the expenses and the remaining value of prepaid insurance in each month. Second, this framework is not suitable for funeral funds, which is one type of insurance commonly found in Thai rural areas. For a household member who is a member of a funeral fund, the amount of monthly payment to the fund depends on the number of fund members who passed away that month. It is a kind of instantaneous informal mutual fund. Furthermore, the coverage length is not predetermined but, rather, depends on the longevity of the member's life.

In Samphantharak and Townsend (2009), insurance premiums and payments to funeral funds are recorded as other (net) expenditure, deducted from or added to household net income in the month of the payment or receipt, respectively. In contrast, we decide to treat insurance premiums and payments to funeral funds as household depletion of insurance coverage. When household members receive compensation from the insurance company, the compensation will not be counted as household income but, for consistency of the income statement and balance sheet, there will now be in the revised accounts an increase in cumulative insurance indemnity as an increase in household wealth.

2.11.5 Land and Land Improvement

While the value of land typically increases over time due to the limited amount of land available in a given area, the value of buildings and other infrastructure is often depreciated. If we combine the value of land and land improvement together and do not depreciate the value of land improvement, we might overestimate the value of household assets and wealth. Therefore, in the revised financial accounts, we report the value of buildings and other infrastructure separately from the value of land, and depreciate the value of improvements net of land accordingly.

2.11.6 Rice Consumption

Households in rural Thailand often buy rice for consumption in bulk, store this as inventory, and then consume gradually out of stock over time. When households make their rice purchases, we observe in the survey both the quantity and the price. On the other hand, when households consume rice from their inventory, we observe only the quantity. Therefore, we need the estimated price of rice to calculate the value of rice consumption.

In Samphantharak and Townsend (2009), the consumption of rice in inventory was treated as if households sell rice at the current market price and buy it back, also at the market price, for consumption. If the market price was higher (or lower) than the average purchase price of the inventory, we treated this as if households received a capital gain (or a capital loss) from storage. The market price of rice was based on the median price from actual transactions within the village for regular rice, or within the province for sticky rice.

However, the estimation of market price could be inaccurate in the area where, or during a period when, there were few transactions, or if the price of rice in a household's inventory differed from the average market price by a large margin (due to the difference in quality), or if there was a large fluctuation in rice price during that period. Therefore, in the revised accounts, we decide to estimate the value of rice consumption based on the quantity of rice consumed and the quantity-weighted average price of rice in the inventory computed using historical acquisition values.

2.11.7   Case Studies

In this subsection, we present several case studies to illustrate the impact of some changes we made upon Samphantharak and Townsend (2009).

(a) Remittances, Gifts, and Transfers Figure 2.9 shows the sources of the change in net wealth of three households in our data between January 1999 and November 2017. As discussed earlier, changes in household net wealth come from four sources: cumulative savings from operations, cumulative savings from non-operations, contributed capital, and cumulative insurance indemnity.

During that period, the net wealth of all three households increased by approximately 380,000 baht. The sources of the increase in net wealth, however, differed across households. For household D, the change in net wealth was driven mainly by cumulative savings from operations (i.e., retained earnings). Both households E and F had negative cumulative savings from operations (i.e., consumed more than what they earned). While the change in net wealth of household E came mostly from cumulative savings from non-operations (i.e., remittances and gifts), the increase in contributed capital (i.e., from the migration of household members) was also an important source of change in net wealth of household F.

Figure 2.10 shows the change in net wealth of households D, E, and F over time. The main source of income for household D is cultivation activity. From the beginning to May 2004, this household also ran a small grocery store but had negative profits in most months. This led to the negative cumulative savings

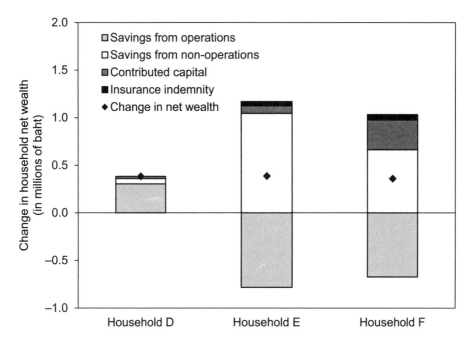

FIGURE 2.9 Decomposition of the change in household net wealth.
Source: Townsend Thai Project; authors' calculations.

from operations. Once the grocery store was closed, the financial situation of
this household improved and the cumulative savings from operations became
positive starting in August 2005. Between March 2007 and July 2008, this
household ran another business (i.e., a clothing stall), which provided additional income for the household.

Household E was a typical elderly household in rural Thailand. As working-
age members moved to work in the cities, the remaining household members
consisted mostly of children and elderly members. Elderly households usually
have little earned income and rely on transfers from working-age members
living outside the household. As seen in Panel (b) of Figure 2.10, the cumulative savings from non-operations (i.e., gifts and transfers) is almost a mirror
image of the cumulative savings from operations (i.e., income less consumption). From October 2009, there were some working-age members moving
back into this household. Therefore, this household started having labor income, and cumulative savings from operations became less negative.

Panel (c) of Figure 2.10 shows the change in net wealth of household
F. While this household was not an elderly household (i.e., consisted of mostly

(a) Household D

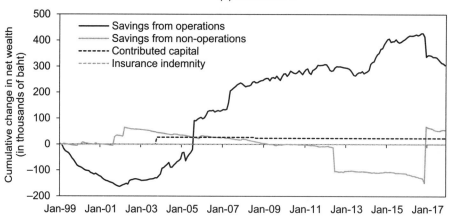

(b) Household E

(c) Household F

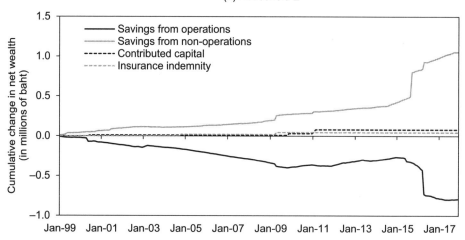
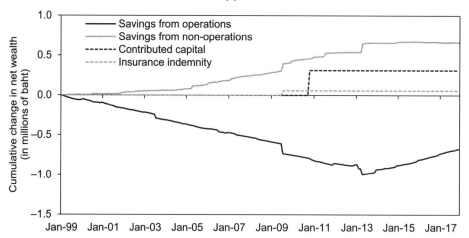

FIGURE 2.10 Cumulative contribution to the change in household net wealth.
Source: Townsend Thai Project; authors' calculations.

working-age members), its cumulative savings from operations was negative in most months. This household ran an auto repair shop that was not very profitable. As a result, in the first decade, this household's income was not enough to cover its consumption, and transfers from outside the household could cover only a fraction of its consumption deficits. In October 2010, two household members moved in and brought assets with them, including a pickup truck, a motorcycle, and a television. These assets increased the household net wealth through an increase in contributed capital. These members also provided labor income as an additional source of income. As a result, household income started to keep up with its consumption and, from May 2013, cumulative savings from operations increased.

(b) Depreciation of Business Assets For the second case study, we consider a household operating a business in Chachoengsao. The main business of this household was running a grocery store. This household also had a second business: making ice cubes for sale. From the beginning, the only business asset owned by this household was the ice-making machine. In December 2000, this household expanded its business by constructing another building on its empty plot of land and acquired refrigerators and shelves. The ice-making business ended in April 2004, when the household traded its ice-making machine for another refrigerator. In April 2009, this household started its third business: selling hot milk and steamed buns. This business ended in July 2011 when household members moved out and took the equipment with them. The business assets of this household included an ice-making machine, refrigerators, a milk boiler, and a bun steamer, all of which have a recovery period of 7 years. The business assets also included a building, which has a recovery period of 37 years.

In the baseline scenario, we follow Samphantharak and Townsend (2009) and assume a 5 percent depreciation rate for all assets. In the alternative scenario, we follow the revised framework and assume that depreciation rates are varied based on the assets' recovery period. As expected, the value of business assets of this household will be lower in the second scenario than in the baseline scenario. In the beginning, the value of business assets of this household is 400,000 baht (approximately 11,000 USD) in both scenarios. At the end, however, the difference in the values of business assets can be as large as 55 percent of the value of business assets in the baseline scenario.

The differences in depreciation rates also affect the business profit. In the beginning, higher depreciation rates under the revised framework led to larger depreciation costs and business expenses, and thus lower business profit. In the last 7 years, however, business profit under the revised framework was higher than that in the baseline scenario even though the depreciation rate was higher. This is because the remaining value of business assets was also lower in the baseline scenario.

(c) Depreciation of Land Improvements Consider a relatively rich household in our data. This household was in the agricultural sector, and the buildings on its land included houses, crop storage buildings, buildings for livestock, and a biogas plant. Again, we compare the value of land improvements of this household in two different scenarios. In the first scenario (baseline), we follow Samphantharak and Townsend (2009) and do not depreciate land improvements. In the second scenario, following the revised framework, we assume that all land improvements had a recovery period of 39 years, and the corresponding depreciation rate was 3.8 percent per year.

As expected, the value of land improvements of this household is lower under the revised framework than in the baseline scenario. More importantly, over the 19-year period, the difference in values could be as large as 1.8 million baht (approximately 53,000 USD) or 30 percent of the value of land improvements in the baseline scenario.

3

Constructing Community-Level Economic Accounts

IN THIS SECTION, we show how to create village-level income and product accounts. This will serve the dual purpose of explaining what is happening at the village aggregated level (i.e., where the data come from) and assessing the impact of counterfactuals at the village aggregated level. A preliminary outline of this work appeared in Paweenawat and Townsend (2012).

To create the village economic accounts, we follow the method described in U.S. Department of Commerce (1985) for constructing the national economic accounts. Each village is considered as a nation. And, as in Samphantharak and Townsend (2009), each household is considered as a business firm. Therefore, to create economic accounts of a household that will be used in the accounts for a village, we follow the steps in creating economic accounts of a business firm from the firm's financial statements. First, we create these economic accounts for each household, one at a time. Then, we create village economic accounts by consolidating all the (sampled) household economic accounts together.

In our survey, when a household reports a transaction, it also reports the name and the village of the person or institution with whom or which it made the transaction. Therefore, we can categorize the transactions as intra-village and inter-village and distinguish between these when we aggregate.

3.1 Some Special Issues for Village Economic Accounts

In the case of national economic accounts, after the accounts of all business firms have been created, one can aggregate them up to get the accounts of the business sector. Since the output of one firm is usually used as the input of other firms, the entries for a net transaction between two business firms are cancelled. Therefore, only investments in the business sector and transactions between the business sector and other sectors remain.

Similarly, village economic accounts can be created by adding the accounts for all households together. However, not all intra-village transactions will be cancelled. The residual intra-village transaction stems from at least three sources. First, in village accounting, households play two roles, as producers and as consumers. In the production account, only the transactions related to products sold by one household in the village and used as inputs by other households in the village would cancel. If the products sold by one household in the village are consumed or used as investments by other households in the village, the related transactions will remain in the production account. Second, sampling error can also create a residual in intra-village transactions. One might miss a pivotal or large household—say one playing the role of intermediary—so substantial that its (unmeasured) transactions are a big part of the village average.[1] Finally, there is conventional measurement error, though if this is independent and identically distributed over households and the number of sampled households is large, it will be small.

3.2   Issue Concerning Consumption

Even though we can categorize most transactions in our survey into intra-village and inter-village, this is not the case for consumption, since, unfortunately, the survey instruments do not ask about trading partners in consumption transactions. Hence—and this is quite unfortunate—we cannot distinguish directly between consumption of village products and consumption of imported goods. However, we can indirectly estimate the consumption of village products by assuming that households in our survey are perfectly representative, as if either we had a representative subsample or we sampled all of them. Since the village's products sold within the village must be either consumed or invested, and since we know the value of the village's products sold within the village and the value of investment of village's products, we can estimate the value of consumption of the village's products as:

$$\textit{Consumption of village's products} = \textit{Village's products sold within the village} \quad (3.1)$$
$$- \textit{Investment of village's products.}$$

---

1. We searched for such households and could not find one.

3.3 Issue Concerning Labor Income

In national economic accounts, wages and salaries that households receive from business firms are not considered as households' production but as input into business firms' production.[2] Again, business firms are envisioned as the main producers in the economy, while households provide the factors of production (such as labor, but also capital via lending, and so on) and buy produced goods for consumption. The only production within the household sector is when a household provides services directly to other households such as childcare and cleaning. This is counted as consumption of the recipient household and income of the producing or supplying household.

In Thai villages, most households also play the role of business firms and engage in production activity as single proprietors. The distinction between household and firm accounts is difficult to make even for narrower wage-earning households. Consider the case in which household A receives a wage payment from household B. If the labor service provided by household A is used in the production activity of household B, this wage payment should in principle be considered as part household B's production, via factor payments. On the other hand, if the labor service provided by household A is for household B's consumption or investment, e.g., a carpenter repairing a house or a mechanic repairing an equipment, this wage payment should be considered as household A's production.

In the survey, when a household member receives labor income, the counterparty's (employer's) name and location are recorded. However, sometimes we do not have information on what the activity is. Therefore, we cannot distinguish between the two cases discussed above.

Consequently, we consider all labor income as the income from household production, as if the household were a proprietor supplying labor services. Indeed, all households are regarded as business firms, and their products include labor services. In sum, when household A receives labor income from household B, we consider this as household A supplying its product (labor service) to household B, and the transaction is recorded as household A's production.

---

2. There are some exceptions, though. For example, households paid as consultants are treated as businesses.

3.4 Owner-Occupied Housing

In national economic accounts, the service flow from owned housing is also recorded as the household's consumption and income, usually measured at an implicit market rental rate. Thus, the service that a household in our survey receives from its own house should ideally be included in consumption and income. However, the estimation of a market rental rate cannot be straight-forwardly obtained from the household survey. Consequently, the current village accounts do not yet include the value of owner-occupied housing.

3.5 Creating Economic Accounts of a Typical Household

Below, we take each of the accounts, one at a time.

3.5.1 Production Account

First, we construct the production account, which is related to the statement of income (see Table 3.1). To create the production account from the statement of income, we first subtract the cost of materials and services used in production from both sides. Note, this expense includes wages paid (to service contractors). Then, we subtract the non-production revenue (i.e., interest revenue, capital gains net of capital losses, and insurance indemnity) from both sides. In this account, we introduce a term called "profit," which is defined as net income before tax less net capital gains and less insurance indemnity. In other words, "profit" is the household's earnings from production.

The sum of terms on the sources side equals the output, which is the value added from production activities (but, again, for us value added does not include paid labor expenses). The terms on the uses side are charges against output, which show where the output goes (disposition into factor payments).

In the model, entrepreneurial profit will be net of capital cost (including own capital), but the agent will also get capital compensation from the capital he owns. In the data, we did not subtract off the cost of own capital from entrepreneurial profit. So, we will overestimate the profit from entrepreneurial activity, though the total income for the household will be the same. This is also true for unpaid labor from household members, overestimating profit but underestimating labor income.

TABLE 3.1. Creating production account from statement of income.

Statement of income	
Uses	Sources
Expenses from production	Revenues from production
Interest expense	Interest revenue
Depreciation	Capital gains
Insurance premium	*Less:* Capital losses
Property tax	Insurance indemnity
Net income before tax	
Charge against revenue	Total revenue

Production account	
Uses	Sources
Interest expense	Revenues from production
Less: Interest revenue	*Less:* Expenses from production
Insurance premium	
Property tax	
Profit	
Net income before tax	
Less: Capital gains	
Plus: Capital losses	
Less: Insurance indemnity	
Charge against output	Output

Source: Adapted from U.S. Department of Commerce (1985) Table 4.

3.5.2 *Appropriation Account*

The appropriation account shows how a household distributes its profits. We can create the appropriation account from the statement of retained earnings. The statement of retained earnings has the net income before tax as the source of funds and has corporate income tax, dividend paid, and addition to retained earnings as the uses of the funds. From the net income before tax, we can create profit, which is earnings from production, by subtracting capital gains (net of capital losses) and insurance indemnity from both sides. On the uses side, we define the term "undistributed profit" to be equal to retained earnings less net capital gains and less insurance indemnity.

TABLE 3.2. Creating saving-investment account from changes in balance sheet.

Change in balance sheet

Uses	Sources
Change in financial assets	Change in current liabilities
Cash	Accounts payable
Deposits	Other borrowing
Accounts receivable	Change in household's net wealth
ROSCA (net position)	Contributed capital
Other lending	Gifts
Change in prepaid insurance	Current retained earning
Change in inventories	
Change in livestock	
Change in fixed assets	
Distribution of net income	Change in liabilities and net wealth

Saving-investment account

Uses	Sources
Change in financial assets	Change in household's net wealth
Change in prepaid insurance	Contributed capital
Change in inventories	Gifts
Change in livestock	Current retained earning
Change in fixed assets	
Plus: Depreciation	
Less: Change in current liabilities	
Gross investment	Gross savings

Source: Adapted from U.S. Department of Commerce (1985) Table 6.

3.5.3 Saving-Investment Account

Table 3.2 shows the construction of the saving-investment account, which considers the changes in household's assets and liabilities. To create the saving-investment account, we start with the changes of items in the balance sheet. Then, we add the depreciation of fixed assets (from the statement of income) to both sides and subtract the change in current liabilities from both sides.

On the left side of the saving-investment account is gross investment, which is the change in current assets plus the change in fixed assets (before deprecia-

TABLE 3.3. Production account of a village in Lopburi.

Production account			
Uses		Sources	
Depreciation	12,714	Revenues from production	192,923
Net interest		*Less:* Expenses from production	82,330
Interest expense			
To within village	776		
To other villages	6,542		
Less: Interest revenue			
From within village	1,455		
From other villages	732		
Insurance premium	241		
Property tax	136		
Profit			
Net income before tax	93,223		
Less: Capital gains	1,043		
Plus: Capital losses	191		
Less: Insurance indemnity	0		
Charge against output	110,593	Output	110,593

Source: Townsend Thai Project; authors' calculations.

tion) less the change in liabilities. On the right side is gross saving, which equals the change in the household's net wealth (before depreciation).

3.6 Village Economic Accounts

Next, we create village economic accounts by aggregating the economic accounts of every household in the village. Tables 3.3–3.4 and Tables 3.5–3.6 show the production account and the saving-investment account of representative villages in Lopburi and in Buriram, respectively. The numbers shown are per-household, averaged over a 7-year period.

Figure 3.1 shows the movements of villages' output over time for all four provinces. Each line represents the output from each village. The outputs of the villages in Chachoengsao have been decreasing over time, while the outputs of the villages in the other three provinces have been increasing.

TABLE 3.4. Saving-investment account of a village in Lopburi.

Saving-investment account			
Uses		**Sources**	
Change in financial assets		Change in village net worth	
Within village	−14,873	Change in contributed capital	
With other villages	55,150	Within village	−347
Change in inventories		With other villages	−835
Within village	33,730	Net transfer	
With other villages	−36,804	Within village	−2,843
Change in livestock		With other villages	24,435
Within village	2,195	Current retained earnings	38,248
With other villages	2,546	Depreciation	12,714
Change in fixed assets			
Within village	610		
With other villages	26,502		
Plus: Depreciation	12,714		
Less: Change in liabilities			
Within village	1,238		
With other villages	−353		
Gross investment	71,373	Gross savings	71,373

Source: Townsend Thai Project; authors' calculations.

TABLE 3.5. Production account of a village in Buriram.

Production account			
Uses		**Sources**	
Depreciation	5,822	Revenues from production	229,115
Net interest		*Less:* Expenses from production	168,239
Interest expense			
To within village	2,502		
To other villages	4,271		
Less: Interest revenue			
From within village	1,397		
From other villages	173		
Insurance premium	317		
Property tax	9		
Profit			
Net income before tax	54,280		
Less: Capital gains	5,024		
Plus: Capital losses	269		
Less: Insurance indemnity	0		
Charge against output	60,876	Output	60,876

Source: Townsend Thai Project; authors' calculations.

TABLE 3.6. Saving-investment account of a village in Buriram.

Saving-investment account			
Uses		Sources	
Change in financial assets		Change in village net worth	
Within village	924	Change in contributed capital	
With other villages	25,639	Within village	−128
Change in inventories		With other villages	239
Within village	−5,019	Net transfer	
With other villages	1,852	Within village	6,226
Change in livestock		With other villages	13,148
Within village	−2,117	Current retained earnings	7,729
With other villages	−3,207	Depreciation	5,822
Change in fixed assets			
Within village	5,824		
With other villages	7,409		
Plus: Depreciation	5,822		
Less: Change in liabilities			
Within village	1,631		
With other villages	2,461		
Gross investment	33,036	Gross savings	33,036

Source: *Townsend Thai Project; authors' calculations.*

Figure 3.2 plots the average share of village income in each province. Based on the estimated factor intensity as above, we classify cultivation as labor-intensive and classify running business, operating fish and shrimp ponds, and livestock as capital-intensive. The results suggest that, in Chachoengsao, the share of income from the capital-intensive sector decreases over time, while the share of labor income increases over time. In Buriram, the share of income from the capital-intensive sector increases over time and the share of income from the labor-intensive sector decreases over time. In Lopburi and Sisaket, the shares of income are flat.

A village's saving-investment account tells us how the village allocates its wealth. When a village has positive savings (i.e., it consumes less than its income), its wealth increases. As mentioned at the individual level, a village can allocate its savings in inventories (including livestock), financial assets (cash, deposits, loans,

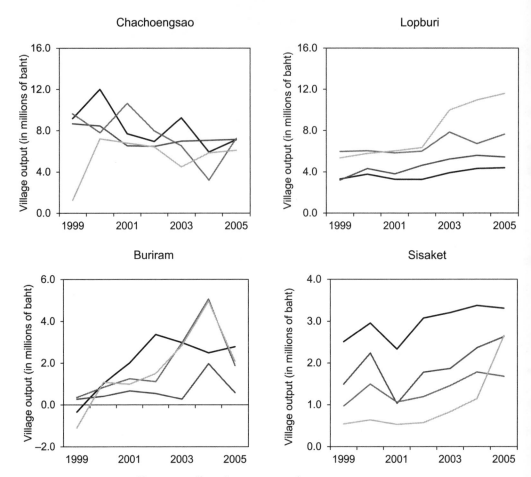

FIGURE 3.1 Change in villages' output in each province over time.
Source: Townsend Thai Project; authors' calculations.

etc.), fixed assets, or gifts (or others' contributed capital).[3] We construct the gifts such that the positive sign means that the village gives out gifts.

Figure 3.3 shows how villages in each province allocate their savings (plus gifts) annually. The line representing financial assets moves closely with the line representing villages' savings. This pattern appears in every village, suggesting that, at a high frequency, the village keeps its wealth in the form of financial assets. But capital also co-moves somewhat.

3. In the saving-investment account, we separate gifts from other contributed capital. Gifts represent transfers from one household to another household. Contributed capital represents the situation when a member of a household moves out and takes some assets with him. However, in this presentation, we group them together.

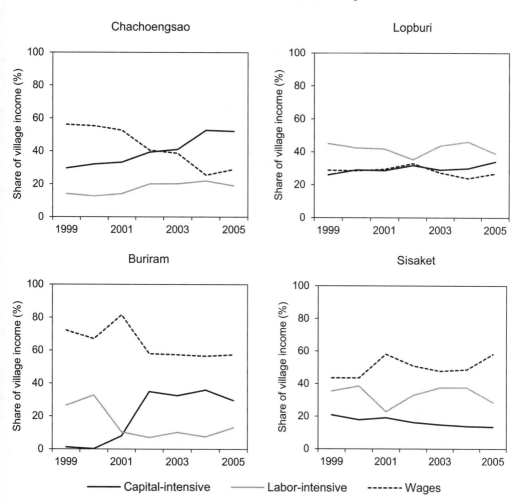

FIGURE 3.2 Average share of villages' income in each province.
Source: Townsend Thai Project; authors' calculations.

3.7 Village Balance of Payments Accounts

Village balance of payments accounts can be constructed from village economic accounts. As discussed earlier, we can separate the transactions into two different groups: within-village and across-village. A within-village transaction is a transaction between two village residents. An across-village transaction is a transaction between a village resident and a nonresident.

To illustrate the within- vs. across-village transactions, we use the following examples. Suppose a household buys 500-baht worth of fertilizer from a store located within the village. This transaction will enter that particular household's

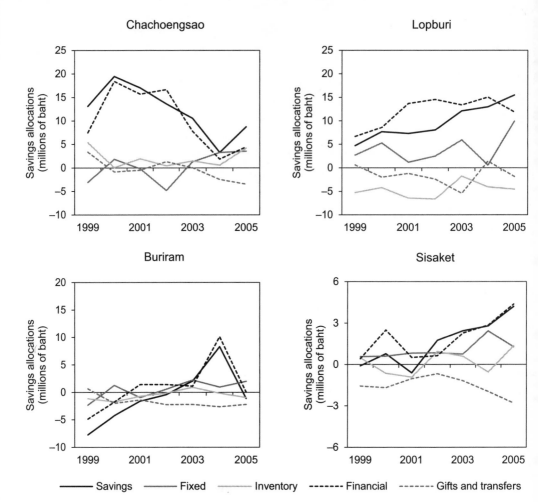

FIGURE 3.3 Allocations of villages' savings in each province.
Source: Townsend Thai Project; authors' calculations.

financial statement as a within-village 500-baht increase in inventory of input and a within-village 500-baht decrease in cash. Similarly, suppose a household sells 1,000-baht worth of rice to someone residing in another village. This transaction will enter that household's financial statement as an across-village 1,000-baht increase in cash and an across-village 1,000-baht decrease in finished-goods inventory.

An across-village increase in fixed assets could be (i) an import of fixed assets, (ii) a re-acquisition of claims on village fixed assets previously held by a village nonresident, or (iii) an acquisition of claims on a fixed asset located in another village. An example of the first case is the import of a machine used in production. An example of the second case is a purchase of land located within the village from a village nonresident. An example of the third case is a purchase of land located in another village from a village nonresident. We use the residential status of the trading partner to distinguish the type of transaction. Also, as discussed above, labor earnings of village residents are considered village production even when employment is outside the village.

Similarly to that of the nation, a village's balance of payments consists of the trade balance, current account, capital account, financial account, and cash reserve. The trade balance records the exports net of the imports of goods (including the ownerships of fixed assets) and services between village residents and nonresidents. The current account measures the transactions of goods, services, and transfers between village residents and nonresidents. In other words, the current account equals the trade balance plus net factor income (interest earned abroad) and transfers to village residents.

The financial account[4] measures the transactions of financial assets between village residents and nonresidents (though, for this, cash is treated as a residual and measured separately). Financial assets include bank deposits, accounts payable, accounts receivable, lending, and borrowing. The capital account measures the changes in ownership of assets due to the migration of household members.

The balance of payments identity is

$$\textit{Current Account} + \textit{Capital Account} + \textit{Financial Account}$$
$$+ \textit{Change in Cash Reserve} = 0. \tag{3.2}$$

Note that, as is standard, a current account surplus is associated with a capital + financial account deficit.

Figure 3.4 shows the balance of payments, accumulated to the provincial level, in four provinces. The current account surplus of the villages in Chachoengsao is decreasing, while the current account surpluses of the villages in Lopburi and Sisaket are increasing. The current account balance of the villages in Buriram increased in every year except for 2005.

The scale of balance of payments accounts in village economies is large, compared to the scale of international economic accounts. For example, a village in Chachoengsao has a current account surplus that is 66% of its gross village product on average. In comparison, Thailand had current account

---

4. By the current standard for national balance of payments accounts, the capital account includes both the capital account and the financial account in our framework.

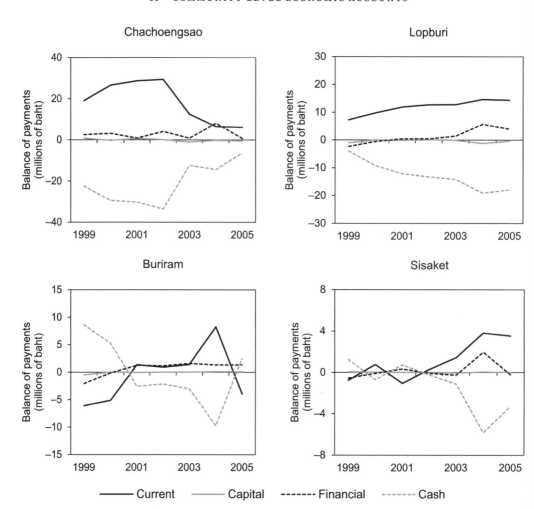

FIGURE 3.4 Villages' balance of payments in each province.
Source: Townsend Thai Project; authors' calculations.

deficits of around 6.7% of its GDP in the pre-1997 crisis and has had a current account surplus of around 4.5% of its GDP in the post-crisis period. The United States has run current account deficits at 4.6% of its GDP on average during the last 10 years. There are international norms for reasonable balance of payments deficits, presumably based on cumulative experience.

4

A Model Economy for
the Thai Data

IN THIS CHAPTER, we create an economic model which we calibrate against the Thai data in order to understand what has happened to regional economies over time and to analyze the counterfactual impact of isolationist policy.

4.1. Relation to the Literature

We have a lot in common with the widely cited, seminal review of Goldberg and Pavcnik (2007), not only in the topic we study but also in the overall conclusions. Goldberg and Pavcnik study the impact of reductions in tariff barriers, arguing for a causal link between trade openness and changes in inequality. But they also believe that by the 1990s, increased capital flows from financial liberalization were playing a co-determining role. They found this worrisome for research purposes, as one is no longer looking at the impact of trade alone. We thus emphasize our attempt to disentangle (through measurement and the model) real trade factors from financial factors. We also study the impact of trade on particular regional economies in Thailand over a period of time, one region at a time, rather than making cross-sectional comparisons. We have panel data from a continuously implemented survey to do this. Goldberg and Pavcnik also abstract from the growth channel and macro dynamics. In contrast, we have some endogenous wealth dynamics, and hence time-varying impacts; on the other hand, we abstract from productivity growth. However, we have variation in total factor productivity (TFP) across firms and regions, and this plays a leading role in our model. Finally, we identify several, diverse channels through which trade and financial openness can have an impact. As Goldberg and Pavcnik (2007) and Feenstra (2010) emphasize, the popular notion that relatively abundant factors in a country would be aided by exports and the consequent increase in factor prices turned out to be naïve. The standard Heckscher-Ohlin predictions do provide intuition but need an adjustment in the context of our model, and data, as well. Their conclusion, and ours, is that attempts to understand, anticipate, or alleviate the distributional effects of within-country openness need to be grounded in a careful study of regional circumstances. We document this extensively.

More recent papers continue to try to exploit exogenous policy variation in conjunction with theory. Brambilla, Lederman, and Porto (2012) study exports, export destinations, and skill utilization by firms. Using the exogenous changes in exports and export destinations brought about by a 1999 Argentine devaluation, they find that Argentine firms exporting to high-income countries hired a higher proportion of skilled workers and paid higher average wages than other exporters (to non-high-income countries) and domestic firms. We too are using exogenous policy variation. In Thailand, in particular, we use variation in credit in the data associated with a government financial intervention (though other things were happening at the same time—we use our model to sort this out).

On the other hand, unlike Brambilla, Lederman, and Porto (2012), we do not focus at all on skills variation within the labor sector, nor the source of demand for these exports. We do have heterogeneity among firms in a given sector in terms of productivity, but not on exports, or not per se. There is, of course, a large and growing literature emphasizing this kind of heterogeneity, for example, Bustos (2011), Melitz (2003), and Verhoogen (2008). Indeed, as reviewed by Harrison, McLaren, and McMillan (2011), the poor performance of the Stolper-Samuelson mechanism has led Feenstra and Hanson (1996), Helpman, Itskhoki, and Redding (2011), Frías, Kaplan, and Verhoogen (2012), and Burstein, Morales, and Vogel (2015) to study different channels through which trade affects the distribution of earnings: outsourcing, labor market frictions, quality upgrading, or capital-skill complementarity. Here we take a different tack and incorporate financing frictions into a 2 × 2 Heckscher-Ohlin model. This is another way to overturn the Stolper-Samuelson mechanism, a point made rather dramatically in Antràs and Caballero (2009) in their model of North-South trade and globalization, though their study was not empirical.

As in the recent paper by Fajgelbaum and Khandelwal (2016), we complement literature that views the distributional impact of international trade as one of the central tasks to be pursued by international economists. Fajgelbaum and Khandelwal (2016) find that trade has relatively adverse effects for low-income consumers in more than half of the countries that they consider and that the distributional effects of trade are often large relative to the aggregate effects. They focus on the demand side and heterogeneity in demand elasticities. For Thailand, we shut down that mechanism entirely and focus instead on the cross-sectional distribution of welfare gains and losses associated with varying factor endowments, varying factor intensities across sectors, and household-specific credit constraints related to wealth. As with the labor mobility literature, we find that occupation shifts can play a role in mitigating adverse impact, or facilitating gains, but the distribution of gains and losses even with this mechanism in place can also be heterogeneous and large.

In emphasizing local within-country impacts associated with initial conditions, our monograph shares much in common which various literatures that take us to the United States. Autor, Dorn, and Hanson (2013) find impacts on local labor markets from rising Chinese import substitutes (unemployment, lower labor force participation, and reduced wages), which account for up to one quarter of declines in manufacturing employment. We, too, find for Thailand impacts on factor prices and occupation, from changes in relative prices arguably associated with international and interregional trade. We show, in fact, that relative prices of manufacturing and agricultural goods move considerably in the period we study. Related is Hakobyan and McLaren (2016), who find, using U.S. Census data for 1990–2000 at a quite disaggregated level, the NAFTA-induced effects on U.S. wages by industry and by geography, measuring each industry's vulnerability to Mexican imports and each locality's dependence on vulnerable industries. They find large distributional effects (larger than aggregate welfare effects estimated by other authors).

Related in turn are the earlier papers on emerging markets. Topalova (2007) constructs an employment-weighted average tariff for each Indian district to identify the differential effects of local labor market shocks on different locations. Kovak (2013) uses a similar technique for Brazil. These studies indicate significant location-specific effects of trade shocks on wages, which of course implies mobility costs of some sort for workers that prevent them from arbitraging wage differences across locations. We, too, make these explicit assumptions about the local labor market in Thailand, and we, too, document effects on wages. We go beyond these papers in taking an explicitly structural approach, which in turn allows us to conduct a number of counterfactual exercises. Though we stop short of introducing heterogeneity in labor skills—the matching of labor to task and worker-specific capital—we allow heterogeneity across firms. Though we do not have direct costs of adjustment, we do have credit constraints that can prevent expansion in scale. We find with what is in the model an enormous degree of heterogeneity in impact.

There is, of course, increasing interest in using structural models to understand the impacts of policy shocks in the United States and other countries. Donaldson and Hornbeck (2016) study the impact of railroads on American growth using a "market access" approach based on Eaton and Kortum (2002). Morten and Oliveira (2018) use the same approach to study economic integration in Brazil, with new roads connecting to the new capital city, and Bryan and Morten (2018) study aggregate productivity effects of migration in Indonesia. Allen and Arkolakis (2014) feature a versatile general equilibrium framework to study the spatial distribution of economic activity in the United States.

Other studies incorporate dynamics and explore the impact of trade shocks on U.S. labor markets, such as reductions in tariffs associated with NAFTA or the China import shock. Caliendo and Parro (2015) study a multi-sector multi-country model of the impact of NAFTA. Lyon and Waugh (2018) study the impact of the China shock in the United States, motivated by the Autor, Dorn, and Hanson (2013) study mentioned earlier.

There are trade-offs in modeling and techniques when solving for the general equilibrium that have a lot to do with how the heterogeneity is allowed to enter the problem. Specifically, Caliendo and Parro (2015) use the Dekle–Eaton–Kortum dynamic technique with perfect foresight, which allows a certain kind of aggregation—share of income from each sector remains constant across equilibria while a measured counterfactual policy variable changes the level of income from each sector. Their model, focusing on labor migration, does not incorporate a financial sector and hence is not in a position to distinguish between real and financial flows. Lyon and Waugh (2018) feature discrete choice across value functions and differ from the former literature by studying an economy in which households face labor income shocks, incomplete markets, and partial self-insurance achieved over time. The cost of this departure is that they are unable to incorporate geographic and sectoral details due to the computational complexities inherent in their approach. So, though real and financial can be distinguished between, community and regional impacts are not studied.

The study of sufficient assumptions for aggregation and improved computational methods is a very active area of research. Itskhoki and Moll (2018) allow dynamic occupation choice of households running firms or providing labor, both with savings and borrowings, with credit constraints on firms as a linear function of wealth. If there is no persistence in randomly drawn productivities, this allows an aggregation, in that macro variables are simple sums of the micro-level variables. But if productivity shocks have some persistence, as in Moll (2014), then new techniques are needed, though in Moll the new state variables are the shares of wealth at various productivities. Pecuniary fixed costs subtracted from consumption can cause problems, as well. Sraer and Thesmar (2018) show that scaling up small-scale experiments for an entire economy remains tractable if and only if the revenue to capital ratio is independent of general equilibrium conditions, which happens if the sources of distortions are homogeneous of degree 1 and the production functions are Cobb–Douglas. Otherwise, the modeler as analyst has to keep track of the joint distributions of wealth and talent in solving for the general equilibrium, which, though doable in some contexts, as noted, can lead to computationally hard if not infeasible problems in others.

Here, we take two different tracks. First, for the work in Thailand, rather than tie our hands and limit individual and regional heterogeneity so that we can solve for the general equilibrium of the entire economy, we free ourselves by considering counterfactual experiments for small, open regional economies. We calibrate local economies using data from the observed equilibrium path. Relative to this baseline, general equilibrium effects would show up as changing wedges on the relative prices of goods and changing interest rates. We study the impact of such changes. These changes could be generated from the general equilibrium macro effects or from local restrictive policies. From the point of view of the local economy, it does not matter. We can thus feature substantial, realistic individual and local heterogeneity. This results in simultaneous gains and losses across groups, highly nonlinear and non-monotone impacts with sign changes, and orders of magnitude that can be substantial.

4.2 Stylized Facts for Local, Regional, and National Thai Economies

Figure 4.1 shows the average levels of village openness within each province. The black line represents the share of inputs purchased from outside the village, and the grey line represents the share of outputs sold to other villages. Overall, the Central villages are more open than the Northeast villages.

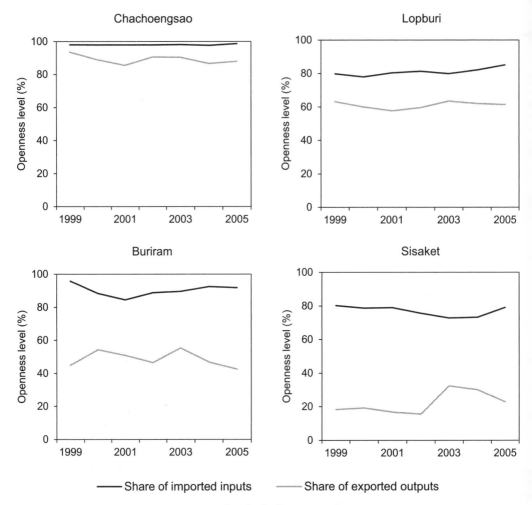

FIGURE 4.1 Average openness level of villages in each province.
Source: Townsend Thai Project; authors' calculations.

4.2.1 *Price Indices, Inflation, and Relative Prices*

The national and regional consumer price indices are shown in Figure 4.2. All price indices increase over time. The price level in the Northeast region increases faster than the price level in the Central region. The model will be in real terms, so we use the inflation data to adjust interest rates and make nominal values real.

Panel (a) of Figure 4.3 shows the retail price indices of the products from livestock (pork loins, eggs, and milk) and the product from cultivation (jasmine rice). We use the price index of the products from livestock to represent the price of capital-intensive goods in our model and use the price index of the

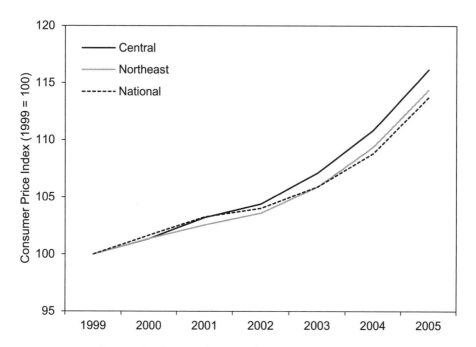

FIGURE 4.2 National and regional price indices.
Source: Thailand Ministry of Commerce; authors' calculations.

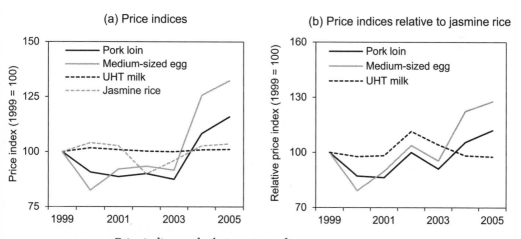

FIGURE 4.3 Price indices and relative price indices.
Source: Thailand Ministry of Commerce; authors' calculations.

cultivation product to represent the price of labor-intensive goods.[1] Panel (b) of Figure 4.3 shows the relative price indices, i.e., the ratio of the price indices of livestock products to the price index of jasmine rice. We find that the relative price of capital-intensive goods is increasing.

We are, however, unable to show province-level figures given the great heterogeneity across provinces already documented. So, we treat the relative price of capital- to labor-intensive goods as something we try to infer though the lens of other observables.

4.2.2   Factor Prices

Figure 4.4 shows the median real wage rates and the median real interest rates in four provinces in the Townsend Thai survey. To get the real interest rate, we subtract the expected (realized) regional inflation from the nominal interest rate. To get the real wage rate, we normalize the nominal wage rate with the regional price index.

First, consider the levels of factor prices. The real wage rates are lower in the Northeast provinces, while the real interest rates are lower in the Central provinces. We now turn to the movements of factor prices over time. Real wage rates in the Central provinces have been increasing, though erratically, while real wage rates in the Northeast provinces have remained constant. On the other hand, real interest rates in the Northeast provinces have converged to those in the Central provinces in recent years.

Figure 4.5 shows the ratios of factor prices in four provinces. The wage-interest ratio increases fastest in Chachoengsao, due mainly to the increasing wage rate in the last two years. Lopburi also experiences the increasing factor price ratio due to the increasing wage rate. While the change in that factor price ratio in Sisaket is about the same size as that in Lopburi, it is driven by the lower interest rate. Buriram has the smallest change in the factor price ratio. There is a divergence of factor price ratios across provinces.

---

1. In the data, the income sources for the "capital-intensive" sector are fish and shrimp ponds, livestock, and businesses. Certainly, none of them involve the traditional manufacturing sector. We don't think fish and shrimp ponds are good representatives since they are active in only one province and are declining. Most of the household businesses are either in the service sector (e.g., barber shop) or are small-scale productions (e.g., food stalls or local grocery shops). Therefore, it is hard to choose the price index that represents goods from the business sector. Livestock is the only activity for which we can find the related price index.

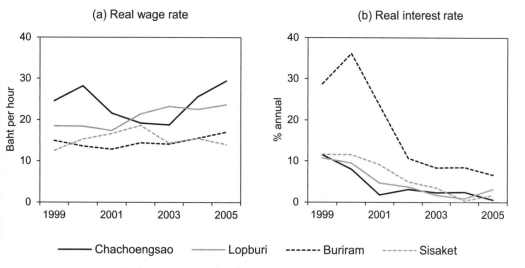

FIGURE 4.4 Real wage rates and real interest rates.
Source: Townsend Thai Project and Thailand Ministry of Commerce; authors'
calculations.

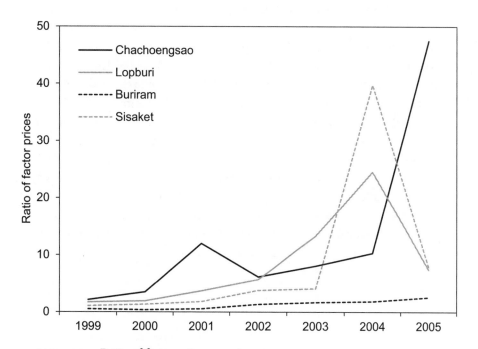

FIGURE 4.5 Ratio of factor prices.
Source: Townsend Thai Project and Thailand Ministry of Commerce; authors'
calculations.

4.3   Comparison to the Thai National Economy

Since the financial crisis in 1997, Thailand has gone through a considerable change in its financial environment, from the devaluation of the Thai baht in 1997, to the decision to change from the monetary targeting framework to the inflation targeting framework in 2000, to the introduction of one-million-baht village funds in 2001, which is one of the largest microfinance programs in the world.[2]

In July 1997, the Thai government decided to change its exchange rate policy from fixed to a managed float. The exchange rate then increased from the pre-float level at 25 baht per U.S. dollar to more than 40 baht per U.S. dollar in January 1998, as shown in Panel (a) of Figure 4.6. Two vertical dash lines indicate the period considered here (1999–2005). The crisis hit Thailand the hardest in 1998, when Thai gross domestic product dropped 10.51% from the previous year. The movement of the Thai GDP over time is shown in Panel (b) of Figure 4.6. The unemployment rate rose to the level of 4.35% in 1998, before it continuously declined (see Panel (c) of Figure 4.6).

The balance of payments of Thailand is shown in Figure 4.7. Before the crisis, Thailand consistently ran a trade deficit financed by foreign capital inflows. After the crisis, it faced a sharp reversal of foreign capital inflows. The exporting sectors have benefited from the depreciation of the Thai baht, and Thailand has run a trade surplus since 1998. In addition to the trade balance, we also look at Thailand's level of openness to trade. We use the standard openness measure, namely the ratio of exports and imports to GDP. The openness level has been increasing over time, driven by the increases in both export and import shares (see Figure 4.8).

Under the inflation targeting framework, the Bank of Thailand has managed to keep the inflation rate well below the level under the previous regime. As a result, the interest rate has also come down during the same period (consistently with the rest of the world's rates). Figure 4.9 shows the headline inflation and the interest rate in Thailand from 1990 to 2010.

---

2. As reported in Kaboski and Townsend (2011), the size of the initial fund of this program is about 1.5 percent of the Thai GDP in 2001.

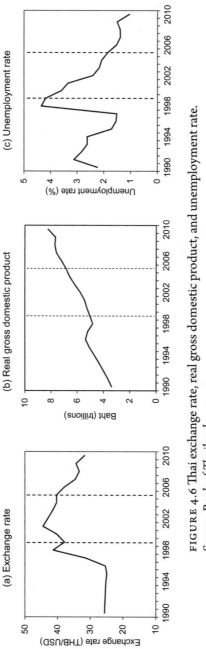

FIGURE 4.6 Thai exchange rate, real gross domestic product, and unemployment rate. *Source: Bank of Thailand.*

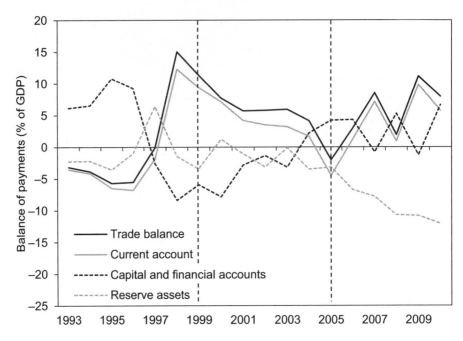

FIGURE 4.7 Thai balance of payments.
Source: Bank of Thailand.

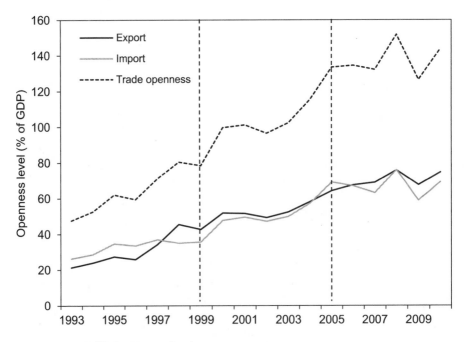

FIGURE 4.8 Thai openness levels.
Source: Bank of Thailand.

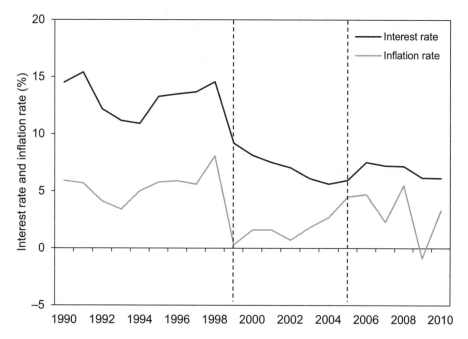

FIGURE 4.9 Thai interest rates and inflation rates.
Source: Bank of Thailand.

4.4 Outline of the Model

Consider a two-good, two-factor trade model with financial friction. The two factors of production are labor and capital. And there are two production sectors, which differ in their factor intensity. Let *a* denote the labor-intensive sector and let *m* denote the capital-intensive sector. In this economy, there is a continuum of infinitesimal agents that are different in their wealth level and in their "entrepreneurial ability." In each period, an agent chooses to be a wageworker or to run a business as an entrepreneur in one of the two sectors. An entrepreneur utilizes the factors of production and produces consumption goods. A worker provides inelastic labor supply[3] $\overline{L}$ at the market wage rate w_t. We assume that workers can move freely across sectors but cannot move across regions. There is, in fact, nontrivial migration, but on the other hand real wages do not converge in the data. Interest rates do.

---

3. The estimated wage elasticities in the data are quite low (see Bonhomme et al., 2012).

4.5 Preference, Entrepreneurial Ability, and Technology

To review, agent i consumes according to the following consumption function:

$$C_{it} = C^* + \gamma(\pi_{it} - C^*), \tag{4.1}$$

where C_{it} is the total consumption of agent i in period t, C^* is the subsistence level of consumption, and π_{it} is the total income of agent i in period t. The total consumption of agent i is the combination of the consumption of goods a and m according to the following function:

$$C_{it} = \left(\frac{C_{it}^a}{\mu}\right)^{\mu} \left(\frac{C_{it}^m}{1-\mu}\right)^{1-\mu} \tag{4.2}$$

where C_{it}^a is agent i's consumption of good a in period t, C_{it}^m is agent i's consumption of good m in period t, and μ is the parameter capturing the share of spending on goods from sector a. We currently assume that $\mu = 0.5$.[4] Since we model our village as small-open economies, the supply of goods from each sector is determined by the global relative price and not by the local demand for each good. Therefore, the equilibrium outcomes of our model are not sensitive to this parameter. The exceptions are the counterfactual example with financial frictions, in which the direction of trade flows depends on the local supply and the local demand for goods; the consumption share affects the local demand, so it also affects the equilibrium outcomes in this counterfactual exercise.

Agents accumulate their wealth by holding a fraction ω of their savings in cash and investing the rest in capital, which is produced by combining goods a and m according to the production function:

$$\Delta K_{it} = \left(\frac{I_{it}^a}{\mu}\right)^{\mu} \left(\frac{I_{it}^m}{1-\mu}\right)^{1-\mu}, \tag{4.3}$$

---

4. While we could use the detailed information about the composition of household consumption in the data to determine consumption shares, this has been deferred. In the model, we use cultivation for the labor-intensive sector, and we use livestock, fish and shrimp, and business for the capital-intensive sector. When we look at consumption data, we have the consumption of food and non-food, which includes the spending on gas, electricity, clothing, etc. Therefore, we need to decide what to do with the consumption of goods that are not related to the village's production.

where ΔK_{it} is the new capital produced, I_{it}^a is agent i's investment of good a in period t, and I_{it}^m is agent i's investment of good m in period t. The price of capital q is therefore equal to

$$q = (p_a)^\mu (p_m)^{1-\mu}, \tag{4.4}$$

where p_a is the price of good a and p_m is the price of good m. The capital will be used as the numéraire, and, therefore, $q = 1$.

4.6 Occupational Choice

An entrepreneur i in sector a with owned capital W_{it} and ability z_i solves the following maximization problem:[5]

$$\max\nolimits_{(K_{it}, L_{it})} p_a A_i K_{it}^{\alpha_K} L_{it}^{\alpha_L} - r_t K_{it} - w_t L_{it} \tag{4.5}$$

subject to the borrowing constraint

$$K_{it} \leq \eta_t W_{it}. \tag{4.6}$$

Let $\pi_t^a(W_{it}, z_i)$ denote the net profit of an entrepreneur i in sector a with owned capital W_{it} and ability z_i in period t. Similarly, an entrepreneur i in sector m with owned capital W_{it} and ability z_i solves the following maximization problem:

$$\max\nolimits_{(K_{it}, L_{it})} p_m B_i K_{it}^{\beta_K} L_{it}^{\beta_L} - r_t K_{it} - w_t L_{it} \tag{4.7}$$

subject to the borrowing constraint

$$K_{it} \leq \eta_t W_{it}. \tag{4.8}$$

Let $\pi_t^m(W_{it}, z_i)$ denote the net profit of an entrepreneur i in sector m with owned capital W_{it} and ability z_i in period t.

As discussed in Chapter 2, with the DRS production function, there exists an optimal business size for each entrepreneur. On the other hand, if the

---

5. As discussed in Chapter 2, we assume that a household's entrepreneurial ability is common across all production activities.

production function has a constant return to scale, only the most productive producers will produce until they reach their borrowing limit. Then, the second-most productive producers will take over, and so on.

Therefore, we can summarize the within-period income of agents in each group as follows:

$$\pi_t(W_{it}, z_i) = \begin{cases} w_t \overline{L} + r_t W_{it} & \text{for a worker} \\ \pi_t^a(W_{it}, z_i) + r_t W_{it} & \text{for an entrepreneur in sector } a \\ \pi_t^m(W_{it}, z_i) + r_t W_{it} & \text{for an entrepreneur in sector } m \end{cases} \quad (4.9)$$

The models with occupational choice and borrowing constraints, like this one, are quite standard in development economics literature (see, for example, Lloyd-Ellis and Bernhardt, 2000; Giné and Townsend, 2004; Jeong and Townend, 2008; or dynamic versions with endogenous saving of Buera, Kaboski, and Shin, 2011).

4.7 Markets for Capital and Labor

In this model, we assume that the market for capital is completely open and the market for labor is completely closed. In equilibrium, the wage rate w_t adjusts so that the local demand for labor equals the local supply of labor. This assumption might seem extreme at first. However, it is not unreasonable in practice. For supporting evidence, we refer back to Figure 4.4, which shows that the differences in interest rates across provinces become smaller over time, while the differences in wage rates do not.

We assume that each household is endowed with 3,461 units of labor per year. This number comes from the Townsend Thai data, in which the median number of household members whose age is above 15 is 2.4, and from the Thai macro data, in which 69.34% of the population aged 15 or above work full-time.[6]

We calibrate the capital endowment across households to match the distribution of their fixed assets in 1999, as noted earlier. Then, we use the cash-to-fixed-asset ratio in 1999 to approximate the initial cash holding in the model. We also assume that the initial distribution of a household's capital is uncorrelated with the household's ability.

---

6. There is very little difference in the demographics across provinces.

4.8 Mechanics of the Model

Borrowing limits and relative prices will jointly determine the occupational choices and the equilibrium wage rate. An increase in borrowing limits will increase the demand for capital and labor for the constrained entrepreneur. This will, in turn, increase the real wage rate.

The effect of increasing the borrowing limit on the decision to become workers vs. entrepreneurs is less obvious. On the one hand, an increase in borrowing limit increases the size and the profits of the constrained businesses. On the other hand, the increasing wage rate makes being a worker more attractive. An increase in borrowing limit also benefits the entrepreneurs in sector m (capital-intensive) more than the entrepreneurs in sector a (labor-intensive).

An increase in relative price, p_m/p_a, will increase the benefit of entrepreneurs in sector m relative to sector a. As entrepreneurs switch from sector a to sector m, the demand for labor will decrease. This is because sector a is labor-intensive, while sector m is capital-intensive. Finally, the decreased demand for labor will lower the real wage rate.

4.9 Calibration

Here we discuss first which variables we can use for calibration and then move on to dynamics.

4.9.1 Calibration Exercises

As we envisioned this model as a trade model with occupational choice subject to financial constraints, the obvious exogenous variables are the interest rate, the relative prices of goods, and the borrowing limit. To summarize what we have mentioned in the introduction and along the way, for the interest rate, we believe we have a good measure of the interest rate in the data, the observed value. Figure 4.10 shows the real interest rates in Lopburi, which we will use as the model's parameters.

For the relative price and the borrowing limit, we do not think we have very good measures. The relative prices are determined at the sector level, but the goods in the capital-intensive and labor-intensive sectors vary by region, and the available price indices are not sufficiently disaggregated, and so do not reflect local variation or shipping costs. Borrowing limits are approximations

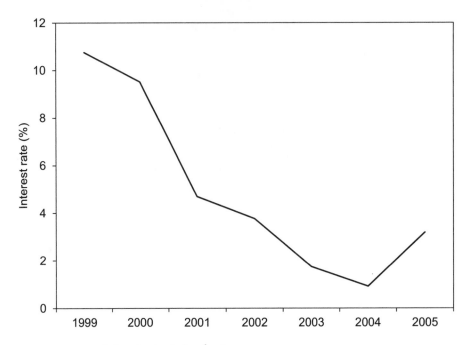

FIGURE 4.10 Interest rates in Lopburi.
Source: Townsend Thai Project; authors' calculation.

to implicit and formal credit contracts, which are not modeled in detail here, either. Therefore, we calibrate the relative price using the profit share from each sector and calibrate the borrowing limit using the wage rate.

4.9.2 Calibration Procedure for the Dynamics

Each year, we adjust the borrowing limit and the relative price jointly to match (i) the real wage rate observed in the data, and (ii) the share of entrepreneurial profits from sector a and sector m, respectively.

Figure 4.11 compares the calibrated borrowing limit from the model with the loan-to-wealth ratio of the median household in Lopburi. The result suggests that the calibrated borrowing limit moves closely with the loan-to-wealth ratio, with an exception in years 1999–2000, which is right after the Asian Financial Crisis.

Figure 4.12 shows the calibrated relative prices in Lopburi. The price of capital-intensive goods increases relative to the price of labor-intensive goods during 1999–2001 and decreases from 2002. The calibrated relative price in this baseline scenario could also include trade costs and other frictions. However,

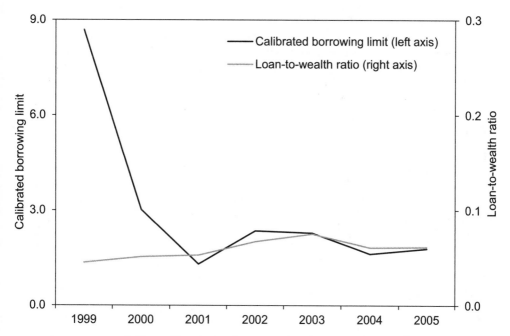

FIGURE 4.11 Calibrated borrowing limits and loan-to-wealth ratios in Lopburi.
Source: Townsend Thai Project; authors' calculations.

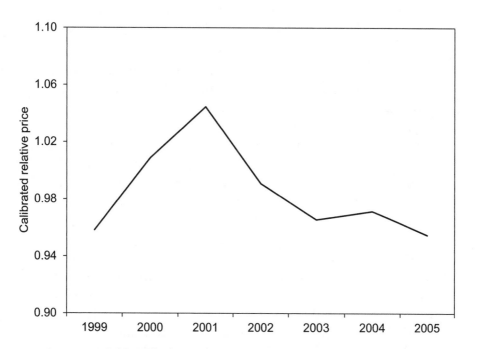

FIGURE 4.12 Calibrated relative prices in Lopburi.
Source: Townsend Thai Project; authors' calculations.

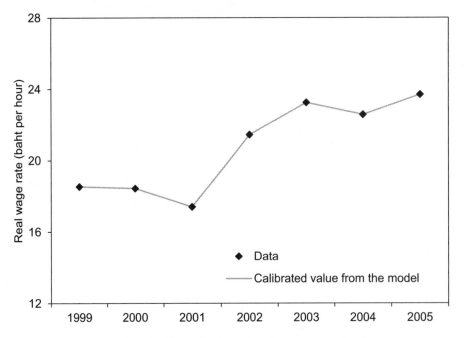

FIGURE 4.13 Actual and calibrated values of real wage rates in Lopburi.
Source: Townsend Thai Project; authors' calculations.

neither the results in this baseline scenario nor those in subsequent counter-factual exercises are affected by these unobserved initial trade frictions. We will discuss this more in Section 4.12.

Figures 4.13 and 4.14 compare the actual and the calibrated real wage rates and the actual and the calibrated shares of profits from the capital-intensive sector, respectively. With two calibrated variables (i.e., borrowing limit and relative price), we can exactly match the two target variables (i.e., wage rate and share of profit).

4.9.3 Calibration Result

Figure 4.15 shows the predicted occupational choices from the calibrated model in Lopburi in 1999. The horizontal axis represents the initial wealth of the household, while the vertical axis represents the household's entrepreneurial ability. The lines in the figures are the boundaries of the sets of households who choose certain occupations. A household can choose to become a worker, an entrepreneur in the labor-intensive sector *a*, or an entrepreneur in the capital-intensive sector *m*. We also distinguish a financially constrained

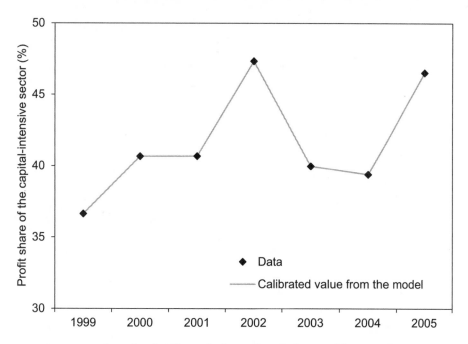

FIGURE 4.14 Actual and calibrated values of profit shares of the capital-intensive sector in Lopburi.
Source: Townsend Thai Project; authors' calculations.

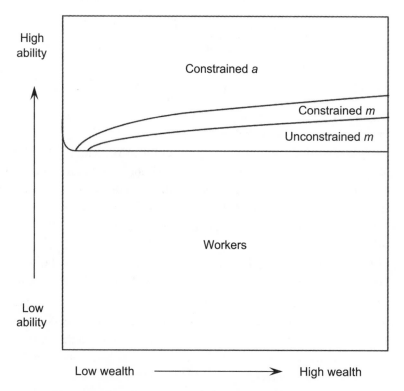

FIGURE 4.15 Predicted occupational choices in Lopburi in 1999.
Source: Authors' calculations.

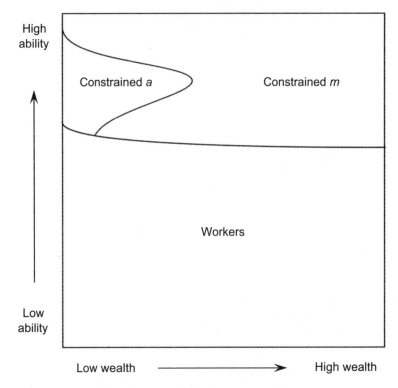

FIGURE 4.16 Predicted occupational choices in Lopburi in 2005.
Source: Authors' calculations.

entrepreneur, whose business could benefit from expansion, from an unconstrained entrepreneur, whose business is at the optimal size. For example, a financially constrained entrepreneur in the labor-intensive sector will be labeled
as "constrained a." The model predicts that households with medium to low
ability will choose to be workers regardless of their wealth level. The households
with high ability will be entrepreneurs. The household's choice of sector is determined by the household's ability rather than the household's wealth level.

Figure 4.16 shows the predicted occupational choices from the calibrated
model in Lopburi in 2005. Again, the households with medium to low ability
will choose to be workers regardless of their wealth level. However, for households with high ability, their wealth now determines the sector in which they
choose to be entrepreneurs. The households with low wealth will choose the
labor-intensive sector a, while the households with high wealth will choose
the capital-intensive sector m. The region of unconstrained entrepreneurs is
compressed to virtually zero.

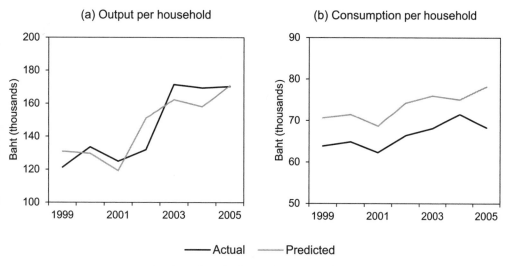

FIGURE 4.17 Actual and predicted values of output and consumption
per household.
Source: Townsend Thai Project; authors' calculations.

4.9.4 Evaluating the Performance of the Model

In this section, we evaluate the performance of the calibrated model by comparing the predicted values of income, consumption, fixed assets, and cash
holdings with those in the data at the village aggregated level. Panel (a) of
Figure 4.17 compares the predicted and the actual values of output per
household in Lopburi. The model can predict the levels reasonably well; the
average output per household in the data over the 7-year period is 146,140 baht
vs. the predicted value of 146,031 baht. Panel (b) of Figure 4.17 compares the
actual and the predicted values of consumption per household in Lopburi.
The model can also predict the level reasonably well (average 66,472 baht
actual vs. 73,462 baht predicted; the actual is a bit lower consistently).

The comparison of the actual and the predicted values of fixed assets per
household in Lopburi is shown in Panel (a) of Figure 4.18. Again, the model can
capture both the level (average 270,030 baht actual vs. 263,826 baht predicted)
and the growth of fixed assets remarkably well. Lastly, Panel (b) of Figure 4.18
compares the actual and predicted values of cash holding per household in
Lopburi. The model slightly underestimates the change in cash holding.

Figure 4.19 compares the actual and the predicted current account balances
in Lopburi. Again, the model can capture the average level of current account
surplus reasonably well (80,206 baht actual vs. 76,273 baht predicted). However,

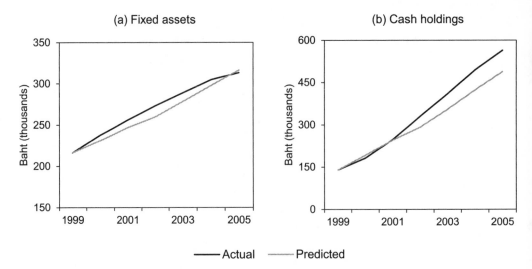

FIGURE 4.18 Actual and predicted values of fixed assets and cash holdings per household.
Source: Townsend Thai Project; authors' calculations.

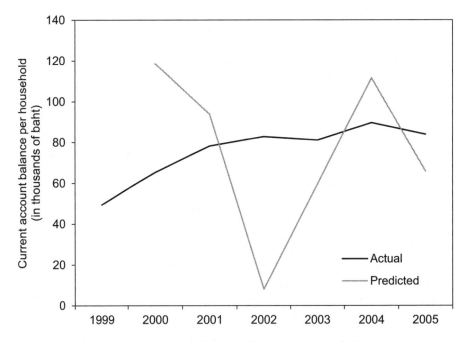

FIGURE 4.19 Actual and predicted values of current account balance per household.
Source: Townsend Thai Project; authors' calculations.

the model predicts that the current account surplus fluctuates much more than what we observe in the actual data.

4.10 The Model through the Lens of Illustrative Micro Data—Our Case Studies

We compare the model's prediction on households' occupation, income, and wealth with the data for our featured case-study households.

4.10.1 Household A

Recall that household A is an average-ability household with very low initial capital level. As a result, the model's prediction is that this household will always be a worker, which is confirmed by the data, as labor income has always been the main source of income for this household. Panels (a) and (b) of Figure 4.20 compare the actual income and consumption of this household with those predicted by the model. The model can predict the average income of household A reasonably well (75,568 baht predicted vs. 70,188 baht actual) but overpredicts the average consumption level (58,369 baht predicted vs. 40,528 baht actual).

Panels (c) and (d) of Figure 4.20 compare the actual values of fixed assets and cash holdings of household A with those predicted by the model. The model can capture the overall growth rate of fixed assets reasonably well, while it underpredicts the growth rate of cash holdings.

4.10.2 Household B

Household B is a high-ability household with intermediate initial capital level. In the data, the main source of income for this household is cultivation activity, which is labor-intensive. However, the model predicts that this household would always choose to be an entrepreneur in the capital-intensive sector.

Panels (a) and (b) of Figure 4.21 compare actual income and actual consumption of household B with those predicted by the model. The model can predict the average level of consumption reasonably well (83,542 baht predicted vs 82,763 baht actual) but underpredict the average level of income (202,126 baht predicted vs. 271,208 baht actual). Moreover, the model cannot capture the fluctuation in income and consumption level. Recall that, here and elsewhere, there are no income shocks in the model.

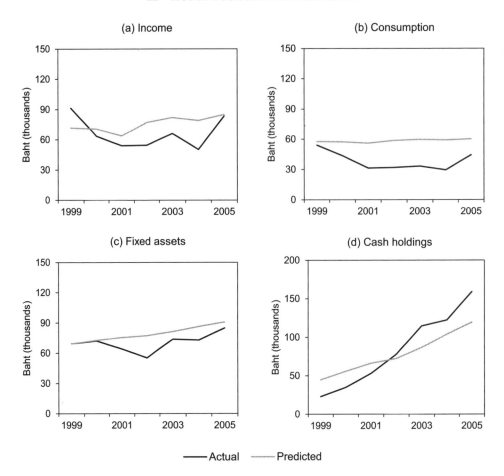

FIGURE 4.20 Actual and predicted values of income, consumption, fixed assets, and cash holdings of household A.
Source: Townsend Thai Project; authors' calculations.

Panels (c) and (d) of Figure 4.21 compare the values of household B's fixed assets and cash holdings in the data with those predicted by the model. As with the case of household A, the model can capture the overall growth rate of fixed assets reasonably well, while it underpredicts the growth rate of cash holdings.

4.10.3   Household C

Household C is a very-high-ability household with very high wealth. In the data, the main source of income for this household is business activity, which is capital-intensive. Indeed, the model correctly predicts that this

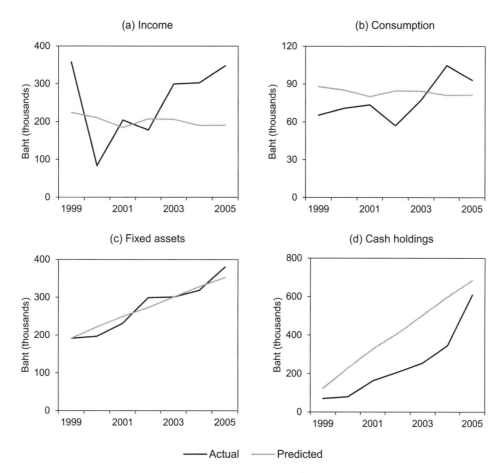

FIGURE 4.21 Actual and predicted values of income, consumption, fixed assets, and cash holdings of household B.
Source: Townsend Thai Project; authors' calculations.

household would choose to be an entrepreneur in the capital-intensive sector.

Panels (a) and (b) of Figure 4.22 compare the actual income and consumption of household C with those predicted by the model. The model can predict the average level of income reasonably well (1,055,052 baht predicted vs. 1,117,568 baht actual) but overpredicts the average level of consumption (253,189 baht predicted vs. 184,561 baht actual). Moreover, the model cannot capture the fluctuation in income and consumption level.

Panels (c) and (d) of Figures 4.22 compare the values of household C's fixed assets and cash holdings in the data with those predicted by the model. For

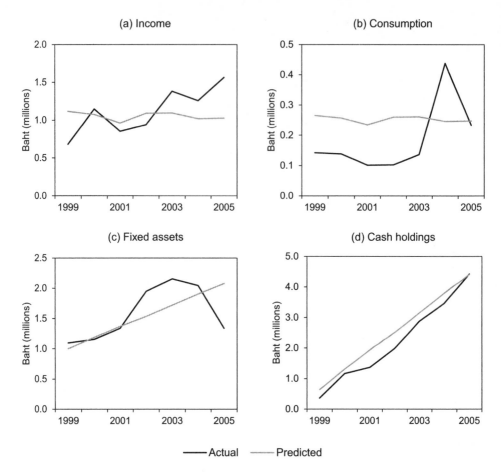

FIGURE 4.22 Actual and predicted values of income, consumption, fixed assets, and cash holdings of household C.
Source: Townsend Thai Project; authors' calculations.

this case study, the model captures the overall growth rate of cash holdings reasonably well, while its prediction errors for the growth rate of fixed assets are erratic.

4.11 Counterfactual Exercise

In this section, we consider two counterfactual exercises. In the first exercise, we try to distinguish between the effects of real and financial factors by keeping one factor at the initial level and varying another factor. In the second exercise, we consider the effects of wedges reflecting frictions for trade, for the financial market, or for both. Finally, we predict what would happen to our case-study households in these counterfactual scenarios.

4.11.1 *Disentangling Real and Financial Factors*

In this exercise, we freeze the relative price ratio at the initial 1999 level and vary the financial variables (i.e., the interest rate and the borrowing limit) using the calibrated values from the baseline scenario. Then, we freeze those financial variables at the initial 1999 levels and vary the relative price. Hence, we are disentangling real and financial forces behind the movement over time through the lens of the model.

4.11.2 *Lopburi*

Figure 4.23 compares the outputs in the baseline scenario with those in the counterfactual scenario. The black line shows the outputs in the baseline scenario, where both real and financial factors are, in effect, playing active roles. The grey line shows the outputs in the counterfactual scenario, where only the real factor (i.e., relative price) is varied. Thus, the difference between the black line and the grey line for the relative price shows the effect of financial factors (i.e., interest rate and borrowing limit). The dashed line shows the outputs in the counterfactual scenario where only the financial factors (i.e., borrowing limit and interest rate) are varied, and the difference between the black line and the dashed line for financial factors shows the effect of the real factor.

In Lopburi, both interest rates and borrowing limits decrease over time (see Figures 4.10 and 4.11). These changes have opposing effects on output. On the one hand, lower interest rates increase entrepreneurial profits and the optimal size of businesses. Therefore, output should be higher. On the other hand, tighter borrowing limits decrease entrepreneurs' ability to borrow and the size of businesses of the constrained entrepreneurs. As a result, output should be lower. The results in Figure 4.23 suggest that the effect of borrowing limits dominates, as the output is lower in the baseline scenario (which includes the effect of financial factors) than in the "only real factor" counterfactual exercise (which excludes the effect of financial factors).

The relative price in Lopburi increases in the first three years and decreases in the last four years. Moreover, the changes in relative price are relatively small

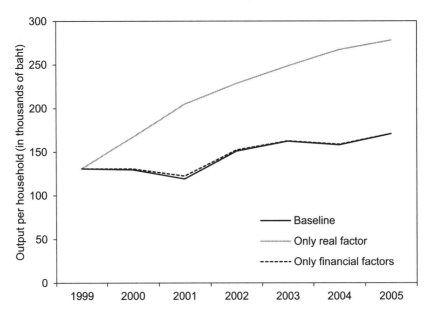

FIGURE 4.23 Outputs in baseline and counterfactual scenarios in Lopburi.
Source: Townsend Thai Project; authors' calculations.

(i.e., within a 5% range). The result suggests that the effect of relative prices is small since the dotted line lies almost on top of the black line.

The changes in interest rates and borrowing limits also have opposing effects on wage rates. On the one hand, lower interest rates increase the amount of capital used and raise the marginal product of labor. Thus, wage rates should be higher. On the other hand, tighter borrowing limits decrease economic activity, which lowers the demand for labor, and lowers wage rates as well. The result in Figure 4.24 suggests that, as in the case of outputs, the effect of borrowing limits dominates.

The level of relative prices in 2000–2004 of the capital-intensive sector good relative to the labor-intensive sector good is higher than the 1999 level. As a result, the change in relative prices should have a negative effect on wage rates. This is because the higher relative price will increase the profits of entrepreneurs in sector m relative to the profits of entrepreneurs in sector a. As the entrepreneurs move from the labor-intensive sector a to the capital-intensive sector m, the aggregate demand for labor decreases. The result in Figure 4.24 confirms this prediction as the wage rates in the "only financial factors" counterfactual scenario are higher than the wage rates in the baseline scenario between 2000 and 2004 that has an increase in the relative price.

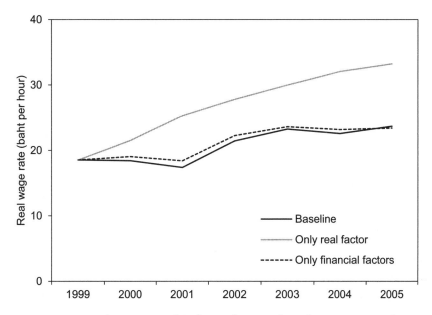

FIGURE 4.24 Real wage rates in baseline and counterfactual scenarios in Lopburi. *Source: Townsend Thai Project; authors' calculations.*

Changes in interest rates and borrowing limits also have opposing effects on the share of profit from each sector. On the one hand, decreasing interest rates benefit the capital-intensive sector m more than the labor-intensive sector a. Therefore, the share of profit from sector m should increase. On the other hand, tightening the borrowing limits affects the constrained entrepreneurs in sector m more than those in sector a, since sector m is more capital-intensive. As a result, the shares of profit from sector m should decrease. Figure 4.25 compares the share of profit from sector m in Lopburi in the baseline scenario with that in the counterfactual scenario. Again, the result suggests that the effect from tightening borrowing limits dominates, since the share of profit from sector m in the baseline scenario is lower than that in the "only real factor" counterfactual scenario that does not have these financial changes.

The effect of the changes in relative price on the share of profit from sector m is straightforward. The relative prices in 2000–2004 are higher than the 1999 level. Therefore, the share of profit from sector m should also be higher in this period. On the other hand, the relative price in 2005 is lower than the 1999 level. Therefore, the share of profit from sector m should be lower in this year.

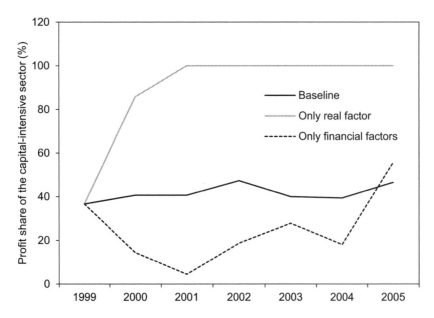

FIGURE 4.25 Shares of profit from the capital-intensive sector in baseline and counterfactual scenarios in Lopburi.
Source: Townsend Thai Project; authors' calculations.

The results in Figure 4.25 confirm this prediction, for example, with the baseline lower in 2005 than the "only financial factors" line.

4.12   Trade and Financial Frictions

In the second counterfactual exercise, we consider the effects of frictions on trade and financial channels, one at a time. For trade frictions, we impose iceberg-type trade costs on the imported goods. The effect of trade costs on relative prices will depend on the types of goods that a village imports. For example, if a village imports good a and exports good m, we assume that trade frictions will lower the relative price of exported good m and increase the price of the imported good a, so the relative price decreases by 1%. On the other hand, if a village exports good a and imports good m, we assume that trade frictions will increase the relative price by 1%.

For financial frictions, we assume that if a village resident lends to a non-village resident, there is a 1% transaction tax. On the other hand, lending to another village resident is risk-free. Therefore, financial frictions by keeping more funds at home will lower the local equilibrium interest rate if a village is a net lender.

4.12.1 *Lopburi*

Since villages in Lopburi export the labor-intensive good a and import the capital-intensive good m under the baseline scenario, trade frictions increase the price of imported good m relative to the price of good a. Panel (a) of Figure 4.26 shows the value of output from each sector in the counterfactual scenario with this trade friction. The level of output from labor-intensive sector a is higher than the level of output from capital-intensive sector m in the first three years. This result suggests that villages in Lopburi can still export goods from sector a despite trade frictions in these years. On the other hand, imposing trade frictions totally shut down trade for this village in the last four years. Therefore, the equilibrium relative price in the last four years is the one that equalizes the local demand for and the local supply of goods from each sector. Panel (b) of Figure 4.26 compares the equilibrium relative prices in the baseline scenario with those in the counterfactual scenario with trade frictions.[7]

Panel (a) of Figure 4.27 shows the local demand and the local supply of capital in the counterfactual scenario with financial frictions. The local supply of capital exceeds the local demand for capital in all years. Therefore, the local interest rates will be lower than the global ones due to financial frictions. We compare the equilibrium interest rates in the baseline scenario and those in the counterfactual scenario with financial frictions in Panel (b) of Figure 4.27.

Panel (a) of Figure 4.28 shows the differences between the levels of output in the two counterfactual scenarios and that in the baseline scenario. While the 1% trade frictions are enough to drive the village into autarky, their effect on the levels of output is quite small. In the counterfactual scenario with financial frictions, the levels of output are higher than those in the baseline scenario in all years and the difference pattern resembles the pattern of borrowing limits. This is because this village is the net lender in all years. Thus, financial frictions lower the local interest rates, which, in turn, lead to entrepreneurs using more capital and producing more output. The size of the output increase will depend

---

7. As discussed in Section 4.9, the relative price under the baseline scenario could include existing trade costs and other frictions. However, these existing trade frictions will not qualitatively affect our counterfactual results. For example, suppose that the baseline price of 0.96 in 1999 already includes 2% trade costs. Since this village exports good a in baseline 1999, the "world" relative price is likely to be 2% lower (i.e., $p_m/p_a = 0.94$). For the counterfactual exercise, in which we impose a 1% trade friction on top of the existing frictions, the village's relative price would be 0.97, which is similar to the level in our current counterfactual exercise. Thus, the counterfactual results remain unchanged.

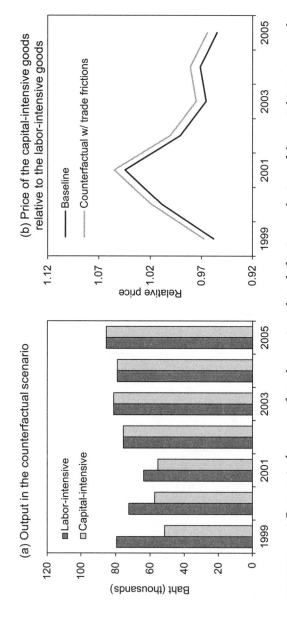

FIGURE 4.26 Outputs in the counterfactual scenario with trade frictions and prices of the capital-intensive goods relative to the labor-intensive goods in the baseline scenario and in the counterfactual scenario with trade frictions.

Source: Townsend Thai Project; authors' calculations.

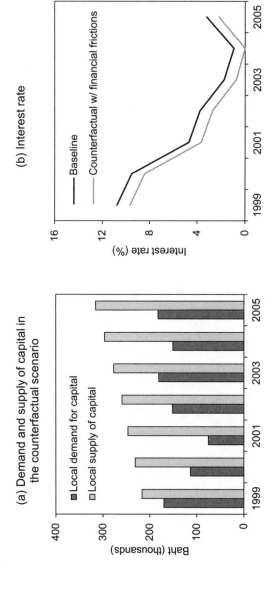

FIGURE 4.27 Demand and supply of capital in the counterfactual scenario with financial frictions and interest rates in the baseline scenario and in the counterfactual scenario with financial frictions.
Source: Townsend Thai Project; authors' calculations.

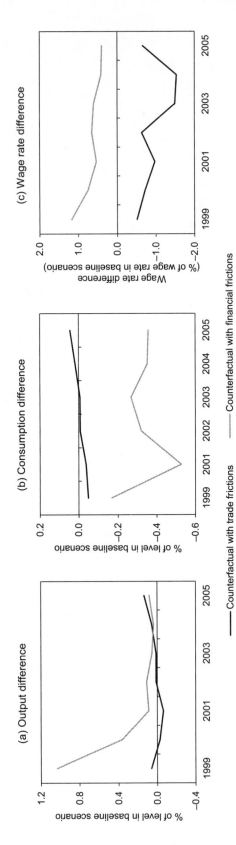

FIGURE 4.28 Differences in output levels, consumption levels, and wage rates in the counterfactual scenarios in comparison to the baseline scenario.

Source: Townsend Thai Project; authors' calculations.

on how much more entrepreneurs can borrow, which is determined by the borrowing limits.

The differences between the consumption levels in counterfactual scenarios and those in the baseline scenario are reported in Panel (b) of Figure 4.28. As in the case of output, trade frictions have a small effect on the average consumption level. Financial frictions have negative effects on consumption levels through the lower interest income.

Both frictions have considerable impact on wage rates, as shown in Panel (c) of Figure 4.28, but in opposite directions. In the counterfactual scenario with trade frictions, wage rates are lower than those in the baseline scenario. As noted earlier, trade frictions increase the relative price of the output of sector m relative to that of sector a in these villages. As a result, the marginal entrepreneurs will move from the labor-intensive sector a to the capital-intensive sector m. Therefore, the local demand for labor decreases, and so do the wage rates. In the counterfactual scenario with financial frictions, the lowered interest rates raise the use of capital and thus raise the marginal product of labor. As the local demand for labor increases, so do the wage rates.

4.12.2 Effects on Households' Occupation and Income

4.12.2.1 COUNTERFACTUAL SCENARIO WITH TRADE FRICTIONS

Finally, we return to our main theme and consider the effects of the counterfactual scenario on the income of agents. Panel (a) of Figure 4.29 shows the income difference between the baseline scenario and the counterfactual scenario with trade frictions in Lopburi in year 1999. To show that the effect of trade frictions could be different across heterogeneous households, we compare three groups of households that have different ability levels: the average-skilled group ($z_i = 0$), the high-skilled group ($z_i = \sigma$), and the very-high-skilled group ($z_i = 2\sigma$). The vertical axis shows the welfare gains and losses measured as the changes in households' total income. The horizontal axis shows the value of households' capital in 1999.

The dashed line shows the change in income of average-skilled and high-skilled households. Since the households choose to be wageworkers in both the baseline scenario and the counterfactual scenario, welfare loss reflects the change in wage income as a fraction of household total income. For wealthier households, the welfare loss becomes smaller since the fraction of interest income becomes bigger.

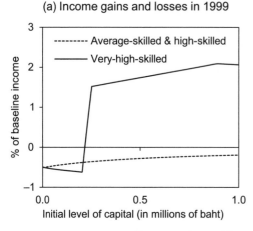

(a) Income gains and losses in 1999

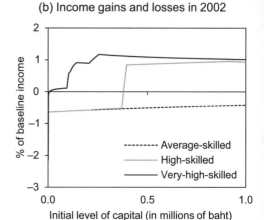

(b) Income gains and losses in 2002

FIGURE 4.29 Income gains and losses from trade frictions for households with different skill levels.
Source: Townsend Thai Project; authors' calculations.

The solid line shows the change in income of very-high-skilled households. For them, the effect of trade frictions on households' income is non-monotonic. We can separate the very-high-skilled entrepreneurs into three groups. The first group consists of households with low wealth (i.e., those with initial capital less than 206,000 baht). The second group consists of households with medium wealth (i.e., those with initial capital between 206,000 and 254,000 baht). Households with high wealth (i.e., those with initial capital more than 254,000 baht) belong to the third group.

The first group of very-high-skilled households chooses to be entrepreneurs in the labor-intensive sector in both the baseline scenario and the counterfactual scenario. For this group, the households' total income decreases because trade frictions lower the price of labor-intensive goods.

The second group switches from being entrepreneurs in the labor-intensive sector in the baseline scenario to being entrepreneurs in the capital-intensive sector in the counterfactual scenario. We observe a positive relationship between the change in welfare and the households' initial wealth for this group.

The third group of very-high-skilled households chooses to be entrepreneurs in the capital-intensive sector in both the baseline scenario and the counterfactual scenario. For this group, the households' total income increases because trade frictions raise the price of capital-intensive goods.

Panel (b) of Figure 4.29 shows the income difference between the baseline scenario and the counterfactual scenario with trade frictions in Lopburi in the

later year of 2002. Again, average-skilled households choose to be wageworkers in both the baseline scenario and the counterfactual scenario, and the welfare loss reflects the decrease in wage rate.

For high-skilled households, we can separate them into three groups. First,
households with low initial wealth (with initial capital less than 370,000 baht)
choose to be workers in both the baseline scenario and the counterfactual
scenario and have welfare loss from the lower wage rate. Second, households
with medium initial wealth (with initial capital between 370,000 and 395,000
baht) switch from being wageworkers in the baseline scenario to being entrepreneurs in the capital-intensive sector. The welfare of households in this
group increases with wealth level. Third, households with high wealth (with
initial capital more than 395,000 baht) choose to be entrepreneurs in the
capital-intensive sector in both the baseline scenario and the counterfactual
scenario. The welfare gain of households in this group reflects the increase in
the price of capital-intensive goods.

For very-high-skilled households, welfare change in 2002 reflects not only
the occupational switch in 2002, but also the effects from previous years caus-
ing a change in the 2002 wealth level. This results in the highly nonlinear pattern of welfare gains and losses.

4.12.2.2 COUNTERFACTUAL SCENARIO
WITH FINANCIAL FRICTIONS

Panel (a) of Figure 4.30 shows the income difference between the baseline
scenario and the counterfactual scenario with financial frictions in Lopburi in
year 1999. In the counterfactual scenario, the interest rate is lower than in the
baseline scenario, while the wage rate is higher. These changes in factor prices
have opposite effects on the welfare of average-skilled and high-skilled
households, who always choose to be wageworkers. On the one hand, a higher
wage rate raises their wage income. On the other hand, a lower interest rate
lowers their interest income. Therefore, households with very low initial
wealth enjoy welfare gain since the effect from a higher wage rate dominates,
while households with higher initial wealth face welfare loss since the effect
from a lower interest rate dominates.

Very-high-skilled households always choose to be entrepreneurs (except for
the poorest ones, which choose to be workers) in both the baseline scenario
and the counterfactual exercise. Therefore, the effects from changing factor prices
on their income are in the opposite direction from those on wageworkers, i.e.,

(a) Income gains and losses in 1999

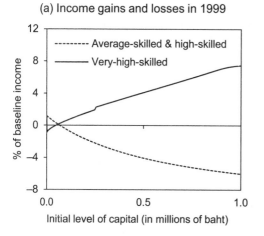

(b) Income gains and losses in 2002

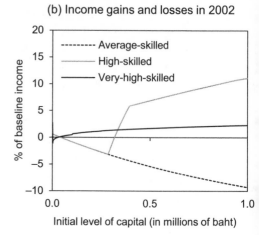

FIGURE 4.30 Income gains and losses from financial frictions for households with different skill levels.
Source: Townsend Thai Project; authors' calculations.

they enjoy a lower interest rate but are hurt by a higher wage rate. The result in Panel (a) of Figure 4.30 suggests that the benefit from a lower interest rate outweighs the cost of a higher wage rate for most households. And those with higher wealth, who used more capital, benefit more from a lower interest rate. Note, in particular, that for relatively high wealth the losses or gains in these experiments can be quite substantial, approaching 8%.

Panel (b) of Figure 4.30 shows the income difference between the baseline scenario and the counterfactual scenario with financial frictions in Lopburi in the year 2002. Again, average-skilled households choose to be wageworkers in both the baseline scenario and the counterfactual scenario, and the welfare loss reflects the decrease in interest income.

High-skilled households with relatively low wealth also choose to be wageworkers in both the baseline scenario and the counterfactual scenario and, therefore, face the same welfare gain/loss as the average-skilled households. Households with medium wealth level (i.e., initial level of capital between 285,000 and 394,000 baht) choose to switch from being workers in the baseline scenario to being entrepreneurs in the capital-intensive sector in the counterfactual scenario. For this group of households, welfare gain increases with their wealth level.

Again, very-high-skilled households always choose to be entrepreneurs, and the result suggests that the benefit from a lower interest rate outweighs the cost of a high wage rate for most households.

Note also that the effect as a percentage of gains and losses can be large. However, in addition to the effects of trade frictions and financial frictions on income level, we also looked at the effects on income inequality across households and found that the effects are small.

4.13 Case Studies

4.13.1 Household A

Recall that household A in our case studies is an average-skilled household with very low initial wealth. Our model predicts that this household will always choose to be a worker in both the baseline scenario and all counterfactual scenarios. Figure 4.31 reports the differences between the net income of household A in the counterfactual scenarios and that in the baseline scenario. Since household A always chooses to be a worker, the two sources of this household's income are wages and interest from savings. And thus, its income will depend only on the wage rate and the interest rate. In the counterfactual scenario with trade frictions, wage rates are lower than those in baseline scenario while interest rates are the same. As a result, the net income of household A in the counterfactual scenario with trade frictions is lower than that in the baseline scenario.

In the counterfactual scenario with financial frictions, wage rates are higher than those in baseline scenario, but interest rates are lower. Since the net income of household A in the counterfactual scenario with financial frictions is lower than that in the baseline scenario, this result suggests that the changes in interest income are larger than the changes in labor income. The change in household A's consumption has a similar pattern to the change in income.

4.13.2 Household C

As household C has very high ability and very high initial wealth, our model predicts that this household will choose to be an entrepreneur in the capital-intensive sector in both the baseline scenario and all counterfactual scenarios. Figure 4.32 reports the differences between the net income of household C in the counterfactual scenarios and that in the baseline scenario. As an entrepreneur in the capital-intensive sector, household C's income will be affected by all the equilibrium prices (wage rates, interest rates, and relative prices). In the counterfactual scenario with trade frictions, relative prices of the

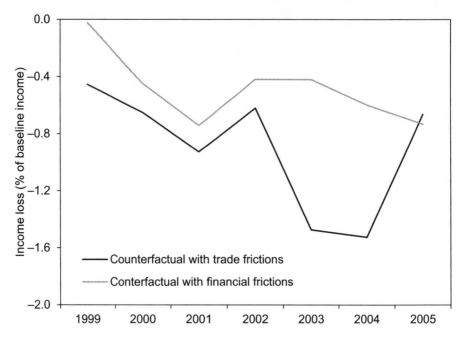

FIGURE 4.31 Household A's income losses from trade and financial frictions.
Source: Townsend Thai Project; authors' calculations.

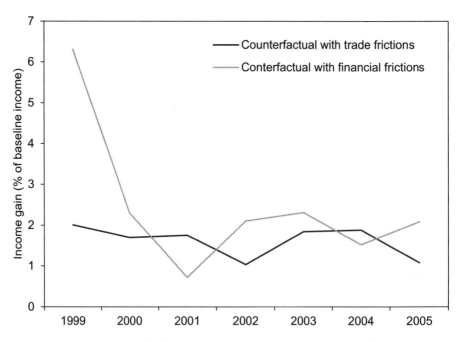

FIGURE 4.32 Household C's income gains from trade and financial frictions.
Source: Townsend Thai Project; authors' calculations.

capital-intensive goods are higher than those in the baseline scenario. In addition, wage rates are lower. Both changes increase the profits of entrepreneurs in the capital-intensive sector. Therefore, the net income of household C in the counterfactual scenario with trade frictions will be higher than that in the baseline scenario.

In the counterfactual scenario with financial frictions, the wage rate is higher than that in the baseline scenario, while interest rates are lower. The benefit of lower interest rates outweighs the cost of higher wage rates, as can be seen from the higher net incomes of household C. Again, the change in household C's consumption has a similar pattern as the change in income.

The changes in income and consumption of household B are similar to those of household C and therefore are omitted in the interest of brevity.

4.14 Regional Comparison: Buriram

In this section, we will briefly describe villages in Buriram and compare them with those in Lopburi. We will also discuss the possible similarities and differences in the outcomes of the counterfactual exercises in these two provinces.

First, Buriram is less capital-abundant in comparison to Lopburi. Figure 4.33 compares the initial distribution of fixed assets in Lopburi and Buriram. Households in Buriram have less capital than households in Lopburi, and the relative scarcity of capital in Buriram is also reflected in factor prices. Figure 4.34 compares the interest rates and the wage rates in Lopburi and Buriram. Not surprisingly, capital-abundant Lopburi has lower interest rates and higher wage rates than the labor-abundant Buriram.

The differences in factor endowments and factor prices across provinces also affect the production activities within the villages. The standard Heckscher-Ohlin model predicts that villages in the Central provinces would have an advantage in producing capital-intensive goods, while villages in the Northeast provinces, labor-intensive goods. We do observe such patterns, at least in the early years. In 1999–2000, almost all of the profit in Buriram comes from labor-intensive activities, as can be seen in Figure 4.35.[8] On the other hand, capital-intensive activities account for 40% of the profit in Lopburi. However, the share of capital-intensive profit in Buriram increases significantly

8. We define growing crops as a labor-intensive activity and define operating fish/shrimp ponds, raising livestock, and operating household businesses as capital-intensive activities.

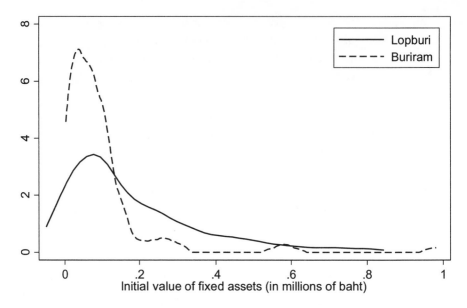

FIGURE 4.33 Initial distributions of fixed assets in Lopburi and Buriram.
Source: Townsend Thai Project; authors' calculations.

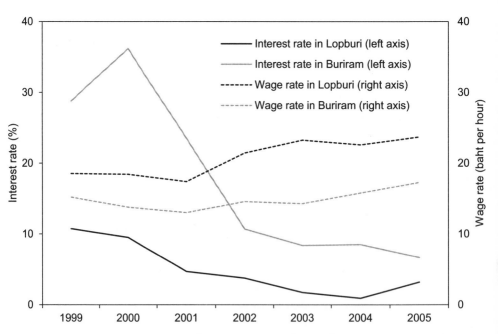

FIGURE 4.34 Interest rates and wage rates in Lopburi and Buriram.
Source: Townsend Thai Project; authors' calculations.

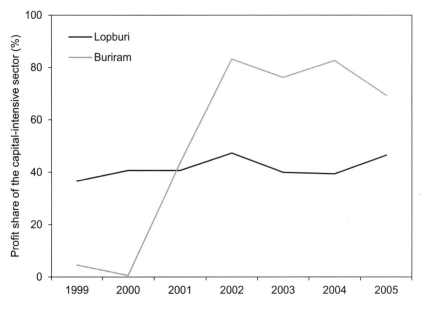

FIGURE 4.35 Share of profits from the capital-intensive sector.
Source: Townsend Thai Project; authors' calculations.

over time, reaches the Lopburi level in 2001, and accounts for 80% of the profit in Buriram from 2002. This change happens at the same time as the sharp drop in the interest rate in Buriram. Thus, the calibration results of Buriram provide a dynamic picture of transition economies.

The difference in occupational compositions between Lopburi and Buriram will also lead to the different outcomes in the counterfactual exercises. For example, suppose that a village in Buriram is also a net lender. In the counterfactual exercise, financial frictions will lower the local interest rate, as in Lopburi. The interest rate decrease will have different effects on households with different occupations (i.e., workers, labor-intensive entrepreneurs, capital-intensive entrepreneurs). More specifically, capital-intensive entrepreneurs will benefit more than labor-intensive entrepreneurs. On the other hand, workers will be negatively affected by the lower interest rate due to the loss in interest income. And, for example, if Buriram has less capital-intensive entrepreneurs than Lopburi (as in 1999–2000), it will be affected less. Thus, counterfactual exercises in Buriram illustrate different outcomes of trade and financial frictions.

5

Taking Integrated Financial Accounts to the U.S.

IN THIS CHAPTER, we assess the degree of integration of the U.S. household surveys by comparing the changes in the balance sheet with the flows in the income statement, both of which are constructed in each of the various household-level surveys.[1] Relative to other countries, the United States has a large amount of high-quality data on household economic behavior. Even the U.S. data, however, were inadequate to inform economic agents and policy-makers sufficiently to avoid the 2007–2008 financial crisis. Many efforts are underway to acquire and develop additional needed data; these efforts include the Eurosystem's Household Finance and Consumption Survey (HFCS), which was inspired partly by the U.S. Survey of Consumer Finances.[2] Other efforts, such as the National Academy of Science's call for substantially revised Consumer Expenditure Surveys, aim to reform existing datasets (Dillman and House, 2013).

U.S. household survey data exhibit several characteristics that limit their effectiveness. The U.S. statistical system (public and private) is decentralized, with each data source specializing in a part of household activity. Although there are often good reasons for specialization, the result is a general lack of comprehensive measurement of household activity. Many datasets are cross-sectional,

1. We gratefully acknowledge permission from Western Economic Association International to reproduce, with edits, Samphantharak, Krislert, Scott Schuh, and Robert M. Townsend (2018), "Integrated Household Surveys: An Assessment of U.S. Methods and an Innovation," *Economic Inquiry* 56 (1): 50–80, Western Economic Association International.

2. For more information on the HFCS, see https://www.ecb.europa.eu/pub/economic -research/research-networks/html/researcher_hfcn.en.html.

which limits their ability to track the behavior of specific households over time, and are gathered infrequently. When data sources are combined in an effort to provide a more comprehensive view of household behavior, the combination of the specialized data sources can create imperfect, if not misleading, views of household economic conditions, due to differences in sampling, measurement, and linkages between microeconomic and aggregate data.[3] These imperfections make it difficult to ascertain from the data the extent and nature of important developments, such as adjustments affecting household balance sheets in the wake of the financial crisis, increases in income inequality, and intergenerational dynamics of household net worth.

We believe an important step forward in understanding household behavior is the development of more reliable and effective measures of household economic activity, both real and financial. Therefore, an overarching goal of this chapter is to describe a comprehensive vision for a practical implementation of household surveys that are integrated with financial statements and payments data, leaving no gaps in measurement and strengthening the theoretical and applied linkages among measures. The main contributions of this chapter are: 1) to assess how well integrated U.S. household surveys are with elements of financial statements for households; and 2) to demonstrate how a diary of U.S. consumer payment choices can be used to construct a new statement of liquidity flows that advances the current state of the art in measuring stock-flow dynamics. Consistent stock-flow dynamics are the key step in creating integrated financial accounts at all levels, including integrated financial accounts in the United States at the macro level. This second step thus takes us closer to realizing the overarching vision of these lectures.

As a first step, we use the Samphantharak and Townsend (2009) framework to assess the degree of integration in leading U.S. household surveys. For each survey considered, we tabulate and juxtapose the data in the form of corporate financial statements applied to the representative U.S. household. We first construct for each survey a harmonized balance sheet, income statement, and

---

3. Carroll, Crossley, and Sabelhaus (2015) present numerous studies showing the various practical and theoretical trade-offs inherent in attempting to use survey data to build economic aggregates, trade-offs that can make comparing results from different surveys extremely challenging. For instance, Crossley and Winter (2015) note the difficulties survey designers can have even in defining the term "household," which can significantly affect the comparability of survey results. Similarly, surveys with a short reference period may underestimate infrequent purchases, while surveys with a long reference period may suffer from recall issues. Two surveys with different reference periods may have comparability issues.

statement of cash flows for a recent time period that matches the survey dates—around 2012—as closely as possible.

Then, we use the estimated U.S. household financial statements to characterize the degree of integration by two distinct measures. *Integration by coverage* reflects the extent to which a survey contains estimates of each line item in the financial statements. All the surveys cover roughly half the income statement items, although most specialize in income or expenditures. However, the coverage of the balance sheet items varies widely across surveys. *Integration by dynamics* reflects the extent to which the statement of cash flows accurately measures the law of motion between stocks (shown in the balance sheet) and flows (shown in the income statement). None of the surveys can provide truly direct statements of cash flows, and all of them make large errors relative to indirect estimates of changes in assets and liabilities.

Our assessment of integration in U.S. household surveys is merely a factual statement of results and is not intended to be a criticism of the surveys or a call for reforming them. We recognize and accept the specialty nature of U.S. surveys, which has the benefit of allowing gains from specialization and achievement of each survey's original goals. For example, the Panel Study on Income Dynamics (PSID) was originally designed to measure poverty and to contribute to its reduction in conjunction with President Lyndon B. Johnson's Great Society programs; the Consumer Expenditure Surveys (CE) were designed to gather data for developing accurate price indices; and the Survey of Consumer Finances (SCF) was designed to measure wealth. Although some of these surveys have evolved over the years, particularly the PSID, others retain their original mandate. Yet the specialization and persistence of the U.S. surveys does leave gaps in measurement that can only be overcome by comprehensive integration of the surveys with financial statements. Ironically, because the PSID and the SCF are so highly regarded, they are adopted as the gold standard elsewhere in the world, for example, in China and Europe, thus propagating essentially the same gaps in these other regions' surveys as in their U.S. counterparts.

A second step of this chapter is to use the Federal Reserve Bank of Boston's 2012 Diary of Consumer Payment Choice (DCPC) to demonstrate how consumer payment diary surveys can improve the dynamic integration of surveys.[4] The DCPC directly measures several, but not all, components of the law

---

4. Separately, Schuh (2018) reports that the DCPC produces estimates of U.S. consumer expenditures that greatly exceed those from the Consumer Expenditure Surveys (and diary)

of motion governing the stock-flow relationship between assets and liabilities (balance sheet items) and income and expenditures (income statement items). Because the 2012 DCPC is focused on consumer payments authorized by payment instruments (cash, check, debit or credit card, online banking, and such), it focuses on liquid assets used as payment instruments, including the currency held and used by U.S. consumers. In this respect, the DCPC is similar to the Townsend Thai Monthly Survey (TTMS), which underlies the Samphantharak and Townsend (2009) methodology, where currency is the main household asset and payment instrument in rural Thailand.

The central innovation of this chapter is the construction of a new, more detailed analysis of cash flows at the level of liquid asset accounts, where currency, checking accounts, and other liquid assets are distinguished between and treated separately. By tracking consumer expenditures that are authorized by payment instruments tied to specific types of liquid asset accounts, the DCPC matches expenditures to the sources of money and credit that fund them. This matching cannot be done by surveys that track consumer expenditures at the level of individual products (the Consumer Expenditure Surveys) or at the level of aggregated expenditure categories ("food away from home").

Linking all the liquidity accounts to one another and to the expenditures (or investments) they fund makes it possible to better assess the changing landscape of payments taking place in the United States and industrialized countries as well as in emerging market and low-income countries.[5] This then links back to the need for data to better inform public policy and to provide consumers with the information they need to improve household decision making and economic behavior. More informative financial accounts come from considering payments, and, vice versa, better payments data come from integrated financial accounts.

The conceptualization contribution, a comprehensive statement of liquidity flows, applies not just at the household level, as done here, but also for other sectors such as unincorporated business. Indeed, the financial accounts of the Townsend Thai data do not make this distinction at all. Traditionally in the United States, households are viewed as wage and salary earners, though

---

and that approximately match the National Income and Product Accounts estimates of comparably defined measures of consumption and disposable income.

5. For information about the Federal Reserve's efforts to stimulate innovations in the U.S. payment system, see https://fedpaymentsimprovement.org/.

this assumption in turn can lead to errors, as in the discussion of inequality and imputed wealth in the concluding chapter on U.S. inequality. In any event, nonfinancial and financial corporate businesses are another sector for which a comprehensive statement of liquidity accounts would be of some interest, as it would be as well for broker dealers. Think of recent discussions of liquidity and the U.S. repo market, for example.

5.1 Overview of U.S. Household Surveys

This section describes the main surveys included in this study, which are used to collect data on U.S. household economic conditions (henceforth, "household surveys"). Summary descriptions of these surveys appear in Table 5.1 in order of chronology based on continuous fielding. Five sponsors produce these U.S. surveys:

- **University of Michigan, Institute for Social Research (ISR).** The Michigan ISR sponsors two surveys. First, the biennial Panel Study on Income Dynamics (PSID), which is "the longest running longitudinal household survey in the world" and which includes data on wealth and expenditure as well as other socioeconomic and health factors.[6] Second, the biennial (even-numbered years) Health and Retirement Survey (HRS), which "has been a leading source for information on the health and well-being of adults over age 50 in the United States" for more than 20 years; the HRS includes the biennial Consumption and Activities Mail Survey (CAMS) for tracking household expenditures in "off" years (odd-numbered).[7]
- **U.S. Bureau of Labor Statistics (BLS).** The BLS sponsors the Consumer Expenditure Surveys (CE), comprising "two surveys—the quarterly Interview Survey and the Diary Survey—that provide information on the buying habits of American consumers, including data on their expenditures, income, and consumer unit (families and single consumers) characteristics."[8] "As in the past, the regular revision of the Consumer Price Index (CPI) remains a primary reason for undertaking

6. For more information about the PSID, see https://psidonline.isr.umich.edu/.

7. For more information about the HRS, see http://hrsonline.isr.umich.edu/.

8. For more information about the CE, see http://www.bls.gov/cex/ and http://www.bls .gov/cex/csxovr.htm. The CE dates back to the late 1800s but was not implemented annually until 1980; for details, see https://www.bls.gov/cex/ceturnsthirty.htm.

the Bureau's extensive Consumer Expenditure Survey. Results of the CE are used to select new 'market baskets' of goods and services for the index, to determine the relative importance of components, and to derive cost weights for the market baskets."

- **Federal Reserve Board.** The Board sponsors the Survey of Consumer Finances (SCF), "normally a triennial cross-sectional survey of U.S. families. The survey data include information on families' balance sheets, pensions, income, and demographic characteristics. Information is also included from related surveys of pension providers and the earlier such surveys conducted by the Federal Reserve Board." The SCF collects some consumer expenditures directly.[9]

- **U.S. Census Bureau.** The Census Bureau sponsors the Survey of Income and Program Participation (SIPP), "the premier source of information for income and program participation. SIPP collects data and measures change for many topics including: economic well-being, family dynamics, education, assets, health insurance, childcare, and food security."[10]

These surveys were selected because of their quality and breadth of coverage of U.S. household financial conditions, including their relatively large numbers of detailed questions pertaining to the line items of household financial statements (assets, liabilities, income, or expenditures). None of the surveys considers all relevant financial conditions because none was designed to do so. Thus, no single survey is fully integrated with financial accounting statements and no single survey alone can provide complete estimates of household financial conditions.

When combined, however, these U.S. household estimates come closer than any single dataset available today to providing a comprehensive assessment of U.S. household financial conditions. These surveys were also chosen because, except for the HRS, they are representative of U.S. consumers.[11] However, the

9. For more information about the SCF, see http://www.federalreserve.gov/econresdata/scf/scfindex.htm.

10. For more information about the SIPP, see http://www.census.gov/sipp/.

11. The HRS includes consumers aged 50 years and older and thus includes households with relatively high income and assets, making it more representative of all U.S. consumers than other surveys that focus on subsets of the population, such as low-income consumers. Two non-representative surveys merit analogous analysis but are not included here because they focus on selected low- and moderate-income (LMI) U.S. consumers. One is the U.S. Financial Diaries

surveys are implemented with different samples of households (or consumers) and, in some instances, substantively different questions, so their estimates are not necessarily comparable.

We reiterate that each survey has its own particular purposes or goals and that none is intended to provide a comprehensive, integrated set of household financial conditions as described in Samphantharak and Townsend (2009). The CE, for example, is primarily intended to produce data on a wide range of consumption expenditures that aid in the construction of the CPI. In contrast, the SCF primarily tracks details of assets and liabilities plus income from all sources but does not track all consumer expenditures. The PSID aims to estimate most income and expenditures but also focuses on collecting data on social factors and health, a practice that might be beneficial for every survey and data source. In any case, the PSID's breadth limits the amount of detail it can obtain on income and expenditure, so it does not obtain a comprehensive estimate of balance sheet items. For all of these reasons, the analysis in the next section does not expect or presume to find an individual integrated financial survey, nor does it recommend that any of these surveys change what it is currently doing.

Table 5.1 summarizes the key characteristics of the selected U.S. household surveys in terms of their basic features, survey methodologies, and sampling methodologies. Surveys are listed in columns in chronological order (left to right) based on their initial years of continuous production. The oldest is the PSID, which dates back to the 1960s, while the newest, the SCPC and the DCPC, are less than a decade old. Most of the surveys are conducted relatively infrequently, ranging from quarterly (the CE and the SIPP) to triennially (the SCF). Although it gathers detailed daily diary data when it's fielded, the official DCPC has been implemented only three times in five years. The date of statistical calculations refers to the period used to estimate the elements of the household financial statements, as discussed later in the monograph. The rows of the table are grouped into sections related to the survey methodology and the sampling methodology. For further comparison, the table also shows corresponding information about the TTMS.

(USFD), produced jointly by the Center for Financial Services Innovation (CFSI) and the NYU Wagner Financial Access Initiative. For more information, see http://www .usfinancialdiaries.org/. The other is the National Asset Scorecard for Communities of Color (NASCC), which is very similar to the PSID. For more information, see https://socialequity .duke.edu/research/wealth, Hamilton et al. (2015) and Munoz et al. (2015).

Survey methodologies vary widely across the surveys along several dimensions. One obvious distinction is the mode: survey (PSID, CE-S, SCF, HRS, SIPP, and SCPC) versus diary (CE-D, DCPC) or "diary survey." This distinction is complicated by the fact that modes also vary for each type of survey or diary, including paper surveys, paper diaries (or memory aids), online surveys—with or without assistance—and interviews; some surveys use mixed-mode strategies. A key differentiating factor among surveys is whether they collect data based on respondents' recall, where the recall period can vary in length from a period of one week to one year, or based on respondents' recording the data, where the recording period is typically one day. Recall-based surveys are more susceptible to memory errors and aggregation errors (over time and variable types). Some sponsors field their own survey (Michigan ISR), while others outsource to vendors (for example, the SCF uses NORC, formerly called the National Opinion Research Center).

The sampling methodologies are relatively similar across surveys. All surveys aim to provide estimates that are representative of some U.S. population measure, except the HRS, which is limited to older households. The main reporting unit varies across surveys from individual consumers to entire households, with some surveys obtaining information about the household from just one member—an important choice that can significantly affect the results of the survey. The surveys also differ in whether the samples are drawn as independent cross-sections or as longitudinal panels. The precision of survey estimates varies widely because sample sizes range from 2,000 to 52,000 reporting units.

Estimates of economic and financial activity for consumers and households are influenced heavily by at least two major factors: (1) heterogeneity in the survey specifications, sampling methodologies, and data collection methodologies; and (2) variation across surveys in the content, scope, and nature of questions about real and financial economic activity. Therefore, the reader should not expect estimates of income, expenditures, or wealth from the surveys to coincide. Instead, there might be large discrepancies in estimates of economic and financial activities even if the conceptual measures are similar. Differences in target populations can naturally produce large differences in economic and financial measures. But even more subtle survey design differences, such as recall versus recording, can produce large differences in the estimated measures. With regard to survey content and questions, even minor differences in wording can elicit differences in measured concepts between surveys. Similarly, the level of aggregation—collecting data on just the total or on the

TABLE 5.1. Overview of U.S. surveys and diaries and TTMS.

	PSID	CE-S/D	SCF	SIPP	HRS/CAMS	S/D-CPC	TTMS
Sponsor	University of Michigan	BLS	Federal Reserve Board	Census Bureau	University of Michigan	Boston Fed	MIT
Vendor	University of Michigan	Census Bureau	NORC/ University of Chicago	Census Bureau	University of Michigan	RAND/University of Southern California	Thai Family Research Project
Frequency	Biennial	Monthly	Triennial	Quarterly	Biennial	Yearly/irregular	Monthly
Period	1968–present	1980–present	1983: Q1–present	1983: Q4–present	2008–present	2012, 2015	1998–present
Statistical calculations	2011, 2013	2011, 2012	2009, 2012	2010, 2011	2010, 2012	2011, 2012	2012
				Questionnaires			
Observation unit	U.S. family unit	U.S. consumer units	U.S. primary economic units	U.S households	U.S. households	U.S. consumers and households	Thai households
Mode(s)	Interview	Interview, diary	Interview	Interview	Interview, mail	Interview, diary	Interview
Data collection	Recall	Recording, recall	Recall	Recall	Recall	Recording (1 day), recall (1 year)	Recall
Measurement period	Past year	Daily expenditures (diary), or past year (survey)	"Average" week for expenditures, past year for income	Past month, past 4 months, or past year	Past year	Daily payments (DCPC), or "typical" week, month, year (SCPC)	Past month

(continued)

	Sampling						
Target Population	Total U.S. non-institutional	Total U.S. non-institutional	Total U.S. non-institutional	Total U.S.	U.S. ages 50+ non-institutional	Age 18+ non-institutional	Rural and semi-urban households
Sampling Frame	Survey Research Center national sampling frame	U.S. Census Bureau Master Address File	NORC National Sampling Frame and IRS data	U.S. Census Bureau Master Address File	Panel of adults born 1931–1941	RAND ALP, USC UAS, GfK Knowledge Networks	Initial village census
Sample size	~10,000	~7,000	~6,000	14,000–52,000	9,000–15,000	~2,000	~800
Longitudinal panel	4 consecutive quarters	14 days	None	2.5–4 years	Fixed	3-day waves tied to SCPC annual panel	1998–present

Notes: CE-S: https://www.bls.gov/cex/csxsurveyforms.htm#interview; CE-D: https://www.bls.gov/cex/csxsurveyforms.htm#diary; TTMS: http://townsend-thai.mit.edu/about/; SIPP: http://www.census.gov/programs-surveys/sipp/about.html; PSID: https://psidonline.isr.umich.edu/; SCPC: https://www.atlantafed.org/banking-and-payments/consumer-payments/survey-of-consumer-payment-choice; DCPC: https://www.atlantafed.org/banking-and-payments/consumer-payments/diary-of-consumer-payment-choice; SCF: https://www.federalreserve.gov/econresdata/scf/scfindex.htm; HRS/CAMS: https://hrs.isr.umich.edu/about.

Source: Reproduced from Table 1 in Samphantharak, Schuh, and Townsend (2018).

sum of the parts of the total (and then adding them up)—can have dramatic effects on estimates of the total values across surveys.

To summarize a key feature of Samphantharak and Townsend (2009) that will be used to assess U.S. surveys, the reconciled financial statements must exhibit the following accounting identities: (1) in the balance sheet, the household's total assets must be identical to its total liabilities plus total wealth or net worth; (2) the increase in household wealth in the balance sheet over the period must be identical to the household's savings (adjusted for unilateral transfers); that is, it must be identical to a household's net income from the income statement minus consumption; and (3) the increase in the household's cash holdings in the balance sheet must be identical to the household's net cash inflow in the statement of cash flows, summing over all sources. Both sides of every accounting identity are measured.

5.2 Details of the Statement of Cash Flows

Because the dynamic accounting of linkages between stocks and flows is central to the chapter, we provide a more detailed discussion of this topic. The statement of cash flows (CF) provides an accounting of cash received and cash paid during a particular period of time, thereby providing an assessment of the operating, financing, and investing activities of the firm (or household).

The first step in constructing a cash flow statement is to define the term "cash." Despite the label, it is important to remember from the outset that currency is typically only part of this. For advanced industrial economies such as the United States, standard corporate financial statements tend to focus cash flow on the concept of "cash and cash equivalents" (CCE):

- **Cash**. Currency (coins, notes, and bills)[12] and liquid deposits at banks and other financial institutions, including demand deposits, other checkable deposits, and savings accounts. This measure is similar to the broad measure of money known as M2.[13]

---

12. Currency could also refer to foreign currency, such as euros, or even private virtual currency, such as bitcoin, but we abstract from these because the holdings of these currencies by U.S. households are small and their liquidity is less than that of sovereign currency.

13. Recent innovations in the U.S. payment system include nonbank financial companies that take deposits and make payments, such as PayPal and general purpose reloadable (GPR) prepaid cards, such as Green Dot, NetSpend, and Bluebird. In some cases, these nonbank companies act as agents between banks and households and deposit the money they receive into

- **Cash Equivalents**. Short-term investments with a maturity of three months or less that can be converted into cash quickly, easily, and inexpensively (high liquidity, low risk). None of the surveys identify cash equivalents separately from similar investments of longer maturity. Examples include 3-month Treasury bills versus 1-year Treasury bonds and 3-month versus 6-month certificates of deposit.[14]

Once cash is defined, cash flows for that defined concept (CCE) can be calculated to account for the operating, investing, and financing activities of the firm (or household).[15] In particular, the statement of CF includes three main parts:

- CF from production (or operating activities),
- CF from investing activities (consumption and investment),
- CF from financing.

In theory, the statement of CF provides an exact linkage between flows in the income statement and changes in stocks on the balance sheet. To verify this, the statement of CF compares measured cash flows with the measured changes in assets and liabilities from the balance sheet. Total CF is simply the sum of component flows,

$$CF_t = CF_t^p + CF_t^v + CF_t^f, \tag{5.1}$$

where superscript p denotes production (operating activity), v denotes investing activity, and f denotes financing activity. If all financial statement items are measured accurately and constructed comprehensively, this estimate from

bank accounts. However, tracking the actual location of these assets is difficult and is attempted only in the CPC due to its focus on payments. For most households, bank deposits are the main type of cash, but nonbank deposits are becoming more common for some households, especially unbanked and lower-income households.

14. Some cash-flow statements focus on "current assets," which is CCE plus other assets that can reasonably be expected to be converted into cash (or cash equivalents) within about a year. Some current assets are primarily attributable to business activity, which is not in the scope of U.S. financial surveys or covered well by them and is therefore excluded. These assets include accounts receivable, inventories, marketable securities, prepaid expenses, and other liquid assets. In theory, these items apply to household finance, but it would require significant changes in the scope and methodology of the U.S. surveys to include them.

15. The material in this section draws heavily from Imdieke and Smith (1987).

the statement of CF should exactly match the change in the stock of cash from the balance sheet,

$$CF_t = \Delta A_t^C = A_t^C - A_{t-1}^C, \qquad (5.2)$$

where A_t^C denotes the asset value (end of period t) of cash and cash equivalents (superscript C). If these CF identities were to hold exactly using data from a survey, then that survey would be fully dynamically integrated with financial statements. In practice, however, measurement of financial statement items is neither exact (due to measurement error) nor comprehensive in actual surveys (due to failure to include all items), so we expect to observe errors in the CF identities above (that is, we expect to see less-than-full dynamic integration). One logical measure of the degree to which survey estimates are integrated across time (dynamically) is

$$CF_{error} = 100 \times \frac{CF_t - \Delta A_t^C}{A_{t-1}^C}, \qquad (5.3)$$

which is expressed as a percentage of lagged cash. Smaller CF errors (in absolute value) are interpreted as indicating better dynamic integration of a survey.[16]

This analytical linkage between cash flows (also on the income statement if the cash basis rather than the accrual basis is used) and the stock of cash (balance sheet items) can be disaggregated into the linkages between individual liquid assets (stocks) in CCE and the gross flows among them. Henceforth, our language assumes that the cash basis is used, but our analysis remains valid for the accrual basis, since the real difference between the cash and accrual bases is only the labeling of the transaction; for example, goods sold create an accounts receivable that is not necessarily cash and that does not appear on the statement of cash flows if the latter does not recognize accounts receivable as CCE. Nevertheless, the sale would be recognized as creating an increase in an asset (an accounts receivable item).

To see the point about disaggregation, let A_{kt}^C denote the end-of-period dollar value of a liquid asset in CCE from the balance sheet, where subscript k denotes the account/type of liquid asset (currency, demand deposits, and such) and subscript t denotes the discrete time period (such as month, quarter, or year). Liabilities, L_{kt}, are defined analogously and primarily represent various types of loans; in principle, liabilities can be viewed as negative-valued assets.[17]

Let D_{kdt} denote the dollar value of deposits into account k on day d (nearly continuous), and W_{kdt} the withdrawals.[18] Gross cash flows in period t are the sums across all daily flows into and out of an asset type:

$$D_{kt} = \sum_{d=1}^{N_t^d} D_{kdt} \text{ and } W_{kt} = \sum_{d=1}^{N_t^d} W_{kdt}. \tag{5.4}$$

Asset deposits include primarily income of all types (including any capital gains and losses from holding CCE), transfers of another type of asset (or liability) into the account, or unilateral gifts received. Asset withdrawals include primarily payments for goods and services (consumption expenditures or capital goods investment), transfers to another type of asset, or unilateral gifts given. Again, liability flows are defined analogously.

Individual assets are governed by the following law of motion between periods $t-1$ and t:

$$A_{kt}^C = A_{k,t-1}^C + D_{kt} - W_{kt} \tag{5.5}$$

$$\Delta A_{kt}^C = D_{kt} - W_{kt}. \tag{5.6}$$

Individual liabilities are governed by an analogous law of motion where the liability "return" is primarily interest paid.

Finally, the disaggregated cash flows for each CCE type of asset include some that net to zero when aggregated across all k accounts. For example, if a consumer withdraws \$100 in currency $k=1$ from a checking account $k=2$, then $D_{1dt} = W_{2dt}$. For this reason, it is informative to track the flows among types of asset (and liability) accounts when analyzing the cash flow behavior of households. For some types of asset accounts, such as a checking account, withdrawals can be made with multiple payment instruments, such as checks,

17. Assets and liabilities are owned by individual consumers, denoted by subscript i, who are members of a household, denoted by subscript h. Agent identifiers are suppressed for simplicity because the following discussion assumes aggregation occurs across all agents eventually.

18. The day-specific flows are net of intraday deposits and withdrawals, so this accounting could occur even more frequently (hourly or even by the minute) to obtain further insight into cash flows.

debit cards, and various electronic bank account payments. Thus, the gross flows between accounts can be further disaggregated by the type of payment instrument used to authorize the flow.[19]

5.3 Assessment of Integration in U.S. Household Surveys

This section evaluates the content and structure of the main U.S. household surveys—excluding the SCPC and DCPC, which are not designed to be general surveys of household finance—in relation to corporate financial statements. As noted earlier, no U.S. survey is fully integrated with financial statements in a manner consistent with the Samphantharak and Townsend (2009) framework. However, all of the U.S. surveys contain questions that provide estimates of many of the relevant stocks and flows in financial statements. Therefore, the Samphantharak–Townsend framework can be used to organize the survey data into estimates of a representative (average) U.S. household's financial statements: a balance sheet, an income statement, and a statement of cash flows. The remainder of this section presents those estimates for each survey and analyzes the results.

The tables in this section report estimates of U.S. financial statements from the surveys. Each statement contains nominal dollar-value estimates for the line-item elements from each survey, aggregated to the U.S. average per household, with the sampling weights provided by the survey programs.[20] Selected aggregate measures are supplemented with medians. The line items (rows) of each financial statement reflect our best effort to combine survey concepts into reasonably homogeneous measures.[21] Where necessary and feasible, some survey concepts fall into the "other" categories; tables are footnoted extensively to clarify their details. To the extent possible, all economic concepts from each survey are included in the statements. However, the question

19. This discussion and conceptualization apply even if a survey does not have disaggregated data. Some notion of cash is implicitly being used. That said, one can imagine how errors, in particular, discrepancies between the income statement and the balance sheet, could arise.

20. This conversion is necessary because of differences in the sampling units. For surveys that do not use households as the reporting unit, we sum across all reporting units to get the U.S. total and then divide by a common estimate of the number of households from the March Current Population Survey (CPS).

21. This classification naturally involves some discretion as to the grouping and especially the level of aggregation. The latter affects the quantitative measure of integration later, but can be made higher or lower for alternative analyses.

wording and concept definitions can vary significantly across surveys, so detailed estimates fall short of perfect harmonization. To ensure proper handling of data, we have provided our preliminary results and software programs to managers or principal investigators of each survey and offered them the opportunity to evaluate and correct our analysis.[22]

Juxtaposing estimates of the financial statements for each survey provides two benefits. First, and independently of the Samphantharak and Townsend (2009) methodology, the financial statements provide valuable information about the relative magnitudes of real and financial economic conditions estimated by each survey. Differences between survey estimates can be large in absolute and relative terms because of the absence of perfect harmonization, as noted above. The aggregate estimates may also diverge due to significant differences in survey or sampling methodologies, described in Section 5.2, or due to differences in the coverage of statement line items, described below. In any case, the comparison of estimates reveals the relative strengths and weaknesses of each survey in measuring household economic conditions.

Second, juxtaposing the estimates facilitates the quantitative assessment of how well each survey's questions integrate with the elements of the household financial statements. The degree of integration can be evaluated by at least two standards: 1) the coverage of items in the statements; and 2) the dynamic interaction between stock and flow concepts. With regard to coverage, we can further quantify two types of coverage: 1) the percentage of detailed line items estimated by the survey; and 2) the aggregate dollar values of the estimates. As an example of the first of these coverage measures, suppose that a balance sheet concept had 10 detailed items and one survey estimated eight of them while another estimated only two of them. Then, the first survey has broader coverage (80 percent versus 20 percent). However, line-item coverage is not necessarily an accurate indicator of value coverage. If a survey had two estimates of the 10 balance sheet items, and if each one was an estimate of the aggregate of five of the detailed items (for example, short-term assets and long-term assets), then the survey might produce a very high percentage of the total

---

22. We again thank the staff members of each survey program who did so. This comparison is painstaking and difficult for one survey, much less several, and it is a challenge even for the survey managers. Thus, we view our results in this section as preliminary and welcome further development and improvement of the analysis. To this end, we are making underlying data and software programs available to the public, and we invite other researchers to refine and expand our analysis.

value of assets even though it didn't include an estimate of each of the 10 items. Still, estimating the aggregate value of five items without estimating each individual item is prone to producing biased estimates due to the adverse effects of recall and reporting errors. The juxtaposed estimates reveal the extent to which this kind of aggregation effect appears in the survey estimates.

5.3.1 Balance Sheets and Income Statements

Balance sheets constructed from the U.S. surveys appear in Tables 5.2-a (assets) and 5.2-b (liabilities). The asset and liability estimates are reported as current market values to the best of our ability, although it is not always possible to be certain of the type of valuation reported by respondents. Assets are divided into financial and nonfinancial categories, with financial assets further divided into highly liquid current assets (short-term) and assets with other terms and liquidity (long-term). For financial assets, surveys usually obtain market values explicitly or by assumption; where they distinguish between *face* value and *market* value (for example, for a U.S. government savings bond) the latter is reported. For nonfinancial assets, the valuation issue is almost the same, except the potential distinction is between market value and *book* value.[23] For housing assets, the surveys generally ask for the current (market) value of homes, but we cannot be sure they do not report the purchase price, which is the book value. For business assets, all surveys ask for the current (market) value, although the form of the question varies and may use analogous terms (for example, "sale price"). Liabilities are the current outstanding balances for debt, not the original loan amounts. Liabilities are divided into categories of revolving debt, characterized by an indefinite option to roll over the liability, and non-revolving debt. Because the maturity of debt is generally not known from the surveys and the term varies by debt contract within a category, the nonhousing debt categories are listed in rough order of liquidity from most to least liquid.

All the surveys report an estimate of total assets, shown in Table 5.2-a. U.S. households own average assets worth as much as $632,246, according to the

---

23. There are some trade-offs between using book value and using market value. For illiquid assets (of any type) that are rarely traded, market value is not readily available. Subjective assessments of value are prone to having measurement errors. In such cases, conservative accounting practices value the assets at historical cost. In contrast, mark-to-market requirements may be more appropriate when markets are thick, and volatility is not excessive.

TABLE 5.2-A. U.S. surveys: Balance sheets—Assets, various dates.

	PSID	CE	SCF	HRS	SIPP
Assets	422,616	226,314	632,246	556,295	351,702
Median	151,000		170,600	240,000	67,113
Financial assets	163,376	65,537	262,168	205,461	160,651
(% of assets)	(39)	(29)	(41)	(37)	(46)
CURRENT ASSETS	95,883	65,115	140,176	125,898	102,642
Cash	29,850	30,849	30,354	34,733	12,434
Currency			12		
Government-backed currency			12		
Private virtual currency					
Bank accounts	29,850	30,849	30,342	34,733	536
Checking accounts		17,239	12,660		536
Savings accounts		13,610	17,682		
Other deposit accounts			0		11,898
Other current assets	66,033	34,266	109,822	91,165	90,208
Certificates of deposit			4,994	9,354	
Bonds		408	8,227	14,860	3,376
Mutual funds/hedge funds			40,964		18,830
Publicly traded equity	56,335	33,858	48,874	66,951	
Life insurance	9,698		6,763		68,002
LONG-TERM INVESTMENT	67,493	422	121,992	79,563	58,009
Retirement accounts	67,493		97,007	79,563	54,759
Annuities			5,490		
Trusts/managed investment accounts			13,773		
Loans to people outside the HH		422	5,722		361
Other important assets					2,889
Tangible (physical) assets	259,240	160,777	362,445	336,951	191,051
(% of assets)	(61)	(71)	(57)	(61)	(54)
Business	51,404		108,760	55,006	25,921
Housing assets	188,992	160,777	234,187	264,500	154,795
Primary residence	149,211	149,760	170,159	190,818	147,855
Other real estate	39,781	11,017	64,028	73,682	6,940
Vehicles	18,844		19,498	17,445	10,335
Unknown assets			7,633	13,883	
(% of assets)			(1)	(2)	

Notes: Table entries are average dollar values for the survey's unit of observation, approximately a household. Assets and liabilities are stocks dated as of the time of the survey, generally the end of the year. Sampling weights provided by each survey were used in calculating the average values in accordance with the survey's data documentation. A more detailed data appendix and the Stata programs used to construct the tables are available at https://www.bostonfed.org/about-the-boston-fed/business-areas/consumer-payments-research-center.aspx. Data sources: Panel Study of Income Dynamics (PSID) 2013, Consumer Expenditure Survey (CE) 2012, Survey of Consumer Finances (SCF) 2013, Health and Retirement Survey (HRS) 2012, and Survey of Income and Program Participation (SIPP) 2011.

Source: Reproduced with edits from Table 2 in Samphantharak, Schuh, and Townsend (2018).

TABLE 5.2-B. U.S. surveys: Balance sheets—Liabilities, various dates.

	PSID	CE	SCF	HRS	SIPP
Liabilities	82,288	73,668	112,306	64,614	61,979
Median	18,800		23,000	5,600	3,750
Revolving debt	2,671	4,512	2,185		2,661
(% of liabilities)	(3)	(6)	(2)		(4)
Credit cards/charge cards	2,671	4,447	2,096		
Revolving store accounts		65	89		
Non-revolving debt	79,617	69,156	110,121	64,614	59,318
(% of liabilities)	(97)	(94)	(98)	(100)	(96)
Housing	67,506	58,143	87,223	58,584	
Mortgages for primary residence	54,856	52,559	63,889	48,984	
Mortgages for investment real estate or second home	12,650	3,086	19,598	4,440	
HELOC/HEL		2,498	3,556		
Loans for improvement			180	5,160	
Loans on vehicles	4,310	3,926	4,508		3,707
Education loans	6,507		5,788		
Business loans			10,317		5,338
Investment loans (e.g., margin loans)			289		102
Unsecured personal loans					
Loans against pension plan			288		
Payday loans/pawn shops					
Other loans	1,294	7,087	1,708	6,030	50,171
Net worth (equity)	340,328	152,646	519,940	491,681	289,723
Cumulative gifts received					
Cumulative savings					

Notes: Table entries are average dollar values for the survey's unit of observation, approximately a household. Assets and liabilities are stocks dated as of the time of the survey, generally the end of the year. Sampling weights provided by each survey were used in calculating the average values in accordance with the survey's data documentation. A more detailed data appendix and the Stata programs used to construct the tables are available at https://www.bostonfed.org/about-the-boston-fed/business-areas/consumer-payments-research-center.aspx. Date sources: Panel Study of Income Dynamics (PSID) 2013, Consumer Expenditure Survey (CE) 2012, Survey of Consumer Finances (SCF) 2013, Health and Retirement Survey (HRS) 2012, and Survey of Income and Program Participation (SIPP) 2011.

Source: Reproduced with edits from Table 2 in Samphantharak, Schuh, and Townsend (2018).

SCF, and less than half that amount, $226,314, in the CE survey. The HRS estimate of $556,295 is close to the SCF estimate, despite being limited to older consumers. The breakdown of asset types is similar for all the surveys. Financial assets generally account for less than half of asset values, 29 to 41 percent, despite variation in the number and type of detailed asset categories. Tangible (physical) assets represent the majority of asset values. Within financial assets, cash accounts for roughly $30,000 for all but the SIPP, where it accounts for roughly $12,000, most of which is held in bank accounts. Only the SCF contains an estimate of currency, but even that is not a direct estimate of actual currency holdings of the household.[24] Overall, estimates of balance sheet assets are relatively comprehensive for all surveys, as shown by their similar aggregate values and by the breadth of coverage across detailed asset categories. The SCF is the most comprehensive, with asset estimates in every category except short-term assets other than bank accounts (checking and savings); the PSID, HRS, and SIPP are almost as comprehensive as the SCF. The CE is much less comprehensive and has considerably lower asset values.

All the surveys also report an estimate of total liabilities. U.S. households have average liabilities ranging across the surveys between $61,979 and $112,306, much lower than the value of total assets and exhibiting less variation than assets across surveys. Housing debt is by far the largest portion of liabilities, ranging from $58,143 to $87,228 in all surveys where it is reported. The HRS asks specifically only about housing-related debt, with a catch-all question for other loans. The SIPP does not permit an exact estimate for housing-related debt, but the "other loans" category most likely includes some housing-related debt. While estimates of balance sheet liabilities are somewhat comprehensive for most surveys, they are not as comprehensive as the estimates of assets. The aggregate values vary less and there is less line-item coverage across detailed categories of liabilities. Once again, the SCF is the most comprehensive, with liability estimates in nearly every category. The PSID is almost as comprehensive as the SCF. The other surveys are less comprehensive, although in different ways. Given the estimates of total assets and

24. Respondents to the SCF report actual currency holdings only if they choose to do so in an optional response about other assets, and this category also includes "cash" that is not currency, like prepaid cards. The SCF estimate is very small relative to the amount reported in Greene, Schuh, and Stavins (2016) from the SCPC, which indicates average total cash holdings per consumer of $207 (excluding large holdings, which represent the top 2 percent but are not estimated precisely).

total liabilities, household net worth ranges from $152,646 in the CE to $519,940 in the SCF.

Income statements constructed from the U.S. surveys appear in Table 5.3. Income is divided into two main categories: compensation of employees (the most common source of U.S. household income) and other income. The latter includes income from all types of businesses owned and operated by households. Expenditures also are divided into two main categories: production costs and taxes. As explained above, the production costs of households are expenditures associated with businesses operated directly by a U.S. household; these businesses include sole proprietorships, partnerships, and certain Limited Liability Corporations (LLCs).[25] For U.S. households with a business, it would be natural to apply corporate financial accounting to income (revenue) and expenses, as in Samphantharak and Townsend (2009). However, none of the surveys provides sufficient information about household business activity, so we use the simpler approximation of revenues as "income" to accommodate the majority of U.S. households without a business. Furthermore, all income statement estimates are reported on a cash basis of accounting, so revenues and expenses are reported for the period when the cash is received (income) or paid out (expenditures), because this method is the primary way data are collected in the U.S. surveys.

All of the surveys report an estimate of total income (revenue). U.S. households received an average total income of $61,431 to $83,863 per year. Estimates of labor income are even more similar across the surveys, ranging only between $42,377 and $53,623, essentially all of which is wages and salaries. Estimates of other income types vary more, ranging between $9,816 and $37,402, but account for less than one quarter of total income, except for the HRS estimates of 45 percent of total income. Overall, income estimates are the most comprehensive and consistent portion of the household financial statements across the surveys, most likely because employment compensation is widespread among U.S. households and the data are relatively easy to collect. Estimates of income other than employment compensation are less uniform across the surveys due to the unavailability of some detailed line-item categories.

Although three surveys (the PSID, CE, and SCF) have estimates of business income, none of them provides much information about household business expenditures. They ask few, if any, questions about household business activity

25. For more information about these business structures and their tax implications, see https://www.irs.gov/businesses/small-businesses-self-employed/business-structures.

TABLE 5.3. U.S. surveys: Income statement, various dates.

	PSID	CE	SCF	HRS	SIPP
Income	67,187	65,316	83,863	79,779	61,431
Median	44,500	46,774	45,000	46,300	45,396
Labor income	53,623	51,543	53,192	42,377	48,767
(% of total income)	(80)	(79)	(63)	(53)	(79)
Wages and salaries	53,473	51,543	53,192		
Professional practice or trade	113				
Other labor earnings	37				
Production Income	3,748	3,075	11,347		1,144
(% of total income)	(6)	(5)	(14)		(2)
Business income (self-employment)	2,472	2,926	11,347		
Rent	1,276	149			1,144
Other income	9,816	10,698	19,324	37,402	18,176
(% of total income)	(15)	(16)	(23)	(47)	(30)
Interest, dividends, etc.	2,206	1,204	6,682	18,093	
Government transfer receipts	1,302	5,812	10,670	12,415	7,294
Other transfer receipts, from businesses	131			423	
Other transfer receipts, from persons		380	372		
All other income	6,177	3,302	1,600	6,471	10,882
Expenditures	1,837	4,345	2,007	0	22,487
Production costs					
(% of total expenditures)					
Depreciation					
Capital losses					
Business expenses					
Cost of labor provision					
Cost of other production activities					
Taxes	1,837	4,345	2,007	2,798	
(% of total expenditures)	(100)	(100)	(100)		
Employment taxes	2,508	585			
Other taxes	1,837	1,837	2,007	2,213	
Net income	65,350	60,971	81,856	79,779	38,944

Notes: Table entries are average dollar values for the survey's unit of observation, approximately a household. Income and expenses are reported for the prior 12 months, or annualized where necessary. Sampling weights provided by each survey were used in calculating the average values in accordance with the survey's data documentation. A more detailed data appendix and the Stata programs used to construct the tables are available at https://www.bostonfed.org/about-the-boston-fed/business-areas/consumer-payments-research-center.aspx. Data Sources: Panel Study of Income Dynamics (PSID) 2013, Consumer Expenditure Survey (CE) 2012, Survey of Consumer Finances (SCF) 2013, Health and Retirement Survey (HRS) 2012, and Survey of Income and Program Participation (SIPP) 2011.

Source: Reproduced with edits from Table 3 in Samphantharak, Schuh, and Townsend (2018).

(aside from the mere existence of a home business). No survey has an estimate of production costs for household businesses. Only three surveys with business income have estimates of taxes (these estimates average less than $5,000 per household), and only the CE reports employment taxes. Tax expenditures are those paid directly by households and do not include taxes deducted by employers or paid by third parties on behalf of households.

Given their estimates of total income and total expenditures, all of the surveys provide estimates of net income (income less expenditures), which range from $60,971 (CE) to $81,856 (SCF), as shown at the bottom in Table 5.3. The HRS does not collect data on expenses, so its net income equals total income. Net income is similar to income in the other surveys because expenditures are relatively small (taxes only). Household net income is treated as retained earnings that are distributed to household members for consumption and investment expenditures, which are recorded in the statement of cash flows (described below).

5.4   Quantifying Integration by Coverage

We wish to characterize the degree to which surveys are integrated with household financial statements in terms of coverage. We propose to develop the criteria for measuring this kind of integration by quantifying the extent to which a particular household financial survey covers (includes) the breadth of the line items in standard balance sheets and income statements. There are at least two dimensions along which integration by item coverage could be measured using the estimates from the preceding subsection. One is the fraction of detailed line items for which a survey provides estimates ("line-item coverage"). Another is the fraction of the total dollar value of all line items estimated by a survey ("value coverage"). The two measures are independent and not necessarily highly correlated. A survey could cover most items in the financial statements but underestimate them significantly; likewise, a survey might cover only a small number of items but obtain very-high-value estimates if the items covered include mainly the highest-valued items. The latter situation may occur when a survey only collects data on two aggregate subcategories (such as short-term and long-term assets) but collects none on the detailed line items within each subcategory.

We construct the measure of line-item coverage as follows. We define the range of each financial statement as the number of the most detailed line items (rows) from the tables earlier in this section. Then, we count the number of line items (rows) for which each survey provides a dollar-value estimate. The coverage estimate of integration is the proportion of line items estimated relative to the total number of line items. We call this the "item-coverage ratio," and we construct two separate ratios, one for the balance sheet and one for the income statement. This measure reflects only the extensive margin of coverage because it does not account for the magnitude of the dollar values in each line item; thus, it may not give a complete reflection of coverage for total assets, liabilities, income, or expenditures.

We construct the measure of value coverage analogously, as follows. We use the nominal dollar values for each individual line item in the statements to construct the aggregate total values (sum of all individual items) for each statement and divide the aggregate value by the best available per-household estimate of the relevant metric for the U.S. population. For the balance sheet, we use total assets and total liabilities from the flow of funds accounts as the denominator. For the income statement, we use personal income from the National Income and Product Accounts (NIPA). The "value-coverage ratio" represents survey coverage of the intensive margin of coverage. The difference between the two types of ratios reflects the extent to which a survey's coverage of financial statements is more integrated in its intensive or extensive coverage of financial statements. To the extent that one wishes to construct accurate estimates of aggregate U.S. household financial conditions, the dollar-value ratio may be more important.

Figure 5.1 provides scatter plots of the item-coverage ratio (diamonds) and value-coverage ratio (squares) for the balance sheet and income statement. The feasible range of both ratios is $[0, 1]$, with the upper end indicating that a survey has estimates of every single item in the corresponding financial statement. Recall that the ratios are independent and may not be highly correlated. Thus, the item-coverage ratio does not necessarily reflect how well a survey produces aggregate estimates of the data, and the value-coverage ratio does not necessarily reflect how well a survey covers the number of line items in the financial statements. Also, we make one important adjustment to the income statement ratios to adjust for the application to households. As shown in the next subsection, household consumption and durable goods investment are listed in the statement of cash flows rather than the income statement. However, for the purpose of quantifying the overall coverage of household income and total household expenditures, i.e., both business-related

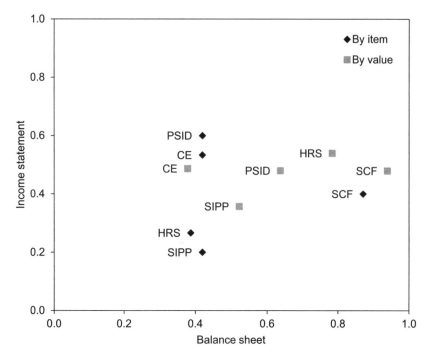

FIGURE 5.1 Financial statement line-item coverage ratios for U.S. surveys.
Source: Reproduced from Figure 3 in Samphantharak, Schuh, and Townsend (2018).

expenditures and household consumption or investment expenditures, we
include all types of expenditures in constructing the coverage ratios for the
income statements.

None of the U.S. surveys is completely integrated (ratio of 1.0) with aggregate
financial conditions for either statement, as can be seen from Figure 5.1. In fact,
no survey has either type of coverage ratio that is greater than 0.6 for both financial statements. However, four of the five balance sheet ratios are greater
than 0.5 (except CE) and four of the five income statement ratios are about
0.5 (except SIPP). The key differences across surveys occur in both types of
coverage ratios for the balance sheets. The SCF has nearly complete value coverage of the balance sheet (above 0.9 by value) and the HRS has a value ratio of
about 0.8 (by value). Most surveys have item-coverage ratios of about half
of the balance sheet line items except the SCF, which covers the vast majority of
line items. Variation across surveys is less in the item-coverage ratios for income statements.

5.5 Quantifying Integration by Dynamics

We also wish to characterize the degree to which surveys are integrated with household financial statements in terms of dynamics. Our proposed criterion for measuring this kind of integration is a quantification of the extent to which the estimated stock-flow identity holds in the survey estimates of household financial statements. The statement of cash flows is well suited to quantifying this measure of integration because it provides the linkage between the income statement (flows of income and expenditures) and *changes* in the balance sheet (stocks of assets and liabilities), assuming all stocks and flows are measured exactly and comprehensively. As explained in Section 5.3, however, the cash-flow error that arises in practice quantifies how well the balance sheet and income statement are integrated over time. Cash-flow errors represent consequences of incomplete item coverage of financial statements, as well as various forms of mismeasurement of the items in the financial statements.

Table 5.4 reports estimates of the statements of cash flows for each survey. Starting with net income (from the income statement), the estimated change in cash flows is the sum of three types of cash flows: from production, from consumption and investment, and from financing. To construct these statements, we have to estimate the elements of the cash flows from financing using estimated changes in the relevant assets and liabilities from the prior-period balance sheet. This methodology produces a cash-flow estimate that is a residual difference between net income and net cash flows, rather than a direct measure of the gross cash flows in and out of the balance sheet, because the latter are not available from the U.S. surveys. For comparison, we estimate the change in cash holdings directly from the current and prior-period balance sheets.[26]

The degree of dynamic integration is defined as the difference (error) between the estimated cash flow variables and the change in cash holdings estimated from the current and prior period balance sheets, expressed in dollar terms and as a percentage of the lagged stock of cash. We call this the "internal" cash-flow error because it is calculated using only the survey's estimates of stocks and flows. However, cash holdings from any particular survey may differ from the actual aggregate U.S. estimate of cash holdings (from the flow of funds), so these errors may not accurately represent the true degree of integration.

---

26. The duration of the preceding period varies according to the frequency of the surveys, from one quarter (CE) to three years (SCF).

TABLE 5.4. U.S. surveys: Statement of cash flows.

(Cash Defined as Current Asset)	PSID 2010–2012	CE 2011–2012	SCF 2010–2013	HRS 2010–2012	SIPP 2010–2011
Net income (+)	65,350	60,971	81,856	79,779	38,944
Adjustments:					
Depreciation (+)	0	0	0	0	0
Change in accounts receivable (−)	0	0	0	0	0
Change in accounts payable (+)	0	0	0	0	0
Change in inventory (−)	0	0	0	0	0
Change in other (not cash) current assets (−)	0	0	0	0	0
Consumption of household-produced outputs (−)	0	0	0	0	0
Cash flows from production	65,350	60,971	81,856	79,779	38,944
Consumption expenditure (−)	−43,766	−44,849	−28,850	−45,073	−22,487
Capital (durable goods) expenditure (−)	0	0	0	0	0
Cash flows from consumption and investment	−43,766	−44,849	−28,850	−45,073	−22,487
Transfers to/from long-term investments	−362	0	1,231	0	0
Lending (−)	0	−151	1,359	50	4,452
Borrowing (+)	4,230	8,089	−4,349	−3,757	−8,988
Net gifts received (+)	0	0	0	0	0
Cash flows from financing	3,868	7,938	−1,759	−3,707	−4,536
Change in cash holding (from statement of cash flows)	25,452	24,060	51,247	31,000	11,921
Change in cash holding (from statement of balance sheet)	3,091	17,770	3,843	1,678	−18,622
Cash flows error	22,362	6,290	47,404	29,322	30,543
Internal error	25%	13%	37%	24%	25%
External error	30%	8%	61%	39%	42%

Notes: Table entries are average dollar values for the survey's unit of observation, approximately a household. Cash flows are at a yearly rate and are constructed with the most recent prior data available. Sampling weights provided by each survey were used in calculating the average values. A more detailed data appendix and the Stata programs used to construct the tables are available at https://www .bostonfed.org/about-the-boston-fed/business-areas/consumer-payments-research-center.aspx. Data sources: Panel Study of Income Dynamics (PSID) 2010–2013, Consumer Expenditure Survey (CE) 2011–2012, Survey of Consumer Finances (SCF) 2010–2013, Health and Retirement Survey (HRS) 2010–2012, and Survey of Income and Program Participation (SIPP) 2010–2011.

Source: Reproduced with edits from Table 4 in Samphantharak, Schuh, and Townsend (2018).

Therefore, we also include the change in household cash holdings from the flow of funds (same for each survey) and construct errors in the survey cash-flow estimates relative to the actual flow of funds cash to get a better measure of dynamic integration. We call this the "external" cash-flow error.

As measured by their ability to track stock-flow identities in the statements of cash flows, the U.S. surveys exhibit relatively weak dynamic integration, and the degree of integration varies widely across surveys. The absolute value of the internal cash-flow error ranges from $6,290 (CE) to $47,404 (SCF). Note that these errors are just one estimate in a time series of errors that could be estimated, and other errors might be smaller in absolute value during other periods. However, the sheer magnitude of these internal errors suggests significant gaps in tracking household financial conditions over time, even within the self-contained estimates of a particular survey.[27] The cash-flow errors are reported in percentage terms relative to the two benchmarks: (1) the lagged cash stock from the survey's balance sheet (internal error); and (2) the lagged cash stock from the flow of funds aggregate benchmark data (external error). The internal errors are relatively large, ranging from about 13 percent to 37 percent of lagged cash (CE and SCF, respectively). The survey estimates of cash flows are generally less than the external benchmark: all but one of the external cash-flow errors are even larger in absolute value, ranging from about 8 percent to 61 percent of lagged cash.

5.6 DCPC

Moving beyond the U.S. household surveys, we now focus on another type of U.S. survey that offers improved integration with financial statements and reflects better measurement of certain aspects of household economic conditions.

The Boston Fed's Consumer Payments Research Center (CPRC) sponsors the annual Survey of Consumer Payment Choice (SCPC) and the occasional Diary of Consumer Payment Choice (DCPC), both of which measure consumer adoption of payment instruments and deposit accounts and the use of

27. In principle, it would be interesting to compare the coverage ratios with the cash-flow errors to quantify the relationship between them. However, with an estimate at only one point-in-time of coverage and dynamic integration for a handful of surveys, such an analysis would be premature. With more data on cash-flow errors over time, it might be feasible to conduct such an analysis.

instruments. Originally, the SCPC and DCPC were not integrated like the CE but were developed independently; they are now being integrated. The SCPC collects only the number of payments, while the DCPC also tracks the dollar values. Both provide data on cash and (in later years) checking accounts plus revolving credit. The SCPC contains very limited information about household balance sheets.

The DCPC is a relatively narrow consumer survey that is administered to U.S. consumers and is focused on payment choices. The DCPC includes currency and is unique in this respect among the U.S. surveys that we analyze here. The DCPC also features other means of payment, for example, payments that use deposit accounts, although it does not track the level of these deposits. The DCPC strives to measure payments activity comprehensively and does not aim to cover financial statement line items widely. For these reasons, comparisons of line-item coverage ratios between these surveys are not meaningful, nor are comparisons with the U.S. surveys.

5.6.1 Measuring Cash Flows CPC Survey Instruments

The 2012 SCPC and 2012 DCPC are related but independent instruments that were implemented around October 2012 with a common sample of respondents from the RAND Corporation's American Life Panel (ALP). The SCPC is an approximately 30-minute online questionnaire that collects data on consumer adoption and use of bank accounts and payment instruments. The DCPC is a three-day mixed-mode survey with daily recording of payments in a paper memory aid (or other form) plus three daily online questionnaires to input memory-aid data plus answer additional questions based on recall within the day. In 2012, most respondents took the SCPC before their randomly assigned three-day period during October, but some respondents completed the SCPC after the DCPC. The order did not affect survey responses because the instruments are independent.

Cash holdings (stock) data are collected by the SCPC and the DCPC, which are related but distinctly different types of survey instruments, as described in Section 5.2. The SCPC obtains estimates of cash held by respondents on their person ("pocket, purse, or wallet") or on their property (home, car, or elsewhere).[28] The 2012 DCPC obtained estimates of currency (no coins) held

---

28. Measuring cash in "pocket, purse, or wallet" is an approximate method of identifying actual "transactions balances" of cash. Although it does not ask the respondent for these bal-

by respondents on their person on each of the four nights of the diary, asking the respondent to report amounts by denomination of the bills ($1, $2, $5, $10, $20, $50, and $100) and in total (summed for them in the online questionnaire).[29] In October 2012, U.S. holdings of currency on person were on average $56 per person with a median value of $22.

Cash flows—deposits and withdrawals (payments)—are collected by the SCPC and DCPC as well. With regard to cash withdrawals made for expenditures (payments), the SCPC obtains estimates of the number of cash payments "in a typical period [week, month, year]," whereas the DCPC more precisely obtains estimates of the number and value of each cash payment (expenditure) made during a three-day period. Both the SCPC and the DCPC collect data on the number and value of cash withdrawals from bank accounts and other sources. However, because cash withdrawals are relatively rare for most consumers, the DCPC does not obtain estimates that are as comprehensive for individual consumers as does the SCPC, which asks for "typical" currency withdrawals during a longer time period than three days. Only the DCPC tracks currency deposits to bank accounts and other sources plus other unusual currency activity (conversion of currency to/from other assets, exchanging of coins for bills, and such).

Two additional differences between the SCPC and the DCPC have important implications for their cash data. First, while both surveys ask respondents to record their cash holdings at the time of the survey, the SCPC allows respondents to estimate their holdings, while the DCPC requires respondents to count their cash on person (bills only, no coins) by reporting the number of bills of each denomination, and the online DCPC questionnaire assists respondents in summing the value of their cash holdings. As a result, the SCPC cash holdings data exhibit more rounding (to the nearest $5, $10, or $20) and approximation than the DCPC data. Second, the SCPC collects data on cash payments based on respondents' recall of their typical behavior, while the

---

ances directly, it is a relatively objective and easy method of collecting these data. An alternative approach is to ask for "transactions balances" directly, as in the Survey of Household Income and Wealth in Italy (http://www.eui.eu/Research/Library/ResearchGuides/Economics /Statistics/DataPortal/SHIW.aspx). The SCPC also estimates U.S. consumer holdings of cash balances "on their property" (house, car, etc.), and some of this cash may be intended (eventually) for use in transactions as well. However, it is unclear whether respondents have an appropriate understanding of transactions balances or provide accurate estimates of them.

29. See Fulford, Greene, and Murdock (2015) for an analysis of $1 bills and Greene and Schuh (2014) for an analysis of $100 bills.

DCPC collects data that respondents record in essentially real time at the point of payment. Recall-based estimates of payments are likely to be inferior to recorded estimates due to potential errors from memory loss and time aggregation. For more information about the DCPC and its advantages in measuring consumer expenditures, see Schuh (2018).

5.6.2 Measurement by Recall versus Recording

By way of summarizing the material so far, we describe the main advantage of the Townsend Thai Monthly Survey (TTMS) over the U.S. surveys and the innovation in the DCPC relative to the TTMS. The main advantage of the TTMS is that it aims to achieve complete integration with household financial statements by line-item coverage and by stock-flow dynamics. To see this point, consider the following illustrative system of equations that reflects the subset of the TTMS financial statement estimates for the cash-flow dynamics of M1 liquid assets:

$$\widetilde{\Delta A_{1t}} = \widehat{D_{1t}} - \widehat{W_{1t}} + \eta_{1t} \tag{5.7}$$

$$\widetilde{\Delta A_{2t}} = \widehat{D_{2t}} - \widehat{W_{2t}} + \eta_{2t} \tag{5.8}$$

$$\widetilde{A_1} = \widetilde{A_{1t}} + \widetilde{A_{1t}}, \tag{5.9}$$

where the two assets, $k = \{1, 2\}$, are currency (1) and demand deposits (2), and η denotes a composite measurement error. An overhead circumflex ("hat") denotes a variable that is estimated directly by the survey (TTMS). The exception is that the TTMS does not directly collect cash holdings *every* period, unlike the DCPC. Instead, the TTMS makes an estimate of the initial stocks, $\widehat{A_{1,0}}$, $\widehat{A_{2,0}}$, and then uses these stock-flow identities to impute the estimates of cash stocks in subsequent periods, denoted by an overhead tilde ($\sim$). In the imputation procedure, the TTMS enforces the constraints imposed by the principles of integration, such as $\widetilde{A_{kt}} \geq 0$, and makes judgmental adjustments where necessary.

Another type of measurement error likely occurring in the TTMS cash-flow estimates arises from recall-based low-frequency (monthly) estimates of cash flows. As noted, recall errors may occur from memory loss due to time aggregation over the days of the month or over the number of cash deposits and withdrawals (payments). To see this, note that monthly currency withdrawals,

$$W_{1t} = \sum_{d=1}^{D_t} \sum_{k=1}^{K_t} W_{1kdt}, \tag{5.10}$$

are the sum over all opportunities and days, where $28 \leq D_t \leq 31$ and $K_t \geq 0$. Like most U.S. surveys, the TTMS obtains an aggregate recall-based estimate of monthly cash withdrawals, $\widehat{W}_{1t}$, from deposits to currency, without measuring each individual cash withdrawal, W_{1kdt}. The same measurement issue holds for currency deposits, which are less frequent and thus may be measured with less error.

By comparison, daily payment diaries like the DCPC represent an innovation in the measurement of stock-flow dynamics by recording high-frequency (daily) cash flows. For example, the DCPC obtains an estimate of each individual cash withdrawal, $\widehat{W}_{1kdt}$, by type, so the DCPC estimate of aggregate monthly cash withdrawals is the sum of individual withdrawal estimates,

$$\overline{W_{1t}} = \sum\nolimits_{d=1}^{D_t} \sum\nolimits_{k=1}^{K_t} \widehat{W_{1kdt}}, \qquad (5.11)$$

denoted by an overhead line (-). Therefore, if high-frequency (daily) recorded estimates of cash flows are more accurate than low-frequency (monthly) recall-based estimates, then we expect that

$$|\overline{W_{1t}} - W_{1t}^*| < |\widehat{W_{1t}} - W_{1t}^*|, \qquad (5.12)$$

at least on average, if not period-by-period as well. Consequently, the DCPC estimates of the stock-flow law of motion for currency,

$$\Delta A_{1t} = \overline{D_{1t}} - \overline{W_{1t}} + \mu_{1t}, \qquad (5.13)$$

are likely to be a better measure than those from the TTMS for the reasons enumerated above: (1) the DCPC estimates of monthly currency flows are sums of individual opportunity-day flows; and (2) the DCPC estimates of currency holdings are obtained each period, not derived from an initial condition (estimate) using the estimated flows. In this sense, the DCPC estimates improve the integration of surveys with financial statements and offer the opportunity for enhanced analysis of household behavior, as demonstrated below.

5.7 An Innovation toward Better Integration

Payment diaries can produce estimates of cash flows that directly link individual asset and liability accounts to cash flows via the payment instrument, rather than just linking aggregate categories of assets and liabilities to aggregate categories of cash flows. The remainder of this section describes the linkage between the balance sheet and payment instruments and then presents a new analysis of cash flows by account.

5.7.1 Payment Instruments and Balance Sheet Accounts

Table 5.5 depicts the linkage between payment instruments and their associated balance sheet accounts: assets and liabilities. Payments are funded (settled) by one of two broad types of accounts: money (asset) and credit (liability). Money includes transactions balances, or M1 (currency plus checking accounts), plus certain non-transaction balances, which are part of M2. The latter are savings, but in some cases can support a limited number of payments directly from or to the account (account-to-account, or A2A, transfers). Payments funded by money are usually settled instantly (with cash) or with delays of at most a couple of days. Alternatively, credit accounts fund payments that are settled much later; non-revolving credit accounts (charge cards) require consumers to repay their debt during a certain period (typically a month), while revolving credit accounts (credit cards) offer consumers the option of rolling over some of the debt (up to a credit limit) to the future indefinitely in exchange for incurring interest charges. Monetary assets and unused credit limits are the liquidity that fund payments that are tracked by instrument in the DCPC.[30]

The linkage between payment instruments and balance sheet accounts merits additional discussion before our moving ahead. Table 5.5 reveals that in U.S. household balance sheets the linkage is not one-to-one, due to the proliferation of accounts and payment instruments in the U.S. monetary and payment system. This linkage complexity is most evident in the variety of instruments that can access various types of deposit accounts (including savings accounts in M2). In particular, debit cards, various types of checks, and electronic banking methods (OBBP and BANP) all can be used to authorize payment or transfer from different types of accounts. In addition, the linkages depicted in Table 5.5 reflect aggregation of individual accounts within a type of account that the overall pattern does not reveal. For example, the 2012 SCPC indicates that 38 percent of U.S. consumers have more than one demand deposit (checking) account (DDA), and 57 percent of consumers with multiple DDAs have multiple

---

30. Note that deposits into an asset account are similar to reductions in loan accounts, although one is an asset and the other a liability. Likewise, withdrawals from an asset account are similar to increases in loan accounts. But there is a substantive difference, in that asset accounts require deposits before being used, whereas liability accounts can be unfunded initially and repaid later.

TABLE 5.5. Payment instruments and their balance sheet accounts.

Balance Sheet Accounts	Payment Instruments
Assets (money)	U.S. currency, foreign currency,
Currency	private currency (e.g., Bitcoin)
Traveler's check	Traveler's check
Checking accounts owned by consumers (demand and other checkable deposits)	Check (personal or certified), debit card, OBBP, BANP
Checking accounts owned or managed by financial institutions or nonfinancial payment service providers (but may have pass-through deposit insurance for consumers)	Cashier's check, prepaid card, money order
Savings accounts owned by consumers ("non-transactions" accounts in the non-M1 part of M2 with direct payment capability)	Check, debit card, OBBP, BANP
Liabilities (credit)	
Revolving credit	Credit card
Non-revolving credit	Charge card, Text/SMS

Source: *Reproduced from Table 8 in Samphantharak, Schuh, and Townsend (2018).*

debit cards, typically one (per account holder) for each DDA. Consequently, the linkages between accounts and instruments can be disaggregated further to match specific accounts and instruments within the categories of Table 5.5. For example, a consumer (or household) may own two DDAs with a debit card for each; thus, it would be necessary to link DDA #1 to debit card #1, and similarly for the other account and card. The 2012 DCPC accurately measures the linkages between types of accounts and types of instruments (such as DDAs and debit cards), but it does not measure the linkages between specific individual accounts and specific individual instruments.

5.7.2 A Comprehensive Statement of Liquidity Accounts

Given the linkage between accounts and instruments, the DCPC can also link balance sheet accounts (or types of cash stocks) to household expenditures on consumer nondurable goods and services (or types of withdrawal flows).[31]

31. If designed properly, a payments diary also could link balance sheet accounts to the expenditures of household businesses, but we omit these from the discussion because the DCPC instructed respondents to exclude household business payments.

Theoretically, a payment diary could link balance sheet accounts for household capital goods to payments for investment in durable goods, but the 2012 DCPC did not track these concepts. In any case, the payment instrument plays the pivotal role because, for each payment, it directly links the balance sheet—that is, the asset or liability funding the payment—to consumer expenditures broadly defined (more broadly than narrow consumption) for *each* payment transaction.

Our major innovation is the statement of account flows, which is constructed using the DCPC and appears in Table 5.6. The rows in this new type of financial statement are generally formatted as in a statement of cash flows, but separately for each payment account. For example, the first column is the statement of currency flows, which records the inflows and outflows of currency for each type of transaction, starting with currency inflow from production activities (monthly basis) in row A and followed by currency outflow from consumption and investment activities in row B (separating consumption expenditure in row B1 from capital expenditure in row B2). Next, row C and its subsidiary rows report the net currency flows from financing activities and its components: deposits (inflows; the C1 rows) of currency from each other account (DDA, nonfinancial deposit accounts (NFDA), foreign currency, long-term financial assets (LTFA), revolving debt, and other debt) and withdrawals (outflows; the C2 rows) of currency to each of those accounts. The remaining rows compare the changes in currency balances from the statement of currency flows above (row D) with those estimated from the balance sheet (row E), plus an estimate of the error (in value and percentage of prior-period balance, rows F and G, respectively).

Similarly to the statement of currency flows in the first column, the remaining columns of the table represent information for the flows of DDA, NFDA, foreign currency, LTFA, revolving debt, and other debt, with the final column reporting the row sum. This provides the link from aggregate cash to each of the payment mechanisms. Importantly, note that the total net flows concept in row C appears in the last column ("All") as exactly zero by construction, since what goes into one payment account comes from another.

Total average account balances of U.S. consumers declined $1,004 in October 2012, according to the DCPC, as average consumption, at $6,771, exceeded total account flows from production activities, which were $5,767. This change in account balances tabulated from account flows resulted from much larger gross inflows and outflows, as withdrawals, at $8,524, exceeding deposits, which were $7,520. However, the decline in account balances estimated from the statement of account flows was considerably smaller in absolute value than the corresponding change estimated from balance sheet stocks, which was $8,816. Therefore, the statement of account balances suggests that the DCPC is likely incomplete and may have considerable measurement errors, despite its conceptual promise for better integration by dynamics. One obvious area of incompleteness in the statement of account flows is that deposits of income to DDAs are not measured directly, but rather assumed to equal the difference between net income and currency deposits to income.[32]

The statement of account flows exhibits at least two interesting results with economic implications that may be useful for future research in linking real (consumption) and nominal (financial) household choices. First, 99 percent of consumption, at $6,771, is funded by payments from DDAs (65.3 percent), from credit cards (18.4 percent), and from currency (15.3 percent). This result reflects heterogeneity in consumer payment choices, which may have implications for payment systems and for household budgeting and management of liquidity. Second, the gross-flow magnitudes are not small relative to income and consumption, which raises questions about the efficiency of the monetary system and relates to the classic literature on money demand: Why are U.S. households holding relatively large amounts of their liquid assets in payment accounts (just as Thai households hold so much in currency)? Also, it is still not entirely clear why consumers make such large transfers between currency and DDA, two assets that have the same monetary nature (M_1) and are essentially equivalent for the settling of exchange. Evidence from the Survey of Consumer Payment Choice indicates that many U.S. consumers still rate the characteristics of currency (cost, speed, convenience, recordkeeping, and such) highly relative to other payment instruments, and merchant acceptance of those other instruments is still not universal. Nevertheless, these large transfers between currency and DDA likely involve costs that may be reduced by the use of electronic money. Altogether, the account flows provide new data with advantages that potentially offer greater insight than existing data and research do into household financial decision making and, more generally, the optimal design of the payments system.

---

32. Furthermore, the income of individual consumers (the 2012 DCPC respondents) is not estimated directly. We use the 2012 SCPC estimate of household income for the respondent (reported in categorical form rather than in exact dollar amounts) and other data in the SCPC, the DCPC, and the SCF to impute income for the DCPC respondents. This shortcoming was partially addressed in the 2015 DCPC.

TABLE 5.6. DCPC statement of account flows, October 2012.

					Flows Associated with Accounts			
	Currency	DDA	NFDA	Foreign Currency	LTFA	Revolving Debt	Other Debt	All
A. Production (inflows)	388	5,379	NA	NA	NA	NA	NA	5,767
B. Consumption and investment (outflows)	−1,038	−4,422	−58	NA	–	−1,249	NA	−6,771
B.1 Consumption expenditure	−1,038	−4,422	−58	NA	–	−1,249	NA	−6,771
B.2 Capital (durable goods) expenditure	NA	NA	NA	NA	NA	NA	NA	NA
C. Financing	−91	−536	−1	2	NA	−43	669	0
C.1 Deposits (inflows)	498	564	20	2	NA	NA	669	1,753
From currency	–	564	15	2	NA	NA	8	589
From demand deposits	455	–	2	NA	NA	NA	643	1,100
From nonfinancial deposit accounts	21	NA	–	NA	NA	NA	0	21
From foreign currency	0	NA	NA	–	NA	NA	NA	0
From long-term financial assets	NA	NA	NA	NA	–	NA	NA	0
From revolving accounts	22	NA	3	NA	NA	–	18	43
From other debt	NA	NA	NA	NA	NA	NA	–	0
Addendum: Total deposits (inflows)	886	5,943	20	2	NA	NA	669	7,520

(continued)

C.2 Withdrawals (outflows)	−589	−1,100	−21	0	NA	−43	NA	−1,753
To currency	–	−455	−21	0	NA	−22	NA	−498
To demand deposits	−564	–	NA	NA	NA	NA	NA	−564
To nonfinancial deposit accounts	−15	−2	–	NA	NA	−3	NA	−20
To foreign currency	−2	NA	NA	–	NA	NA	NA	−2
To long-term assets	NA	NA	NA	NA	–	NA	NA	0
To revolving accounts	NA	NA	NA	NA	NA	–	NA	0
To other debt	−8	−643	0	NA	NA	−18	–	−669
Addendum: Total withdrawals (outflows)	−1,627	−5,522	−79	NA	NA	−1,292	NA	−8,524
D. Change in account balance (from statement of account flows)	−741	421	−59	2	NA	−1,292	669	−1,004
E. Change in account balance (from balance sheets)	164	NA	NA	NA	−4,501	−673	9,489	−8,816
F. Flow error	905	NA	NA	NA	NA	−619	−8,820	7,812
G. Error (% lagged account balance)	135%	NA	NA	NA	NA	92%	93%	−89%

Source: Reproduced from Table 9 in Samphantharak, Schuh, and Townsend (2018).

5.8   Improvements to the 2015 DCPC

While the 2012 DCPC introduced an innovation to the measurement of currency flows that has enhanced the degree of integration for one type of asset (currency), its coverage of financial statements has been relatively low, due to its limited mission and purpose. However, expanding the DCPC to measure the stocks of other assets from which consumers make payments not only increases coverage and integration but also provides important information for studying payment choices. For example, the analysis of the demand for currency and payment cards (debit and credit) by Briglevics and Schuh (2020) is limited by the lack of data on checking account balances. Also, the results in Schuh (2018) demonstrating the close correspondence between payments and personal income were produced without the benefit of direct measurement of the receipt of income by the DCPC respondents.

Consequently, in 2015 the Boston Fed undertook major improvements to the SCPC and the DCPC that substantially enhanced their integration with household integrated financial statements and the ST methodology. Improvements to the coverage of balance sheets included adding:

- additional short-term liquid assets other than currency, including balances held in checking (DDA) and nonbank deposit accounts, such as prepaid cards, PayPal, etc. (SCPC and DCPC) and
- collection of outstanding debt balances from credit card bill payments (DCPC only).

Improvements to coverage of income and cash-flow statements included adding:

- more intentional and detailed classification of expenditures based on official National Income and Product Accounts (NIPA) definitions of consumption, which increases the precision of the distinction between consumption and non-consumption expenditures (DCPC only),
- collection of the actual dollar values, types, and frequencies of personal income receipts, which will permit direct comparison of aggregate DCPC income with NIPA income (DCPC only),[33] and

---

33. The 2012 DCPC only asked for the days on which income was received by the respondent, not the dollar amount of income of individual respondents. The 2012 and 2015 SCPC asked for total household income in dollar ranges.

- increased precision and information about the timing and nature of bill payments, which will improve the classification of expenditures and expand the capability to link payments to assets and, especially, to liabilities (such as outstanding debt other than credit card debt).

5.9 Related Literature

There are several recent papers that are related to the ideas on data systems from an accounting point of view, in an attempt to get better measurement from survey data, including work in other countries. These papers are complementary in some respects to the chapters of this monograph. But also looking at the details of these papers helps clarify the gaps that remain to be remedied.

The paper by Baker et al. (2022) has the goal of identifying consumption and savings responses to individual circumstances, but consumption is not directly measured; hence the title of the paper. Savings are not directly measured as a flow, either. But there is the basic accounting identity, as emphasized in this chapter, that savings as a flow will show up as changes in assets. That is, savings can be inferred from the existing comprehensive administrative data on assets, covering the entire population. Then, with more data on income, consumption can be imputed. Great data like this exists for Norway, Denmark, and Sweden but only as a snapshot. But high-frequency asset trades, which arguably involve transaction costs, are not seen. An exception is Germany, with data from a commercial bank from 2005–2015 recording 2.6 million trades, 13 million portfolio positions for 58,000 securities and 7,000 retail investors. From this high-frequency data one can infer the degree of imputation error in these countries. Not having all variables can lead to errors of 1.7% to 8% in imputed consumption relative to income, an error that increases with income and wealth, as the stratum of higher income and wealth consists of heavy traders. So high-frequency data can help.

Buda et al. (2022) use e-data from the commercial bank BBV, with 3 billion transactions from 1.8 million bank customers, as the basis for their panel. These e-data were not originally organized into NIPA accounts and categories, so the paper is about doing that as a proof of concept. That withdrawals from accounts are used in consumption is an assumption, as the authors do not have the requisite data. They aggregate up and then compare the result to the actual NIPA numbers, which are close in level and in dynamics, so they have a proof of concept for consumption. They then refer to the underlying micro accounts as distributional accounts, whereas other studies bemoan the absence of distributional accounts corresponding with macro aggregates. The authors can then examine consumption inequality.

Using Norwegian administrative and transaction data, Ring (2021) stresses the importance of wealth flows in contrast to most of the literature that is dedicated to the flows of consumption and income. Wealth consists of measured financial assets marked to market by a third party and imputed housing wealth with a thoughtful approach to the balance sheet. The author wants to quantify the impact of a Norwegian wealth tax, which arguably has income and substitution effects. The data used are tax returns (self-reported and third-party), labor data including employment and unemployment insurance, self-employment data and transfers; all are individual data. Evidently, no accounting identity is applied.

In sum, there is substantial interest, as evidenced by recent empirical work, in filling out and creating more accurate measures of the line items of the various financial accounts. Some of this work uses the relationship between wealth changes and income to impute missing items. However, none of the work creates the integrated financial accounts envisioned in this monograph, when income flows in the income statement and wealth changes from changes in the balance sheet are each created from underlying survey or transactions data and are consistent with each other.

6

U.S. Integrated Macro Accounts

THE CONCEPT OF INTEGRATING income statements and balance sheets is understood and officially recognized among U.S. agencies. Integrated Macroeconomic Accounts for the United States have been created and are available on both the Federal Reserve Board and the Bureau of Economic Analysis, Department of Commerce websites.[1]

6.1 Conceptual Framework

This concept is identical to the one underlying the complete integrated financial accounts in Chapter 2 of Samphantharak and Townsend (2009).

As stated in Bond et al. (2007):

> This article introduces a set of macroeconomic accounts that relate production, income and saving, capital formation, financial transactions, and asset revaluations to changes in net worth between balance sheets for major sectors of the U.S. economy. These new accounts should help economists gain a better understanding of major developments in the U.S. economy by providing a comprehensive picture of economic activity within an integrated framework in which consistent definitions, classifications, and accounting conventions are used throughout the presentation. (Bond et al., 2007, page 14)

Further,

> The full set of integrated macroeconomic accounts were developed as part of an interagency effort to further harmonize the Bureau of Economic Analysis National Income and Product Accounts (NIPAs) and the Federal Reserve Board Flow of Funds Accounts (FFAs) and to bring these accounts

---

1. For the FRB at https://www.federalreserve.gov/apps/fof/FOFTables.aspx, and for the BEA at https://www.bea.gov/data/special-topics/integrated-macroeconomic-accounts.

Balance Sheets

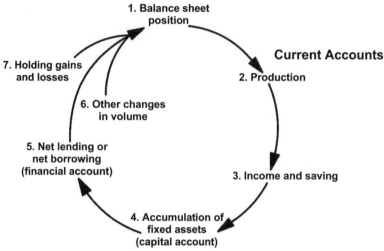

FIGURE 6.1 Sequences of accounts.
Source: Reproduced from Chart 1 in Bond et al. (2007), page 15.

into closer accordance with the national accounting guidelines offered by the international community in the System of National Accounts, 1993 (SNA). (Bond et al., 2007, page 14)

Figure 6.1 explains the sequence of accounts in a schematic.

According to Bond et al. (2007):

> The sequence of accounts for each sector begins with an opening balance sheet, which records the value of assets, liabilities, and net worth (chart 1).
>
> The balance sheet is followed by a sequence of current accounts. The first of these shows the contribution that is made by the sector to gross domestic product both [sic] in terms of the goods and services that are produced and the cost incurred during production. The remainder of these shows how net income that is generated from current production and received by the sector is used to finance consumption and savings.
>
> The current account is followed by two accumulation accounts that separately derive a measure of the net lending or net borrowing position of the sector. The first, a capital account, derives net lending or net borrowing by

subtracting fixed investment from saving that has been carried forward from the current account. [This is from the flows.] The second, a financial account, derives net lending or net borrowing by subtracting the net acquisition of financial liabilities from the net acquisition of financial assets. [This is from the changes in the balance sheet.]

In principle, the value of net lending or net borrowing should be the same in both of the accounts, because saving that is not spent on purchases of fixed assets results in the acquisition of financial assets and because borrowing that is used to finance the purchase of fixed assets results in the incurrence of financial liabilities. However, when compiling the two related accounts, the values for the two measures are almost never equal because of differences in source data, timing of recorded flows, and other statistical differences between data used to create the measures.

The capital and financial accounts are followed by two additional accumulation accounts. The first, an "other changes in volume" account, records changes in net worth that are unrelated to current production or asset revaluation, such as changes due to catastrophic losses or uncompensated seizures of foreign assets and statistical breaks due to substantive changes in sector coverage or details available in key source data. The second, a revaluation account, records changes in the values of assets and liabilities that result from changes in their price.

The sum of fixed investment, net lending or net borrowing, and other changes in net worth from the "other changes in volume" and revaluation accounts fully explains the total change in net worth for the sector, which in turn provides the next opening balance. (Bond et al. 2007, pp. 15–16)

6.2 Discrepancies between Changes in Assets, Stocks, and Savings Flows

The two measures of net lending, or borrowing, are not the same across the accounts as the accounts are created by different agencies using different variables. The data do not come from a single underlying survey that measures financial transaction at the individual household level, i.e., the data are not from ledgers.

The Integrated Macro Account (IMA) uses the capital account measure of net lending or borrowing for the sectoral balance sheets, but the discrepancy between the capital account measure and the financial account measure is recorded in the other changes in the volume account portion of the tables.

TABLE 6.1. Households and nonprofit institutions serving households (in billions of dollars).

	Line	2019	2020	2021
Current account				
Gross value added	1	2,671.2	2,768.3	2,873.2
Less: Consumption of fixed capital	2	600.5	630.9	704.5
Equals: Net value added	3	2,070.7	2,137.4	2,168.7
Compensation paid by households and NPISHs	4	1,012.1	1,048.8	1,094.1
Wages and salaries	5	836.0	860.8	904.0
Employers' social contributions	6	176.1	188.0	190.1
Taxes on production and imports less subsidies	7	208.1	215.6	227.5
Operating surplus, net	8	850.5	873.1	847.1
Net national income/Balance of primary incomes, net	9	16,526.9	16,761.6	17,941.7
Operating surplus, net	10	850.5	873.1	847.1
Compensation of employees (received)	11	11,448.1	11,592.7	12,538.5
Wages and salaries	12	9,324.6	9,457.4	10,290.1
Employers' social contributions	13	2,123.5	2,135.4	2,248.4
Property income (received)	14	4,875.5	4,885.4	5,121.2
Interest	15	1,659.6	1,648.9	1,660.3
Distributed income of corporations	16	3,215.9	3,236.4	3,460.9
Dividends	17	1,460.9	1,448.1	1,543.9
Withdrawals from income of quasi-corporations[1]	18	1,755.0	1,788.3	1,917.1
Less: Uses of property income (interest paid)	19	647.2	589.5	565.2
Net national income/Balance of primary incomes, net	20	16,526.9	16,761.6	17,941.7
Less: Current taxes on income, wealth, etc. (paid)	21	2,198.4	2,236.4	2,661.7
Plus: Social benefits (received)	22	3,089.7	4,187.1	4,546.4
Less: Social contributions (paid)	23	1,424.6	1,450.0	1,540.8
Plus: Other current transfers (received)	24	55.1	44.1	71.0
Less: Other current transfers (paid)	25	209.4	197.9	210.5
Equals: Disposable income, net	26	15,839.4	17,108.5	18,145.9
Less: Final consumption expenditures	27	14,392.7	14,116.2	15,902.6
Equals: Net savings	28	1,446.6	2,992.3	2,243.4
Capital account				
Net savings less capital transfers	29	1,431.5	2,989.4	2,285.5
Net savings	30	1,446.6	2,992.3	2,243.4
Less: Capital transfers paid (net)	31	15.1	3.0	−42.1
Capital formation, net	32	272.0	310.9	427.6
Gross fixed capital formation, excluding consumer durables	33	886.5	955.7	1,146.4
Residential	34	673.0	746.5	925.7
Nonresidential (nonprofit organizations)	35	213.4	209.2	220.6
Less: Consumption of fixed capital	36	600.5	630.9	704.5
Acquisition of nonproduced nonfinancial assets	37	−14.0	−14.0	−14.3
Net lending (+) or borrowing (−), capital account (lines 29–32)	38	1,159.5	2,678.5	1,857.9

TABLE 6.1. (*continued*)

	Line	2019	2020	2021
Financial account				
Net lending (+) or borrowing (−) (line 38)	39	1,159.5	2,678.5	1,857.9
Net acquisition of financial assets	40	2,355.5	3,621.2	2,869.6
Currency and deposits	41	598.7	2,532.2	1,886.1
Currency and transferable deposits	42	24.8	1,980.7	1,097.6
Time and savings deposits	43	575.1	543.7	788.7
Foreign deposits	44	−1.2	7.8	−0.2
Postal savings system deposits	45	0.0	0.0	0.0
Debt securities	46	133.0	−625.4	−867.5
Treasury securities	47	123.8	−347.8	−679.5
Agency- and GSE-backed securities [2]	48	36.2	−298.4	22.6
Municipal securities	49	−63.4	−30.0	−102.4
Corporate and foreign bonds	50	36.4	50.8	−108.1
Loans	51	33.1	113.0	96.4
Short term	52	35.5	114.6	90.4
Long term (mortgages)	53	−2.3	−1.6	6.1
Equity and investment fund shares	54	1,085.3	909.5	1,336.8
Corporate equities	55	288.6	616.3	726.7
Mutual fund shares	56	306.0	−188.4	514.6
Money market fund shares	57	450.9	428.4	101.4
Equity in noncorporate business	58	39.8	53.2	−5.9
Equity investment under Public-Private Inv. Program[3]	59	0.0	0.0	0.0
Insurance, pension, and standardized guarantee schemes	60	496.7	649.0	433.5
Insurance receivables due from property-casualty insurance companies	61	12.0	21.3	40.9
Life insurance reserves	62	16.7	94.2	31.0
Pension entitlements[4]	63	438.2	509.0	325.2
Non-life insurance reserves at life insurance companies	64	15.4	16.2	15.1
Retiree health care funds	65	14.4	8.2	21.4
Other accounts receivable (trade receivables)	66	8.7	42.9	−15.7
Net incurrence of liabilities	67	515.6	625.1	1,241.8
Debt securities (municipals)	68	−2.9	−9.9	−1.6
Loans	69	510.0	628.1	1,235.0
Short term	70	220.6	177.5	394.7
Consumer credit	71	185.2	−12.0	246.0
Depository institution loans n.e.c.	72	11.1	20.5	53.1
Other loans and advances	73	24.3	169.0	95.6
Long term (mortgages)	74	289.4	450.6	840.3
Insurance, pension and standardized guarantee schemes	75	1.5	0.1	1.5
Other accounts payable (trade debt)	76	7.0	6.9	6.9
Addendum:				
Net lending (+) or borrowing (−), financial account (lines 40–67)	77	1,840.0	2,996.1	1,627.9

(*continued*)

TABLE 6.1. (*continued*)

	Line	2019	2020	2021
Other changes in volume account				
Total other volume changes	78	**1,507.8**	**784.5**	**360.5**
Net investment in consumer durable goods	79	256.0	337.5	554.8
Disaster losses	80	0.0	0.0	−19.5
Other volume changes	81	571.4	129.5	55.2
Less: Statistical discrepancy (lines 38–77)[5]	82	−680.5	−317.6	230.0
Revaluation account				
Nonfinancial assets	83	**1,483.3**	**3,049.8**	**5,792.5**
Real estate	84	1,522.2	2,970.1	5,342.3
Equipment	85	−0.6	6.7	14.4
Intellectual property products	86	1.7	7.4	3.3
Consumer durable goods	87	−40.1	65.5	432.4
Financial assets	88	**8,075.6**	**7,981.3**	**10,339.5**
Debt securities	89	194.2	197.0	−122.4
Corporate equities	90	4,124.1	4,400.1	5,081.1
Mutual fund shares	91	1,509.7	1,139.6	1,281.1
Equity in noncorporate business	92	689.9	990.7	2,601.7
Equity investment under Public-Private Inv. Program	93	0.0	0.0	0.0
Insurance, pension, and standardized guarantee schemes	94	1,557.7	1,253.9	1,497.8
Changes in net worth due to nominal holding gains/losses	95	**9,558.9**	**11,031.1**	**16,131.9**
Changes in balance sheet account				
Change in net worth (lines 32+38+78+95)	96	**12,498.2**	**14,805.0**	**18,777.9**
Balance sheet account (end of period)				
Total assets	97	**133,038.9**	**148,465.6**	**168,481.0**
Nonfinancial assets	98	**39,876.9**	**43,580.9**	**50,337.4**
Real estate	99	33,491.0	36,756.7	42,479.8
Consumer durable goods	100	5,731.4	6,134.4	7,121.6
Equipment	101	459.8	482.2	517.4
Intellectual property products	102	194.7	207.5	218.6
Financial assets	103	**93,162.0**	**104,884.7**	**118,143.6**
Currency and deposits	104	**11,086.9**	**13,649.3**	**15,544.3**
Currency and transferable deposits	105	1,201.5	3,182.2	4,280.2
Foreign deposits	106	40.6	48.5	48.2
Time and savings deposits	107	9,844.8	10,418.6	11,215.9
Postal savings system deposits	108	0.0	0.0	0.0
Debt securities	109	**4,369.4**	**3,936.8**	**2,883.4**
Treasury securities	110	1,621.4	1,368.5	590.9
Agency- and GSE-backed securities[2]	111	559.5	237.9	255.2
Municipal securities	112	1,907.2	1,929.6	1,806.0
Corporate and foreign bonds	113	281.4	400.8	231.3

TABLE 6.1. (*continued*)

	Line	2019	2020	2021
Loans	114	**1,141.3**	**1,254.3**	**1,350.7**
Short term	115	1,059.2	1,173.8	1,264.1
Long term (mortgages)	116	82.1	80.5	86.6
Equity and investment fund shares	117	**45,266.1**	**52,733.0**	**63,031.0**
Corporate equities	118	21,081.6	26,122.9	31,940.7
Mutual fund shares	119	10,008.8	10,960.1	12,755.8
Money market fund shares	120	2,273.5	2,701.9	2,803.3
Equity in noncorporate business	121	11,902.2	12,948.1	15,531.1
Equity investment under Public-Private Inv. Program[3]	122	0.0	0.0	0.0
Insurance, pension, and standardized guarantee schemes	123	**31,024.0**	**32,994.0**	**35,032.5**
Insurance receivables due from property-casualty insurance companies	124	603.9	625.2	666.1
Life insurance reserves	125	1,731.3	1,867.0	1,944.9
Pension entitlements [4]	126	28,005.8	29,794.3	31,677.5
Non-life insurance reserves at life insurance companies	127	367.6	383.8	398.9
Retiree Health Care Funds	128	315.4	323.6	345.1
Other accounts receivable (trade receivables)	129	**274.4**	**317.4**	**301.7**
Total liabilities and net worth	130	**133,038.9**	**148,465.6**	**168,481.0**
Liabilities	131	**16,499.7**	**17,121.3**	**18,358.9**
Debt securities (municipals)	132	**211.6**	**201.7**	**200.1**
Loans	133	**15,881.7**	**16,506.3**	**17,737.1**
Short term	134	5,147.6	5,329.8	5,724.5
Consumer credit	135	4,192.2	4,184.9	4,430.8
Depository institution loans n.e.c.	136	350.2	370.7	423.8
Other loans and advances	137	605.2	774.3	869.8
Long term (mortgages)	138	10,734.1	11,176.5	12,012.6
Insurance, pension, and standardized guarantee schemes	139	**36.5**	**36.6**	**38.1**
Other accounts payable (trade debt)	140	**369.9**	**376.7**	**383.7**
Net worth	141	**116,539.3**	**131,344.3**	**150,122.1**

[1] Consists of rental income of tenant-occupied housing and proprietors' income. Quasi-corporations are unincorporated enterprises that function as if they were corporations; they primarily cover their operating costs through sales, and they keep a complete set of financial records.

[2] Government-sponsored enterprises (GSEs) consist of Federal Home Loan Banks, Fannie Mae, Freddie Mac, Federal Agricultural Mortgage Corporation, Farm Credit System, the Financing Corporation, and the Resolution Funding Corporation, and they included the Student Loan Marketing Corporation until it was fully privatized in the fourth quarter of 2004.

[3] Funds invested by financial institutions such as domestic hedge funds through the Public-Private Investment Program (PPIP).

[4] Includes variable annuities, including IRAs, at life insurance companies.

[5] The statistical discrepancy is the difference between net lending or net borrowing derived in the capital account and the same concept derived in the financial account. The discrepancy reflects differences in source data, timing of recorded flows, and other statistical differences between the capital and financial accounts.

NPISHs: Nonprofit institutions serving households.

n.e.c.: Not elsewhere classified.

Source: Reproduced with edits from the Integrated Macroeconomic Accounts for the United States, Table S.3.a, Households and Nonprofit Institutions Serving Households, FRB, https://www.federalreserve.gov/apps/fof/FOFTables.aspx, and BEA, https://www.bea.gov/data/special-topics/integrated-macroeconomic-accounts.

TABLE 6.2. Discrepancy between the capital account measure and the financial account measure for households and nonprofit institutions serving households (in billions of dollars).

	Line	2019	2020	2021
Capital account	38	1,159.5	2,678.5	1,857.9
Financial account	77	1,840.0	2,996.1	1,627.9
Statistical discrepancy	82	−680.5	−317.6	230.0
% Discrepancy		−45.37%	−11.19%	13.20%

Source: Table S.3.a, Integrated Macroeconomic Accounts for the United States, Bureau of Economic Analysis; authors' calculations.

For instance, in the Integrated Macroeconomic Accounts' Table S.3.a, Households and Nonprofit Institutions Serving Households,[2] reproduced in Table 6.1, the capital account net lending or borrowing is recorded on line 38, the financial account measure is noted as an addendum item on line 77, and the discrepancy is recorded on line 82 in the "Other changes in volume account" section.

Table 6.2 above features these lines and computes a percentage difference.

One can see in the last row that the discrepancy ranges from a low of −45% to a high of 13% over the three years. The total other volume changes item for the household sector that is reported on Table S.3.a line 78 (Table 6.1) is also reported in Table S.2.a, Selected Aggregates for Total Economy and Sectors, in the "Total other volume changes" section, line 55.

The other sectoral IMA balance sheets are presented in the same way. The discrepancy for all sectors would be Table S.2.a line 38 less 47, as shown in Table 6.3.

The discrepancy, relatively large, ranges from −548% to 107%. This is not coming from nonfinancial noncorporations, as, by construction, the difference is treated as equity put into the business as an asset change. The discrepancy is coming from the other NIPA sectors: nonfinancial corporation, financial business, federal government, state and local government, and the rest of the world.

2. See Integrated Macroeconomic Accounts for the United States, FRB, https://www .federalreserve.gov/apps/fof/FOFTables.aspx, and BEA, https://www.bea.gov/data/special -topics/integrated-macroeconomic-accounts.

TABLE 6.3. Discrepancy between the capital account measure and the
financial account measure for all sectors (in billions of dollars).

	Line	2019	2020	2021
Capital account	38	−354.0	−383.5	−736.0
Financial account	47	760.6	−116.1	−354.2
Statistical discrepancy		−1,114.6	−267.4	−381.8
% Discrepancy		−548.3%	107.0%	70.0%

Source: Table S.2.a, Integrated Macroeconomic Accounts for the United States, Bureau of Economic
Analysis; authors' calculations.

6.3 Other Sectors

We also reproduce the BEA's Table S.4.a, Nonfinancial Noncorporate
Business,[3] in Table 6.4 to show the separate accounting for nonfinancial noncorporate businesses (the kinds of businesses that can be shown in household
surveys such as the SCF). In this case there are no discrepancies, though this
is by construction. It is assumed that any difference between the income and
the asset side is a transfer to/from households, called "Equity in noncorporate
business" (or proprietors' net investment in the FRB's Financial Account
Table F.103).[4] That is, we do not observe the money that owners of noncorporate businesses put in or take out of their businesses (that is, the flows between
a household and its business).

Net lending in the financial accounts is imposed to match net lending in
NIPA. Line 54 in Table 6.4, "Equity in noncorporate business," is constructed
to make this equality hold. The justification again is as just indicated: as the
amount of money business owners put into their noncorporate business (or
take out of it) is unobserved, any discrepancy we see from business income
and asset changes could reflect a flow between households owning the businesses and the businesses.

As stated in Yamashita (2013), the goals of the IMA are to improve the ability to monitor new developments in the economy for policy making and to

3. See Integrated Macroeconomic Accounts for the United States, FRB, https://www
.federalreserve.gov/apps/fof/FOFTables.aspx, and BEA, https://www.bea.gov/data/special
-topics/integrated-macroeconomic-accounts.

4. See https://www.federalreserve.gov/apps/fof/FOFTables.aspx.

TABLE 6.4. Nonfinancial noncorporate business (in billions of dollars).

	Line	2019	2020	2021
Current account				
Gross value added	1	3,792.9	3,582.0	3,890.0
Less: Consumption of fixed capital	2	351.8	364.8	392.7
Equals: Net value added	3	3,441.0	3,217.2	3,497.3
Compensation of employees (paid)	4	1,204.8	1,172.7	1,296.6
Wages and salaries	5	1,021.5	993.3	1,104.7
Employers' social contributions	6	183.3	179.5	191.9
Taxes on production and imports less subsidies	7	243.3	27.9	92.6
Operating surplus, net	8	1,992.9	2,016.6	2,108.2
Net national income/Balance of primary incomes, net	9	25.4	24.5	26.4
Operating surplus, net	10	1,992.9	2,016.6	2,108.2
Property income (interest received)	11	21.9	20.7	16.4
Less: Uses of property income (paid)	12	1,989.3	2,012.8	2,098.2
Interest	13	273.2	289.5	251.4
Withdrawals from income of quasi-corporations[1]	14	1,714.6	1,722.3	1,844.3
Reinvested earnings on foreign direct investment	15	1.5	1.0	2.4
Rents on land and natural resources	16	—	—	—
Net national income/Balance of primary incomes, net	17	25.4	24.5	26.4
Less: Other current transfers (paid)	18	25.4	24.5	26.4
Equals: Disposable income, net	19	0.0	0.0	0.0
Equals: Net savings	20	0.0	0.0	0.0
Capital account				
Net savings less capital transfers	21	0.0	0.0	5.2
Net savings	22	0.0	0.0	0.0
Less: Capital transfers paid (net)	23	0.0	0.0	−5.2
Capital formation, net	24	82.3	68.4	94.6
Gross fixed capital formation	25	434.1	444.9	491.8
Nonresidential	26	304.4	302.2	323.5
Residential	27	129.7	142.7	168.3
Less: Consumption of fixed capital	28	351.8	364.8	392.7
Change in private inventories	29	0.0	−11.6	−4.5
Net lending (+) or borrowing (−), capital account (lines 21–24)	30	−82.3	−68.4	−89.5
Financial account				
Net lending (+) or borrowing (−) (line 30)	31	−82.3	−68.4	−89.5
Net acquisition of financial assets	32	123.8	486.1	289.4
Currency and deposits	33	49.4	146.8	173.6
Currency and transferable deposits	34	13.9	61.8	78.3
Time and savings deposits	35	35.5	85.0	95.4
Debt securities	36	−3.2	3.0	2.7
Treasury securities	37	−1.1	2.7	2.2
Municipal securities	38	−2.1	0.3	0.5

TABLE 6.4. (*continued*)

	Line	2019	2020	2021
Loans	39	**1.7**	**4.3**	**3.8**
Short term (consumer credit)	40	0.0	0.0	0.0
Long term (mortgages)	41	1.7	4.3	3.8
Equity and investment fund shares	42	**3.8**	**9.3**	**3.6**
Money market mutual fund shares	43	3.5	9.1	2.4
Equity in government-sponsored enterprises[2]	44	0.3	0.2	1.3
Insurance, pension and standardized guarantee schemes[3]	45	**10.0**	**6.9**	**17.2**
Other accounts receivable	46	**62.1**	**315.8**	**88.5**
Trade receivables	47	−89.4	47.1	46.6
PPP subsidies receivable	48	—	134.8	−111.3
Other (miscellaneous assets)	49	151.4	134.0	153.2
Net incurrence of liabilities	50	**206.1**	**554.6**	**378.8**
Loans	51	**113.8**	**428.1**	**261.8**
Short term	52	26.0	194.2	−28.1
Depository institution loans n.e.c.	53	17.4	98.1	−85.4
Other loans and advances	54	8.6	96.1	57.3
Long term	55	87.8	234.0	289.9
Mortgages	56	87.8	234.9	290.0
Foreign direct investment in the U.S.	57	0.0	−1.0	−0.1
Equity and investment fund shares	58	**38.5**	**47.8**	**−21.5**
Equity in noncorporate business	59	34.6	46.3	−21.7
Foreign direct investment in the U.S.	60	3.9	1.4	0.2
Other accounts payable	61	**53.8**	**78.6**	**138.5**
Trade payables	62	−57.0	−27.0	58.0
Taxes payable	63	6.8	13.1	5.0
Other (miscellaneous liabilities)	64	104.0	92.5	75.5
Addendum:				
Net lending (+) or borrowing (−), financial account (lines 32–49)	65	−82.3	−68.5	−89.5
Other changes in volume account				
Total other volume changes	66	**0.0**	**0.0**	**0.0**
Disaster losses	67	0.0	0.0	−12.4
Other volume changes	68	0.0	0.0	12.4
Revaluation account				
Nonfinancial assets	69	**709.5**	**1,000.7**	**2,624.4**
Real estate	70	684.6	948.5	2,477.0
Residential	71	389.1	634.8	1,697.6
Nonresidential	72	295.6	313.7	779.4
Equipment	73	24.4	42.7	93.2
Residential	74	−2.3	6.1	5.8
Nonresidential	75	26.7	36.7	87.4
Intellectual property products	76	4.2	12.3	7.3
Inventories	77	−3.7	−2.8	46.8

(*continued*)

TABLE 6.4. (*continued*)

	Line	2019	2020	2021
Financial assets (debt securities)	78	3.2	3.4	−4.2
Liabilities	79	712.7	1,004.1	2,625.4
Direct investment in the U.S., debt	80	−0.2	−0.1	−0.3
Equity in noncorporate business	81	689.9	990.7	2,601.7
Direct investment in the U.S., equity	82	23.0	13.5	23.9
Changes in net worth due to nominal holding gains/losses	83	0.0	0.0	−5.2
Changes in balance sheet account				
Change in net worth (lines 24 + 30+66 + 83)	84	0.0	0.0	0.0
Balance sheet account (end of period)				
Total assets	85	20,481.1	22,039.8	25,031.6
Nonfinancial assets	86	14,508.6	15,577.7	18,284.3
Real estate	87	13,070.1	14,100.0	16,651.7
Residential[4]	88	7,389.7	8,055.8	9,789.0
Nonresidential	89	5,680.4	6,044.3	6,862.7
Equipment	90	886.5	913.3	1,000.4
Residential	91	56.7	65.7	75.6
Nonresidential	92	829.8	847.6	924.9
Intellectual property products	93	295.6	322.4	347.9
Inventories	94	256.4	242.0	284.3
Financial assets	95	5,972.6	6,462.1	6,747.2
Currency and deposits	96	1,414.8	1,561.6	1,735.2
Currency and transferable deposits	97	331.4	393.2	471.5
Time and savings deposits	98	1,083.4	1,168.4	1,263.8
Debt securities	99	75.9	82.3	80.8
Treasury securities	100	72.1	78.1	76.1
Municipal securities	101	3.8	4.2	4.6
Loans	102	50.7	55.0	58.7
Short term (consumer credit)	103	0.0	0.0	0.0
Long term (mortgages)	104	50.7	55.0	58.7
Equity and investment fund shares	105	120.9	130.2	133.8
Money market mutual fund shares	106	108.1	117.2	119.5
Equity in government-sponsored enterprises[2]	107	12.8	13.0	14.3
Insurance, pension, and standardized guarantee schemes[3]	108	129.0	135.9	153.2
Other accounts receivable	109	4,181.3	4,497.1	4,585.6
Trade receivables	110	763.2	810.3	856.9
PPP subsidies receivable	111	—	134.8	23.4
Other (miscellaneous assets)	112	3,418.1	3,552.1	3,705.3

TABLE 6.4. (*continued*)

	Line	2019	2020	2021
Total liabilities and net worth	113	20,481.1	22,039.8	25,031.6
Net incurrence of liabilities	114	20,481.1	22,039.8	25,031.6
Loans	115	5,986.3	6,413.9	6,675.1
Short term	116	1,741.8	1,936.0	1,907.9
Depository institution loans n.e.c.	117	1,485.4	1,583.5	1,498.1
Other loans and advances	118	256.4	352.4	409.8
Long term	119	4,244.5	4,477.9	4,767.3
Mortgages	120	4,237.5	4,471.9	4,761.6
Foreign direct investment in the U.S.	121	7.0	6.0	5.7
Equity and investment fund shares	122	11,927.0	12,979.4	15,571.4
Equity in noncorporate business	123	11,818.8	12,857.8	15,425.0
Foreign direct investment in the U.S.	124	108.2	121.6	146.4
Other accounts payable	125	2,567.9	2,646.5	2,785.1
Trade payables	126	542.0	515.0	573.0
Taxes payable	127	162.4	175.5	180.5
Other (miscellaneous liabilities)	128	1,863.5	1,956.0	2,031.5
Net worth	129	**0.0**	**0.0**	**0.0**

Notes: Nonfinancial noncorporate business includes noncorporate farms that are excluded from the nonfinancial noncorporate business sector in the financial accounts of the United States. Estimates for 2000 and earlier periods are based on the 1987 Standard Industrial Classification system; later estimates are based on the North American Industry Classification System.

[1] Consists of rental income of tenant-occupied housing and proprietors' income. Quasi-corporations are unincorporated enterprises that function as if they were corporations; they primarily cover their operating costs through sales, and they keep a complete set of financial records.

[2] Government-sponsored enterprises (GSEs) consist of Federal Home Loan Banks, Fannie Mae, Freddie Mac, Federal Agricultural Mortgage Corporation, Farm Credit System, the Financing Corporation, and the Resolution Funding Corporation, and they included the Student Loan Marketing Association until it was fully privatized in the fourth quarter of 2004.

[3] Net equity in reserves of property-casualty insurance companies.

[4] Farm houses are included in the household sector.

n.e.c.: Not elsewhere classified.

Source: Reproduced with edits from the Integrated Macroeconomic Accounts for the United States, Table S.4.a, Nonfinancial Noncorporate Business, FRB, https://www.federalreserve.gov/apps/fof/FOFTables.aspx, and BEA, https://www.bea.gov/data/special-topics/integrated-macroeconomic-accounts.

facilitate analysis with readily available data. Yamashita (2013) also provides key illustrative examples. One such example is an examination of household debt and leverage prior to the 2007–2008 financial crisis. Some of the more obvious measures of indebtedness in the accounts did not give warning signs, but other measures of leverage did—a valuable lesson learned, and again something that can be monitored with these relatively high-frequency data. Related are the flows across sectors prior to the crisis. Households move from net lenders to net borrowers, but it is important to note that measures include changes in equity holding and other financial assets, that is, net acquisition of financial assets. One can also see which sectors were net lenders, including the rest of the world.

To gauge the role of financial intermediaries in these events, assets can be viewed one at a time and in disaggregated categories. Household net acquisition was largely in long-term borrowing and not in liquid assets (money market accounts, currency, bank deposits, treasury securities). Intermediaries raised capital via the issuance of bonds and equities and by taking deposits. As anticipated, the rest of the world provided much investor financing, acquiring the corporate GSE bonds and equities issued by the financial sector.

6.4 Data from BEA and SCF, Geographically Disaggregated

Data for these tables in the Integrated Macro Accounts come from the two agencies, as noted. On the income side, the BEA Department of Commerce produces regional income and product accounts. From its website <https://www.bea.gov/data/economic-accounts/regional>:

> The regional economic accounts tell us about the geographic distribution of U.S. economic activity and growth. The estimates of gross domestic product by state and state and local area personal income, and the accompanying detail, provide a consistent framework for analyzing and comparing individual state and local area economies.

The distinction between income and product is noteworthy. Essentially, production is measured at the plant-level address as factor payments. Income is measured at the household-level residential location as factor payments received by the household. In the event that a household lives in one state and works in another, e.g., lives in New Jersey and works in New York, data from commuting zones is used to make adjustments. This is but one example of the distinction.

On the asset side, from the FRB's Board of Governors, the balance sheet and flow of funds accounts are not broken into geographic subunits, apart from a relatively new release on debt and housing.[5]

In principle, state-level asset and liability information is available from the Survey of Consumer Finances, but due to concerns of not being representative, these geographic identifiers are not released and thus analysis by researchers is not possible. Hence it is not possible as of today to construct integrated community- or state-level accounts, linking income and asset changes, even after setting aside the discrepancies discussed, as in the national-level integrated accounts.

However, in a hopeful sign, the Federal Reserve Board collaborated to the run the codes that created the balance and income accounts in Samphanth-arak, Schuh, and Townsend (2018), reported in Chapter 5 above, by region, on its internal Survey of Consumer Finance database.[6]

Tables 6.5–6.10 detail those accounts by region.

The codes that created the financial accounts in the PSID can also be run on PSID data to deliver both aggregate-level data and case studies. The PSID data are available down to the county level, with permission, but may not be representative.

5. Household debt by state/region: https://www.federalreserve.gov/releases/z1/dataviz /household_debt/ (taken from Equifax data, the same used by FRBNY). Value of housing stock (for most states, or big region) https://www.federalreserve.gov/releases/efa/geographical -detail-for-owner-occupied-housing-wealth.htm.

6. See also the discussion of coverage in Chapter 5.

TABLE 6.5. Balance sheets by region (2013).

Region	Northeast	North Central	South	West
Assets	751,500	538,500	539,100	824,000
Median	254,200	156,400	145,100	203,400
Currency	0	0	0	0
Checking accounts	14,800	8,400	11,600	17,500
Savings accounts	23,500	13,700	14,100	23,000
Other accounts	0	0	0	0
Certificates of deposit	5,900	6,300	3,400	5,700
Mutual funds	51,700	38,100	30,500	56,000
Stocks	55,500	43,800	43,700	68,000
Bonds	12,300	5,800	6,700	10,100
Retirement accounts	130,100	103,000	72,400	105,700
Life insurance	8,400	7,600	6,000	5,800
Annuities	7,700	5,500	4,700	5,100
Trusts	17,900	17,300	10,400	12,900
Loans to people outside the HH	5,200	5,200	5,000	8,800
Vehicles	17,500	19,200	19,900	20,900
Other financial assets	0	0	0	0
Primary housing	225,700	121,800	138,000	227,400
Other housing	62,500	39,100	54,100	106,900
Business assets	105,200	93,600	110,200	140,900
Other nonfinancial assets	6,600	9,000	7,000	7,500
Liabilities	122,600	104,500	92,900	160,200
Median	26,300	28,100	23,600	26,600
Credit cards	2,300	1,900	1,800	2,700
Other revolving debt	100	100	100	100
Primary mortgage	77,000	50,600	50,700	88,800
Other mortgages	17,300	15,400	13,100	37,000
HELOC	4,400	3,200	3,200	4,400
Loans for improvement	500	100	100	100
Loans on vehicles	4,300	4,100	5,000	4,200
Education loans	6,300	7,600	4,500	5,800
Business loans	5,400	16,800	8,500	11,900
Margin loans	200	100	500	200
Loans against pension plan	400	200	200	300
Other loans	1,300	1,300	2,300	1,700

Source: Federal Reserve Board.

TABLE 6.6. Income statements by region (2013).

Region	Northeast	North Central	South	West
Income	105,800	75,800	78,100	97,100
Median	58,500	45,000	44,500	52,000
Censored income	63,600	53,800	53,500	60,500
Total income	103,500	72,700	75,400	94,400
Wage income	67,700	47,200	45,800	59,800
Business and farm income	11,700	8,500	11,100	12,100
Government transfer	10,700	10,700	10,800	10,400
Child-support alimony	300	400	400	300
Other income	2,200	700	900	2,400
Interest, dividends, etc.	10,100	5,200	6,000	9,100
Expenditure	39,900	30,100	30,500	38,600
Median	28,700	22,100	22,700	27,800
Food	9,000	7,200	8,000	8,300
Housing	13,700	9,000	9,400	15,200
Transportation	1,800	1,800	2,100	1,800
Education	600	500	300	400
Insurance, financial services, and pensions	4,200	3,200	2,600	3,800
Real estate tax	3,600	1,900	1,400	1,800
Miscellaneous	2,100	1,600	1,800	2,100
Charity	1,800	1,700	1,900	2,200

Source: Federal Reserve Board.

TABLE 6.7. Statements of cash flows by region (2013).

Region	Northeast	North Central	South	West
Mean IRA withdrawals	1,600	1,000	900	1,600
Mean—all items	4,700	4,100	3,900	4,700
Median—all items	3,300	3,300	3,200	3,200

Source: Federal Reserve Board.

TABLE 6.8. Balance sheets by region (2016).

Region	Northeast	North Central	South	West
Assets	941,800	702,900	704,100	983,300
Median	255,400	175,700	159,500	233,800
Currency	0	0	100	0
Checking accounts	17,500	12,400	12,300	15,300
Savings accounts	36,800	22,600	17,000	20,900
Other accounts	0	0	0	0
Certificates of deposit	6,400	5,800	2,900	6,300
Mutual funds	104,500	64,900	83,300	79,600
Stocks	88,500	34,700	55,900	67,300
Bonds	13,000	10,200	6,400	12,400
Retirement accounts	169,100	112,100	100,700	112,200
Life insurance	9,000	9,700	6,400	5,100
Annuities	7,500	6,200	7,800	5,800
Trusts	22,500	14,500	15,100	26,600
Loans to people outside the HH	6,200	8,400	6,200	14,800
Vehicles	19,100	20,700	22,300	23,200
Other financial assets	0	0	0	0
Primary housing	248,100	130,700	153,900	264,700
Other housing	73,800	77,200	72,500	119,400
Business assets	112,700	168,800	133,100	200,600
Other nonfinancial assets	5,800	3,800	7,000	7,800
Liabilities	131,900	102,800	111,700	161,100
Median	31,700	28,400	27,500	34,400
Credit cards	2,600	2,300	2,100	2,800
Other revolving debt	100	100	100	100
Primary mortgage	76,400	44,500	50,800	89,800
Other mortgages	16,700	21,100	23,100	34,100
HELOC	5,100	3,000	3,200	3,400
Loans for improvement	200	0	0	100
Loans on vehicles	4,600	5,200	7,000	5,500
Education loans	7,700	7,700	7,400	8,000
Business loans	12,700	13,100	11,700	9,400
Margin loans	700	500	800	600
Loans against pension plan	500	300	200	500
Other loans	1,400	1,900	2,100	3,800

Source: Federal Reserve Board.

TABLE 6.9. Income statements by region (2016).

Region	Northeast	North Central	South	West
Income	125,900	95,600	93,100	101,500
Median	61,500	52,100	50,200	55,500
Censored income	65,500	59,600	56,900	62,800
Total income	124,000	92,500	90,700	98,800
Wage income	81,200	56,100	54,700	60,400
Business and farm income	14,400	14,500	12,400	13,900
Government transfer	13,500	12,100	11,900	12,100
Child-support alimony	300	300	300	400
Other income	900	600	3,600	2,300
Interest, dividends, etc.	12,300	8,800	7,000	9,300
Expenditure	43,200	32,400	33,300	41,200
Median	29,700	22,900	23,600	29,300
Food	8,700	6,900	7,400	8,500
Housing	14,500	9,300	10,800	15,800
Transportation	2,200	2,200	2,600	2,300
Education	600	600	400	500
Insurance, financial services, and pensions	6,000	3,600	3,300	3,800
Real estate tax	3,900	2,000	1,500	2,000
Miscellaneous	1,700	1,400	1,600	2,800
Charity	2,500	3,200	2,600	2,400

Source: Federal Reserve Board.

TABLE 6.10. Statement of cash flows by region (2016).

Region	Northeast	North Central	South	West
Mean IRA withdrawals	2,300	1,500	1,300	1,500
Mean—all items	5,500	4,600	4,300	4,600
Median—all items	3,600	3,500	3,200	3,200

Source: Federal Reserve Board.

7

Construction of Disaggregated Integrated Accounts for the U.S.

THE JUXTAPOSITION of salient policy topics with the importance of measurement has been emphasized in Chapter 1. We emphasized the limitations of current data in the United States for analysis of inequality, the impact of Chinese imports on the United States and its sectoral decline of manufacturing, and the tracking of the impact of COVID-19 and related policy responses.

The subsequent chapters featured what can be done when data is available, assessing the impact of import quotas and financial distortions through the lens of consistent integrated financial accounts in an emerging market country, Thailand. The data and financial accounts were described in Chapter 2, the construction of regional Integrated Macro Accounts in Chapter 3, and the calibrated model for analysis in Chapter 4.

We then returned to limitations of the U.S. information infrastructure, assessing micro surveys in Chapter 5 and integrated macro accounts in Chapter 6.

In this final chapter we propose specific concrete steps that can be taken to remedy the U.S. data shortcomings by creating integrated financial statements and constructing integrated regional accounts.

The first, and primary, approach is bottom-up, as if starting from scratch on the ground at the household and SME levels, taking advantage of the marriage of the conceptual frameworks and methods of the Townsend Thai Monthly Survey (TTMS) described in Samphantharak and Townsend (2009), and presented in Chapter 2, and the U.S. Survey and Diary of Consumer Payment Choice (SCPC and DCPC), described in Schuh (2018) and presented in

Chapter 5; but we go beyond these and feature a new multimodal data collection program. The second approach is top-down, starting with existing data sources, and considering how they are utilized, and variables estimated in the construction of the BEA and Federal Reserve Board Integrated Macro Accounts.

7.1 Bottom-Up, Starting on the Ground

As discussed in Chapter 5, the Survey of Consumer Finances (SCF) provides excellent household data for balance sheets, data on some aspects of income, and relatively little data for consumption expenditures and cash flows. The Bureau of Economic Analysis (BEA) provides excellent data for consumption expenditures, consumer durables, and other nonfinancial assets, including some items disaggregated to the community level, but little on financial assets. The PSID, the HRS, the SIPP, and the CEX all provide extensive but not comprehensive data on both assets and income. The goal is to construct continuous, exact cash flows linking the changes in balance sheet line items for assets and liabilities to income and expenditure flows—that is, to obtain *all* elements of these Integrated Household Financial Statements (IHFS) for *each* household in its entirety.

Samphantharak, Schuh, and Townsend (2018), presented in Chapter 5, and Briglevics and Schuh (2020) demonstrate how the Survey of Consumer Payment Choice (SCPC) and the Diary of Consumer Payment Choice (DCPC) produce unique and highly accurate estimates of continuous (daily) cash flows for currency, which can be extended to other assets and liabilities. Remarkably, the TTMS and the DCPC produce data that are essentially the same as transactions data recorded by banks or other financial institutions. Indeed, as was emphasized in the introduction, researchers and policymakers increasingly rely on payments data for assessing shocks, such as the impact of the COVID-19 pandemic crisis, with central banks in many countries leading the charge for nowcasting GDP using specialty, proprietary, and other data sources.

However, because the TTMS and the DCPC are traditional survey-based methods, it is almost surely more efficient and cost-effective to assemble electronic transactions data wherever possible from financial institutions and payment providers. The proposed strategy, outlined in Schuh and Townsend (2020), is multimodal approach that combines surveys, diaries, electronic data, and other methods, following the lead of Angrisani, Kapteyn, and Samek (2018)'s multimodal techniques.

Research on measurement and collection of household financial data shows that such data are difficult to obtain. Survey response rates are notoriously low, privacy concerns are high, and no single method works completely for all consumers and households. Two strategies can be combined to deal with this problem. One is to field a new representative survey for the Survey of Consumer Financial Reporting (SCFR) to gauge the willingness and ability of U.S. households, including those self-employed and running small businesses, to share their financial information. Another is to build relationships with community leaders and the households themselves. This includes initial focus groups, then interviews and finally repeat visits. The latter comes naturally with the goal of a long-term panel (as described in Townsend, Sakuntasathien, and Jordan, 2013).

An obvious strategy is to start with relatively "simple" households characterized by lower income and wealth (thus simpler IHFS) and smaller numbers of household members (lower data collection burden). Locationally, a good choice would be West Virginia, of particular interest due to its residents' struggles with relatively lower income and wealth, its slower economic growth, its industrial restructuring, and its rural-urban divides. Among its population are those left out from the development of the larger national economy, that is, the "victims" of China shocks and manufacturing decline featured in the introduction. Mississippi would be another candidate, where the SEC data show that the use of commercial banks is the lowest in the country. Another set of possible locations would be neighborhoods in major metropolitan areas, though some earlier work on this has been carried out among ethnic communities by the Federal Reserve Banks in Chicago and Minneapolis (Huck et al., 1989; Bond and Townsend, 1989; Toussaint-Comeau et al., 2003).

The long-term goal is to obtain a representative sample of households that each has IHFS data that can be aggregated exactly with sampling weights to produce estimates of IHFS at the regional and national levels. This data set would enable researchers to conduct joint micro and macro analyses of household net worth dynamics and inequality of income and wealth—among other important topics—again as motivated in Chapter 1 of this monograph, but with the type of analysis as conducted in Thailand in Chapter 4.

7.2 Top-Down

The top-down approach is to understand in detail the sources, timing, revisions, and degree of disaggregation used by the Bureau of Economic Analysis and the Federal Reserve Board. The key here is the BEA handbook (BEA, 2020), which presents in detail the assembly of NIPA, input-output, state and local income and product accounts, and the underlying data sources. For the FRB, Batty et al. (2019) focus on distributional accounts and describes the assembly of U.S. Financial Accounts and the Survey of Consumer Finances and their relationship. The goal in this top-down approach is to understand better the construction of Integrated Macro Accounts, with the hope that focused sampling and survey efforts in the bottom-up approach can reduce the relatively large errors and omissions described in Chapter 6. Closely related, and the middle ground where top-down and bottom-up come together, is the construction of integrated regional financial accounts. In particular, electronic data from financial institutions and employers in bottom-up micro surveys should overlap, if not be coincident, with data sources used by the BEA and the FRB for the integrated national accounts. Data on transaction partners would link household respondents both to other actors and sectors that are key to aggregated regional accounts, as in Chapter 3, and to the balance of payment flows needed to quantify financial adjustments that are part of current account identities.

The development of disaggregated economics accounts for Denmark as featured in Andersen et al. (2022) shows the potential of this kind of work. The authors rely on several types of data: customer data from Danske Bank with information about individual customer transactions such as payments and transfers; administrative data from a range of government registers, such as the population, income, and employment registers; and housing, health, and securities statistics. They use these different types of data to disaggregate the flows between consumers, producers, and the government described in the national accounts to the level of region-by-industry cells. Thus, for example, one can quantify rural-to-urban interactions and the impact of export demand shocks at the micro level. Here, in this chapter, we are proposing the goal of doing something like this in the United States, in general equilibrium, but with the techniques from Chapter 3 on the construction of community-level financial accounts and the conceptualization from Chapter 6 for integrated macro accounts in which balance sheet changes and income flows are consistent as much as possible from existing data sources.

7.3 Conclusion

This monograph has featured important policy issues, the importance of measurement, the inadequacy of the U.S. information infrastructure, and what can be done with integrated household and regional accounts. Specific steps to remedy the situation in the United States are outlined. What remains is a national commitment to implementation.

Appendix

A. Data Annex

A.1 Thai Macroeconomic and Household Data

TABLE A.1. Sources of Thai macroeconomic and household data.

Data	Database	Source	Frequency
Price indices	Economic and Trade Indices Database (ETID)	Trade Policy and Strategy Office, Ministry of Commerce	Monthly
Exchange rates	Financial Markets (FM_FX_001)	Bank of Thailand	Monthly
Real GDP	Economic and Financial (EC_EI_027)	Bank of Thailand	Annual
Unemployment rates	Economic and Financial (EC_RL_009)	Bank of Thailand	Monthly
Balance of payments	Economic and Financial (EC_XT_013) – Discontinued (EC_XT_049) – Current	Bank of Thailand	Quarterly
Interest rates	Financial Markets (FM_RT_001)	Bank of Thailand	Monthly
Inflation	Economic and Financial (EC_EI_027)	Bank of Thailand	Annual
Townsend Thai Monthly Survey (TTMS)	Robert M. Townsend Dataverse	Townsend Thai Project	Monthly
Household financial accounts	Robert M. Townsend Dataverse	Townsend Thai Project	Monthly

Notes: ETID (https://www.price.moc.go.th/); Bank of Thailand (https://www.bot.or.th/en/statistics .html); Robert M. Townsend Dataverse (https://dataverse.harvard.edu/dataverse/rtownsend).

A.2 BEA Handbook: Concepts and Methods of the U.S. National Income Accounts and Product Accounts

As a reference guide for the reader, here we will summarize the NIPA handbook.[1]

CHAPTER 1 INTRODUCTION

The U.S. National Income and Product Accounts (NIPAs) are a set of economic accounts that provide the framework for presenting detailed measures of U.S. output and income. This chapter introduces the NIPAs by answering several basic questions about their nature and purpose.

Contents: What are the NIPAs? How did the NIPAs originate? How have the NIPAs evolved? How are the NIPA estimates used? How useful are the NIPA estimates? How are the NIPA estimates prepared? Why are the NIPA estimates revised? Where are the NIPA estimates available?

CHAPTER 2 FUNDAMENTAL CONCEPTS

The NIPAs are based on a set of consistent concepts and definitions. This chapter establishes the types and scope of the economic activities that are covered by the NIPA measures, and it describes several of the principal NIPA measures of these activities. It then discusses the classifications used in presenting the NIPA estimates, and it describes the accounting framework that underlies the NIPAs.

Contents: Scope of the Estimates; Production boundary; Asset boundary; Market and nonmarket output; Geographic coverage; Income and saving; GDP and Other Major NIPA Measures; Three ways to measure GDP; Major NIPA aggregates; Principal quantity and price measures; Classification; Sector; Type of product; Function; Industry; Legal form of organization; Accounting Framework; Accounting principles; Conceptual derivation of the NIPAs; and the summary NIPAs.

---

1. Source: https://www.bea.gov/resources/methodologies/nipa-handbook.

CHAPTER 3 PRINCIPAL SOURCE DATA

The NIPAs incorporate a vast amount of data from a variety of public and private sources. This chapter describes the principal source data that are used to prepare the current quarterly NIPA estimates, to prepare the annual revisions of the NIPAs, and to prepare the quinquennia l comprehensive revisions of the NIPAs.

Contents: Source data as determinants of initial release and revision schedules; Source data for the current quarterly estimates; Source data for the annual updates; Source data for the comprehensive updates.

CHAPTER 4 ESTIMATING METHODS

Estimating methods are the steps that are taken to transform source data into estimates that are consistent with the concepts, definitions, and framework of the NIPAs. This chapter briefly describes some of the general methods that are used to prepare the current-dollar, quantity, and price estimates for the NIPAs. An appendix describes some of the statistical tools and conventions that are used in preparing and presenting the NIPA estimates.

Contents: Current-Dollar Estimates Adjustments to the source data; Seasonal adjustment; Moving average; Best level and best change; Interpolation and extrapolation using an indicator series; Three special estimation methods; Commodity-flow method; Retail control method; Perpetual inventory method; Quantity and Price Estimates; Estimates for detailed components; Estimates for NIPA aggregates; Properties of chain-type measures; Appendix to Chapter 4; Calculation of Output and Price Indexes; Adjusting for quality change; Statistical Tools and Conventions; Chained-dollar measures; Contributions to percent change; Annual rates; Growth rates; and Rebasing an index.

CHAPTER 5 PERSONAL CONSUMPTION EXPENDITURES

Personal consumption expenditures (PCE) is the NIPA measure of consumer purchases of goods and services in the U.S. economy. A technical note at the end of the chapter provides additional details on the methodology for a number of key PCE components.

Contents: Definitions and Concepts; Recording in the NIPAs; Overview of Source Data and Estimating Methods; Benchmark-year estimates; Nonbenchmark-year estimates; Current quarterly and monthly estimates;

Quantity and price estimates; Table 5.A—Summary of Methodology for PCE for Goods; Table 5.B—Summary of Methodology for PCE for Services; Technical Note-Special Estimates; New motor vehicles—Net purchases of used motor vehicles; Gasoline and other motor fuel; Rental of tenant- and owner-occupied nonfarm housing; Financial service charges and fees; Securities commissions; Financial services furnished without payment; Life insurance; Property and casualty insurance; Nonprofit institutions serving households.

CHAPTER 6 PRIVATE FIXED INVESTMENT

Private fixed investment (PFI) is the NIPA measure of spending by private business, nonprofit institutions, and households on fixed assets in the U.S. economy. A technical note at the end of the chapter provides additional details on the methodology for several key PFI components.

Contents: Definitions and Concepts; Recording in the NIPAs; Overview of Source Data and Estimating Methods; Benchmark-year estimates; Nonbenchmark-year estimates; Current quarterly estimates; Quantity and price estimates; Table 6.A—Summary of Methodology for Private Fixed Investment in Structures; Table 6.B—Summary of Methodology for Private Fixed Investment in Equipment; Table 6.C—Summary of Methodology for Private Fixed Investment in Intellectual Property Products; Technical Note-Special Estimates; New single-family structures; Used equipment; Intellectual property products.

CHAPTER 7 CHANGE IN PRIVATE INVENTORIES

Change in private inventories is the NIPA measure of the value of the change in the physical volume of inventories owned by private businesses in the U.S. economy. Appendixes at the end of the chapter illustrate the relationship between business and NIPA inventory accounting and the basic steps used in the NIPA inventory calculations.

Contents: Definitions and Concepts; Recording in the NIPAs; Overview of Source Data and Estimating Methods; Benchmark-year estimates; Nonbenchmark-year estimates; Most-recent-year and current-quarterly estimates; Quantity and price estimates; Table 7.A—Summary of Methodology for Change in Private Inventories; Appendix A—Illustration of LIFO and FIFO Accounting Methods and Their Relationship to NIPA Accounting; Appendix B: Illustration of NIPA Inventory Calculations.

CHAPTER 8 NET EXPORTS OF GOODS AND SERVICES

Net exports of goods and services is the difference between U.S. exports of goods and services, the NIPA measure of the portion of U.S. production that is provided to the rest of the world, and imports of goods and services, the NIPA measure of the portion of U.S. expenditures that is accounted for as foreign-produced goods and services.

Contents: Definitions and Concepts; Recording in the NIPAs; Overview of Source Data and Estimating Methods; Benchmark-year and nonbenchmark-year estimates; Current quarterly estimates; Adjustments and other differences between the NIPA and ITA estimates; Quantity and price estimates; Table 8.A—Summary of Methodology for Exports of Goods and Services; Table 8.B—Summary of Methodology for Imports of Goods and Services.

CHAPTER 9 GOVERNMENT CONSUMPTION EXPENDITURES AND GROSS INVESTMENT

Government consumption expenditures and gross investment is the NIPA measure of the portion of final expenditures that is accounted for by the government sector. In the NIPAs, government is treated as both a consumer/investor and a producer of goods and services.

Contents: Definitions and Concepts; Recording in the NIPAs; Overview of Source Data and Estimating Methods; Benchmark-year and nonbenchmark-year estimates; Current quarterly estimates; Quantity and price estimates; Table 9.A—Summary of Methodology for Government Consumption Expenditures; Table 9.B—Summary of Methodology for Government Gross Investment.

CHAPTER 10 COMPENSATION OF EMPLOYEES

Compensation measures the total income—both wages and salaries and supplements to wages and salaries—earned by employees in return for contributing to production during an accounting period.

Contents: Definitions and Concepts; Recording in the NIPAs; Overview of Source Data and Estimating Methods; Annual estimates; Current quarterly estimates; Table 10.A—Summary of Methodology for Wages and Salaries; Table 10.B—Summary of Methodology for Employer Contributions for Pension and Insurance Funds; Table 10.C—Summary of Methodology for Employer Contributions for Social Insurance; Appendix A—NIPA Measures of Employment and Hours.

CHAPTER 11 NONFARM PROPRIETORS' INCOME

Nonfarm proprietors' income provides a comprehensive and consistent economic measure of the income earned by all U.S. unincorporated nonfarm businesses.

Contents: Definitions and Concepts; Recording in the NIPAs; Overview of Source Data and Estimating Methods; Annual (except most-recent-year) estimates; Most-recent-year estimates

Current quarterly estimates; Table 11.A—Summary of Methodology for Nonfarm Proprietors' Income; Technical Note-Adjustments to IRS Source Data for Nonfarm Proprietors' Income.

CHAPTER 12 RENTAL INCOME OF PERSONS

Rental income of persons reflects the income earned by persons for the provision, to others, of their property.

Contents: Definitions and Concepts; Recording in the NIPAs; Overview of Source Data and Estimating Methods; Benchmark year estimates; Non-benchmark annual estimates; Current quarterly estimates; Table 12.A—Summary of Methodology Used to Prepare Estimates of Rental Income of Persons.

CHAPTER 13 CORPORATE PROFITS

Corporate profits represent the portion of the total income earned from current production that is accounted for by U.S. corporations. A technical note at the end of the chapter describes the BEA's adjustments to the Internal Revenue Service's tax return data.

Contents: Definitions and Concepts; Recording in the NIPAs; Overview of Source Data and Estimating Methods; Annual (except most-recent-year) estimates; Most-recent-year estimates; Current quarterly estimates; Table 13.A—Summary of Methodology for Corporate Profits; Technical Note—Adjustments to IRS Tax Return Data; Appendix—Domestic Gross Corporate Value Added and Related Measures.

A.3 Integrated Macro Accounts: Interactive Data

Instructions for the reader on how to begin using the data and finding data formulas and underlying sources for the IMA as described here: https://www .bea.gov/data/special-topics/integrated-macroeconomic-accounts.

First, here is list of the tables: https://www.federalreserve.gov/apps/fof /Guide/z1_tables_description.pdf.

Next, go to the financial accounts guide and choose a particular table of interest: https://www.federalreserve.gov/apps/fof/FOFTables.aspx. For example, click on Table S.5.a for nonfinancial corporate business, which leads to https://www.federalreserve.gov/apps/fof/DisplayTable.aspx?t=s.5.a.

Next, pick a line item such as wages paid, to find sources: https://www.federalreserve.gov/apps/fof/SeriesAnalyzer.aspx?s=FA10602 0001&t=S.5.A&suf=A, where one can see the underlying source is from BEA, https://www.federalreserve.gov/apps/fof/SeriesAnalyzer.aspx?s=FU10602 0001&t=S.5.A&bc=S.5.A:FA106020001&suf=A.

As another example, to see entries in the flow of funds, choose a table labeled F and scroll down to find them. For example, click on F.103 nonfinancial corporate business. To see from where that line comes, click on the series name (e.g., FA106060005) to get: Series analyzer for FA106060005 = + FA09 6060005 − FA796060005 − FA266060005. Pick the top line FA096060005 and click one more time to get to this: https://www.federalreserve.gov/apps/fof /SeriesAnalyzer.aspx?s=FA096121073&t=F.103&bc=F.103:FA096060005 &suf=Q, to get to the underlying source data for corporate dividends paid (from BEA).

REFERENCES

Agrawal, Sarthak, and David Phillips. 2020. "Catching Up or Falling Behind? Geographical Inequalities in the UK and How They Have Changed in Recent Years." *IFS Deaton Review*, August 2, 2020. https://ifs.org.uk/publications/catching-or-falling-behind-geographical -inequalities-uk-and-how-they-have-changed. Accessed 7/12/21.

Allen, Treb, and Costas Arkolakis. 2014. "Trade and the Topography of the Spatial Economy." *Quarterly Journal of Economics* 129 (3): 1085–1140.

Andersen, Asger L., Emil Toft Hansen, Kilian Huber, Niels Johannesen, and Ludwig Straub. 2022. "Disaggregated Economic Accounts." NBER Working Paper No. 30630.

Angrisani, Marco, Arie Kapteyn, and Swaroop Samek. 2018. "Real Time Measurement of Household Electronic Financial Transactions in a Population Representative Panel." Working paper.

Antràs, Pol, and Ricardo J. Caballero. 2009. "Trade and Capital Flows: A Financial Frictions Perspective." *Journal of Political Economy* 117 (4): 701–744.

Autor, David H., David Dorn, and Gordon H. Hanson. 2013. "The China Syndrome: Local Labor Market Effects of Import Competition in the United States." *American Economic Review* 103 (6): 2121–2168.

Baker, Scott R., R. A. Farrokhnia, Steffen Meyer, Michaela Pagel, and Constantine Yannelis. 2020. "Income, Liquidity, and the Consumption Response to the 2020 Economic Stimulus Payments." NBER Working Paper No. 27097.

Baker, Scott R., Lorenz Kueng, Steffen Meyer, and Michaela Pagel. 2022. "Consumption Imputation Errors in Administrative Data." *Review of Financial Studies* 35 (6): 3021–3059.

Batty, Michael, Jesse Bricker, Joseph Briggs, Elizabeth Holmquist, Susan McIntosh, Kevin Moore, Eric Nielsen, Sarah Reber, Molly Shatto, Kamila Sommer, Tom Sweeney, and Alice Henriques Volz. 2019. "Introducing the Distributional Financial Accounts of the United States." Finance and Economics Discussion Series No. 2019-017, Board of Governors of the Federal Reserve System.

Bond, Charlotte Anne, Teran Martin, Susan Hume McIntosh, and Charles Ian Mead. 2007. "Integrated Macroeconomic Accounts for the United States." *Survey of Current Business* 87 (2): 14–31.

Bond, Philip, and Robert Townsend. 1989. "Formal and Informal Financing in a Chicago Ethnic Neighborhood." *Economic Perspectives* 20 (4): 3–27.

Bonhomme, Stéphane, Pierre-André Chiappori, Robert M. Townsend, and Hiroyuki Yamada. 2012. "Sharing Wage Risk." Working paper.

Brambilla, Irene, Daniel Lederman, and Guido Porto. 2012. "Exports, Export Destinations, and Skills." *American Economic Review* 102 (7): 3406–3438.

Briglevics, Tamás, and Scott Schuh. 2020. "This Is 'What's in Your Wallet' . . . and Here's How You Use It." West Virginia *University Economics Faculty Working Paper No. 20-04.* https://researchrepository.wvu.edu/econ_working-papers/45

Bryan, Gharad, and Melanie Morten. 2018. "The Aggregate Productivity Effects of Internal Migration: Evidence from Indonesia." Working paper.

Buda, Gergely, Stephen Hansen, Tomasa Rodrigo, Vasco M. Carvalho, Álvaro Ortiz, and José V. Rodríguez Mora. 2022. "National Accounts in a World of Naturally Occurring Data: A Proof of Concept for Consumption." Cambridge Working Papers in Economics No. 2244.

Buera, Francisco J., Joseph P. Kaboski, and Yongseok Shin. 2011. "Finance and Development: A Tale of Two Sectors." *American Economic Review* 101 (5): 1964–2002.

Bureau of Economic Analysis. 2020. "Concepts and Methods of the U.S. National Income and Product Accounts." BEA.gov. https://www.bea.gov/resources/methodologies/nipa-handbook. Accessed 8/22/21.

Burstein, Ariel, Eduardo Morales, and Jonathan Vogel. 2015. "Accounting for Changes in Between-Group Inequality." NBER Working Paper No. 20855.

Bustos, Paula. 2011. "Trade Liberalization, Exports, and Technology Upgrading: Evidence on the Impact of MERCOSUR on Argentinian Firms." *American Economic Review* 101 (1): 304–340.

Caliendo, Lorenzo, and Fernando Parro. 2015. "Estimates of the Trade and Welfare Effects of NAFTA." *Review of Economic Studies* 82 (1): 1–44.

Carroll, Christopher D., Thomas F. Crossley, and John Sabelhaus, eds. 2015. *Improving the Measurement of Consumer Expenditures.* Chicago and London: University of Chicago Press.

Charles, Kerwin K., Erik Hurst, and Mariel Schwartz. 2018. "The Transformation of Manufacturing and the Decline in U.S. Employment." NBER Working Paper No. 24468.

Chetty, Raj, John N. Friedman, Nathaniel Hendren, Michael Stepner, and the Opportunity Insights Team. 2020. "The Economic Impacts of COVID-19: Evidence from a New Public Database Built Using Private Sector Data." NBER Working Paper No. 27431.

Collins, Daryl. 2005. "Financial Instruments of the Poor: Initial Findings from the Financial Diaries Study." *Development Southern Africa* 22 (5): 717–728.

Cox, Natalie, Peter Ganong, Pascal Noel, Joseph Vavra, Arlene Wong, Diana Farrell, and Fiona Greig. 2020. "Initial Impacts of the Pandemic on Consumer Behavior: Evidence from Linked Income, Spending, and Savings Data." Becker Friedman Institute Working Paper No. 2020-82.

Crossley, Thomas F., and Joachim K. Winter. 2015. "Asking Households about Expenditures: What Have We Learned?" In *Improving the Measurement of Consumer Expenditures,* edited by Christopher D. Carrol, Thomas F. Crossley, and John Sabelhaus. Chicago and London: University of Chicago Press.

de Mel, Suresh, David McKenzie, and Christopher Woodruff. 2008. "Returns to Capital in Microenterprises: Evidence from a Field Experiment." *Quarterly Journal of Economics* 123 (4): 1329–1372.

Dillman, Don A., and Carol C. House, eds. 2013. *Measuring What We Spend: Toward a New Consumer Expenditure Survey.* Washington, D.C.: National Academies Press.

Donaldson, Dave, and Richard Hornbeck. 2016. "Railroads and American Economic Growth: a 'Market Access' Approach." *Quarterly Journal of Economics* 131 (2): 799–858.

Eaton, Jonathan, and Samuel Kortum. 2002. "Technology, Geography, and Trade." *Econometrica* 70 (5): 1741–1779.

Ehrlich, Daniel, Masao Fukui, and Robert M. Townsend. 2021. "Trade-Financial Linkages and Regional Risk-Sharing." Working paper, MIT.

Fajgelbaum, Pablo D., and Amit K. Khandelwal. 2016. "Measuring the Unequal Gains from Trade." *Quarterly Journal of Economics* 131 (3): 1113–1180.

Feenstra, Robert C. 2010. *Offshoring in the Global Economy: Microeconomic Structure and Macroeconomic Implications. Ohlin Lectures Series.* Cambridge: MIT Press.

Feenstra, Robert C., and Gordon H. Hanson. 1996. "Foreign Investment, Outsourcing and Relative Wages." In *The Political Economy of Trade Policy: Papers in Honor of Jagdish Bhagwati*, Robert C. Feenstra, Gene M. Grossman, and Douglas A. Irwin, eds., 89–127. Cambridge, MA: MIT Press.

Frías, Judith A., David S. Kaplan, and Eric Verhoogen. 2012. "Exports and Within-Plant Wage Distributions: Evidence from Mexico." *American Economic Review* 102 (3): 435–440.

Fulford, Scott, Claire Greene, and William Murdock III. 2015. "U.S. Consumer Holdings and Use of $1 Bills." Federal Reserve Bank of Boston Working Paper No. 15.

Garbinti, Bertrand, Jonathan Goupille-Lebret, and Thomas Piketty. 2018. "Income Inequality in France, 1900–2014: Evidence from Distributional National Accounts (DINA)." *Journal of Public Economics* 162 (June): 63–77.

Giné, Xavier, and Robert M. Townsend. 2004. "Evaluation of Financial Liberalization: A General Equilibrium Model with Constrained Occupation Choice." *Journal of Development Economics* 74 (2): 269–307.

Goldberg, Pinelopi Koujianou, and Nina Pavcnik. 2007. "Distributional Effects of Globalization in Developing Countries." *Journal of Economic Literature* 45 (1): 39–82.

Greene, Claire, and Scott Schuh. 2014. "U.S. Consumers' Holdings and Use of $100 Bills." Federal Reserve Bank of Boston Working Paper No. 14-3.

Greene, Claire, Scott Schuh, and Joanna Stavins. 2016. "The 2014 Survey of Consumer Payment Choice: Summary of Results." Federal Reserve Bank of Boston Working Paper No. 16-3.

Grosh, Margaret, and Paul Glewwe, eds. 2000. *Designing Household Questionnaires for Developing Countries: Lessons from Fifteen Years of the Living Standard Measurement Study, Volumes 1–3.* Washington, DC: World Bank.

Hakobyan, Shushanik, and John McLaren. 2016. "Looking for Local Labor Market Effects of NAFTA." *Review of Economics and Statistics* 98 (4): 728–741.

Hamilton, Darrick, William Darity, Jr., Anne E. Price, Vishnu Sridharan and Rebecca Tippet. 2015. "Umbrellas Don't Make It Rain: Why Studying and Working Hard Isn't Enough for Black Americans." Insight Center for Community Economic Development Report.

Harrison, Ann, John McLaren, and Margaret McMillan. 2011. "Recent Perspective on Trade and Inequality." *Annual Review of Economics* 3 (1): 261–289.

Hart, Oliver. 1995. *Firms, Contracts, and Financial Structure.* Oxford: Clarendon Press.

Helpman, Elhanan, Oleg Itskhoki, and Stephen Redding. 2011. "Trade and Labor Market Outcomes." NBER Working Paper No. 16662.

Hildebrand, Nikolaus. 2019. "The Rise of Finance: 1850–2015." PhD dissertation, Massachusetts Institute of Technology.

Huck, Paul, Sherrie L. W. Rhine, Philip Bond, and Robert Townsend. 1989. "Small Business Finance in Two Chicago Minority Neighborhoods." *Economic Perspectives* 23 (2): 46–62.

Imdieke, Leroy F., and Ralph E. Smith. 1987. *Financial Accounting*. First edition. New York: John Wiley & Sons.

Itskhoki, Oleg, and Benjamin Moll. 2018. "Optimal Development Policies with Financial Frictions." Working paper.

Jeong, Hyeok, and Robert M. Townsend. 2008. "Growth and Inequality: Model Evaluation Based on an Estimation-Calibration Strategy." *Macroeconomic Dynamics* 12 (S2): 231–284.

Kaboski, Joseph P., and Robert M. Townsend. 2011. "A Structural Evaluation of a Large-Scale Quasi-Experimental Microfinance Initiative." *Econometrica* 79 (5): 1357–1406.

Kovak, Brian K. 2013. "Regional Effects of Trade Reform: What Is the Correct Measure of Liberalization?" *American Economic Review* 103 (5): 1960–1976.

Levinsohn, James, and Amil Petrin. 2003. "Estimating Production Functions Using Inputs to Control for Unobservables." *Review of Economic Studies* 70 (2): 317–341.

Lim, Youngjae, and Robert M. Townsend. 1998. "General Equilibrium Models of Financial Systems: Theory and Measurement in Village Economies." *Review of Economic Dynamics* 1 (1): 59–118.

Lloyd-Ellis, Huw, and Dan Bernhardt. 2000. "Enterprise, Inequality and Economic Development." *Review of Economic Studies* 67 (1): 147–168.

Lyon, Spencer G., and Michael E. Waugh. 2018. "Quantifying the Losses from International Trade." Working paper.

Melitz, Marc J. 2003. "The Impact of Trade on Intra-industry Reallocations and Aggregate Industry Productivity." *Econometrica* 71 (6): 1695–1725.

Moll, Benjamin. 2014. "Productivity Losses from Financial Frictions: Can Self-Financing Undo Capital Misallocation." *American Economic Review* 104 (10): 3186–3221.

Morduch, Jonathan, and Rachel Schneider. 2017. *The Financial Diaries: How American Families Cope in a World of Uncertainty*. Princeton and Oxford: Princeton University Press.

Morten, Melanie, and Jaqueline Oliveira. 2018. "The Effects of Roads on Trade and Migration: Evidence from a Planned Capital City." Working paper.

Munoz, Ana Patricia, Marlene Kim, Mariko Chang, Regine O. Jackson, Darrick Hamilton, William A. Darity Jr. 2015. "The Color of Wealth in Boston." *Federal Reserve Bank of Boston Joint Publication with The New School*.

Pawasutipaisit, Anan, Archawa Paweenawat, Krislert Samphantharak, Narapong Srivisal, and Robert M. Townsend. 2010. "Constructing Financial Statements from Integrated Household Surveys: Questionnaires to Computer Code." Technical note.

Pawasutipaisit, Anan, and Robert M. Townsend. 2011. "Wealth Accumulation and Factors Accounting for Success." *Journal of Econometrics* 161 (1): 56–81.

Paweenawat, Archawa, and Robert M. Townsend. 2012. "Village Economic Accounts: Real and Financial Intertwined." *American Economic Review* 102 (3): 441–446.

Piketty, Thomas, Emmanuel Saez, and Gabriel Zucman. 2018. "Distributional National Accounts: Methods and Estimates for the United States." *Quarterly Journal of Economics* 133 (2): 553–609.

Ring, Marius A. K. 2021. "Wealth Taxation and Household Saving: Evidence from Assessment Discontinuities in Norway." Working paper.

Roy, Andrew D. 1951. "Some Thoughts on the Distribution of Earnings." *Oxford Economic Papers* 3 (2): 135–146.

Rutherford, Stuart. 2002. "Money Talks: Conversations with Poor Households in Bangladesh about Managing Money." Finance and Development Research Programme Working Paper No. 45, University of Manchester.

Ruthven, Orlanda. 2002. "Money Mosaics: Financial Choice & Strategy in a West Delhi Squatter Settlement." *Journal of International Development* 14 (2): 249–271.

Samphantharak, Krislert, Scott Schuh, and Robert M. Townsend. 2018. "Integrated Household Surveys: An Assessment of U.S. Methods and an Innovation." *Economic Inquiry* 56 (1): 50–80.

Samphantharak, Krislert, and Robert M. Townsend. 2009. *Households as Corporate Firms: An Analysis of Household Finance Using Integrated Household Surveys and Corporate Financial Accounting.* New York, NY: Cambridge University Press.

Schuh, Scott. 2018. "Measuring Consumer Expenditures with Payment Diaries." *Economic Inquiry* 56 (1): 13–49.

Schuh, Scott, and Robert M. Townsend. 2020. "Starting from Scratch: A Multi-mode Approach to Collecting Micro Data for Fully Integrated United States Household Financial Statements." Working paper, MIT.

Smith, Matthew, Owen Zidar, and Eric Zwick. 2019. "Top Wealth in the United States: Estimates and Implications for Taxing the Rich." Working paper.

Sraer, David, and David Thesmar. 2018. "A Sufficient Statistics Approach for Aggregating Firm-Level Experiments." NBER Working Paper No. 24208.

Stickney, Clyde P., and Roman Weil. 2003. *Financial Accounting: An Introduction to Concepts, Methods, and Uses.* 10th edition. Mason, OH: Thomson/South-Western.

Topalova, Petia. 2007. "Trade Liberalization, Poverty and Inequality: Evidence from Indian Districts." Chapter 7 in *Globalization and Poverty*, Ann Harrison, ed. Chicago: University of Chicago Press, pp. 291–336.

Toussaint-Comeau, Maude, Robin Newberger, Jason Schmidt, Art Rolnick, and Ron Feldman. 2003. "Credit Availability in the Minneapolis-St. Paul Hmong Community." Working paper, Federal Reserve Bank of Minneapolis.

Townsend, Robert M., Sombat Sakuntasathien, and Rob Jordan. 2013. *Chronicles from the Field: The Townsend Thai Project.* Cambridge, MA: MIT Press.

Udry, Christopher. 1994. "Risk and Insurance in a Rural Credit Market: An Empirical Investigation in Northern Nigeria." *Review of Economic Studies* 61 (3): 495–526.

U.S. Department of Commerce. Bureau of Economic Analysis. 1985. "An Introduction to National Economic Accounting." Methodology Paper Series MP-1. Washington, DC: GPO.

Verhoogen, Eric. 2008. "Trade, Quality Upgrading and Wage Inequality in the Mexican Manufacturing Sector." *Quarterly Journal of Economics* 123 (2): 489–530.

Wikipedia. 2021. "Yellow Vests Movement." Wikepedia.org. https://en.wikipedia.org/wiki/Yellow_vests_movement#cite_note-populist-65. Accessed 5/12/21.

Yamarik, Steven. 2013. "State-Level Capital and Investment: Updates and Implications." *Contemporary Economic Policy* 31 (1): 62–72.

Yamashita, Takashi. 2013. "BEA Briefing: A Guide to the Integrated Macroeconomic Accounts." *BEA Survey of Current Business* 93 (4): 12–27.

INDEX

Page numbers in italics indicate figures and tables.

THE GORMAN LECTURES IN ECONOMICS

Richard Blundell, Series Editor

Terence (W. M.) Gorman was one of the most distinguished economists of the twentieth century. His ideas are so ingrained in modern economics that we use them daily with almost no acknowledgment. The relationship between individual behavior and aggregate outcomes, two-stage budgeting in individual decision making, the "characteristics" model which lies at the heart of modern consumer economics, and a conceptual framework for "adult equivalence scales" are but a few of these. For over fifty years he guided students and colleagues alike in how best to model economic activities as well as how to test these models once formulated.

During the late 1980s and early 1990s, Gorman was a Visiting Professor of Economics at University College London. He became a key part of the newly formed and lively research group at UCL and at the Institute for Fiscal Studies. The aim of this research was to avoid the obsessive labeling that had pigeonholed much of economics and to introduce a free flow of ideas between economic theory, econometrics, and empirical evidence. It worked marvelously and formed the mainstay of economics research in the Economics Department at UCL. These lectures are a tribute to his legacy.

Terence had a lasting impact on all who interacted with him during that period. He was not only an active and innovative economist, but he was also a dedicated teacher and mentor to students and junior colleagues. He was generous with his time and more than one discussion with Terence appeared later as a scholarly article inspired by that conversation. He used his skill in mathematics as a framework for his approach, but he never insisted on that. What was essential was a coherent and logical understanding of economics. Gorman passed away in January 2003, shortly after the second of these lectures. He will be missed, but his written works remain to remind all of us that we are sitting on the shoulders of a giant.

Richard Blundell, University College London and
Institute for Fiscal Studies